AT&T

C Language Interfaces

H. Garrett Long, Editor
AT&T Data Systems Group

Prentice Hall, Englewood Cliffs, New Jersey 07632

Library of Congress Catalog Card Number: 88-61900

Production supervision: Karen Skrable Fortgang
Manufacturing buyer: Mary Ann Gloriande

IMPORTANT NOTE TO USERS
While every effort has been made to ensure the accuracy of all information in this
publication, AT&T assumes no liability to any party for any loss or damage caused by
errors or omissions or by statements of any kind in *C Language Interfaces*, its updates,
supplements or special editions, whether such errors are omissions or statements resulting
from negligence, accident or any other cause.

AT&T further assumes no liability arising out of the application or use of any product or
system described herein; nor any liability for incidental or consequential damages arising
from the use of this publication.

AT&T disclaims all warranties regarding the information contained herein, whether
expressed, implied or statutory, including implied warranties of merchantability or fitness
for a particular purpose.

AT&T makes no representation that the interconnection of products in the manner
described herein will not infringe on existing or future patent rights, nor do the
descriptions contained herein imply the granting of license to make, use
or sell equipment constructed in accordance with this description.

AT&T reserves the right to make changes without further notice to any products herein to
improve reliability, function or design.

The text for this publication was processed with `troff` software on an Amdahl 5870
computer running UNIX System V. The `troff` output was networked with `uucp`
software to an AT&T 3B20 computer running UNIX System V to drive an APS-5
phototypesetter.

UNIX is a registered trademark of AT&T. APS-5 is a trademark of AUTOLOGIC, Inc.
Amdahl is a trademark of Amdahl Corporation.

Printed in the United States of America

10 9 8 7 6 5 4 3 2

ISBN 0-13-109661-3

Prentice-Hall International (UK) Limited, *London*
Prentice-Hall of Australia Pty. Limited, *Sydney*
Prentice-Hall Canada Inc., *Toronto*
Prentice-Hall Hispanoamericana, S.A., *Mexico*
Prentice-Hall of India Private Limited, *New Delhi*
Prentice-Hall of Japan, Inc., *Tokyo*
Simon & Schuster Asia Pte. Ltd., *Singapore*
Editora Prentice-Hall do Brasil, Ltda., *Rio de Janeiro*

Contents

Contents

Contents

Contents

Environment   285

Glossary   329

Appendices   347

Index   373

Introduction

NAME

intro — introduction to *C Language Interfaces*

DESCRIPTION

C Language Interfaces answers the needs of programmers developing software that can be ported in source-code form between different computer systems supporting UNIX System V. These programmers need a single reference that identifies the components of UNIX System V and defines the source-code interfaces and the run-time behavior of those components.

C Language Interfaces contains a series of *component interface definitions*, each of a page or more in length, that present the source-code interfaces and the run-time behavior for components of UNIX System V including operating system routines, general library routines, system data files, special-device files and other features of the UNIX System V environment. The component interface definitions specify the functionality of components without stipulating the implementation; they exclude the details of how UNIX System V implements these components and concentrate on defining the external features of a standard computing environment rather than the internals of the operating system, such as the scheduler or memory manager.

The component interface definitions in *C Language Interfaces* draw heavily on material from Volumes I, II & III of the *System V Interface Definition*, Issue 2, which describes the feature/functionality of UNIX System V Release 3.0. The *System V Interface Definition* applies to computer systems ranging from personal computers to mainframes, and defines a computing environment that is independent of any particular computer hardware. Software conforming to the *System V Interface Definition* lets users take advantage of changes in technology and choose the computer system that best meets their needs from among many manufacturers while retaining a common computing environment.

Only the *System V Interface Definition* represents the official statement by AT&T of the requirements for systems conforming to the System V standard.

C Language Interfaces organizes the component interface definitions to better serve the needs of the working programmer than does the *System V Interface Definition* which serves a different set of purposes; however, anyone seeking the definitive statement about the required feature/functionality of the components of the System V computing environment should consult the latest issue of the *System V Interface Definition*.

C Language Interfaces uses the same naming conventions for component interface definitions as that used by the *System V Interface Definition*. This should aid anyone who might wish to look up a component interface definition in the *System V Interface Definition* that corresponds to one in this book. In particular, *C Language Interfaces* follows the *System V Interface Definition* by identifying each UNIX System V component as a member of the Base System or one of a series of Extensions to the Base System.

The *System V Interface Definition* uses pairs of letters to designate the Base System and the Extensions as follows:

BA	Base System
KE	Kernel Extension
NS	Network Services Extension
BU	Basic Utilities Extension
AU	Advanced Utilities Extension
AS	Administered Systems Extension
SD	Software Development Extension

The title of each component interface definition combines the name of the component or group of components, such as READ or BESSEL, with a suffix of the form (*XX_YYY*), where *XX* designates the Base System or Extension the component belongs to as shown above, and *YYY* designates the component type as shown below:

CMD	commands or utilities
OS	system service routines
LIB	general library routines
ENV	environmental components

The titles of component interface definitions may use the following suffixes:

(BU_CMD)	Basic Utilities
(AU_CMD)	Advanced Utilities
(AS_CMD)	Administered Systems Utilities
(SD_CMD)	Software Development Utilities
(NS_CMD)	Shared Resource Utilities
(BA_OS)	Base System Routines
(KE_OS)	Kernel Extension Routines
(NS_OS)	Network Services Routines
(BA_LIB)	Base Library Routines
(NS_LIB)	Network Services Library
(SD_LIB)	Software Development Library
(AS_ENV)	Administered Systems Environment
(BA_ENV)	Base System Environment
(KE_ENV)	Kernel Extension Environment
(NS_ENV)	Network Services Environment

C Language Interfaces arranges component interface definitions in alphabetical order by title, which appears in the upper corners of each page of a component interface definition. Some component interface definitions cover several commands, functions or other UNIX System V components; thus, components defined along with other related components share the same component interface definition title. For example, references to `calloc` cite MALLOC(BA_OS) because the function `calloc` is described with the function `malloc` in the component interface definition entitled MALLOC(BA_OS).

Each component interface definition is a page or more in length and follows the same structure. The headings are listed below, but not all appear in each component interface definition.

NAME	name of component and statement of purpose
SYNOPSIS	C language or Command-level interface
DESCRIPTION	feature/functionality and run-time behavior
RETURN VALUE	value returned by the component
ERRORS	possible error conditions
FILES	names of files used
USAGE	guidance on use
EXAMPLES	examples and sample usage
SEE ALSO	list of related components
CAVEATS	future developments and directions

The component interface definitions are similar in format to traditional AT&T UNIX System V manual pages, but have been extended or modified as follows:

- A section entitled CAVEATS has been added to report on anticipated changes in functionality and general directions of expected development.

- A section entitled USAGE has been added as a guide to the expected or recommended usage of certain components.

C Language Interfaces specifies the run-time behavior for each component of UNIX System V, but not the implementation. All machine-specific or implementation-specific information was removed, and all implementation-specific constants replaced by symbolic names [see implementation-specific constants in VOCAB(BA_DEF)]. These symbolic names always appear in curly brackets (e.g., {PROC_MAX}) and correspond to those the November 1985 draft of the **IEEE P1003** Standard defines to be in a `<limits.h>` header file; however, they must *not* be read as symbolic constants defined in header files.

Some Extensions need other Extensions (e.g., Advanced Utilities need Basic Utilities) and may change how components in the Base System or other Extensions work. Any such effects are described in the Environment section on pages entitled EFFECTS(XX_ENV) [see EFFECTS(KE_ENV)]. Portable software should avoid using any features or side-effects not explicitly defined.

The SYNOPSIS summarizes the component interface; it compactly represents the order of any arguments for the component, the type of each argument (if any) and the type of value the component returns. For a C language function, the SYNOPSIS closely resembles the C language declaration of the function and its arguments. For example, the SYNOPSIS for the macro feof is:

```
#include <stdio.h>

int feof(fp)
FILE *fp;
```

The DESCRIPTION for feof states that it is implemented as a macro, and the SYNOPSIS for feof shows that:

- The macro feof requires the header file stdio.h

- The macro feof returns a value of type int

- The argument fp is a pointer to an object of type FILE

To use feof in a program, you need only write the macro call, preceded at some point by the #include control line, as in:

```
#include <stdio.h>    /* include definitions */
...
main()
{
    FILE *infile;      /* define a file pointer */
    ...
    while (!feof(infile)) {   /* until end-of-file */
        /* operations on the file */
    }
}
```

The SYNOPSIS specifies only the return value of a component, not the form of declaration; thus, the format of a SYNOPSIS only resembles, but does *not* duplicate, the format of C language declarations. To show that some components take varying numbers of arguments, a SYNOPSIS uses additional conventions not found in actual C function declarations:

- Text in courier represents source-code typed just as it appears.

- Text in *italic* usually represents substitutable argument prototypes.

- Square brackets [ ] around arguments indicate optional arguments.

- Ellipses ... indicate that the previous arguments may repeat.

- If the type of an argument may vary, the SYNOPSIS omits the type.

For example, the SYNOPSIS for the function printf is:

```
#include <stdio.h>

int printf(fmt [ , arg ... ] )
char *fmt;
```

This SYNOPSIS for printf shows that the argument arg is optional, may be repeated and is not always of the same data type. The DESCRIPTION in the component interface definition provides any remaining information about the function printf and the arguments to it.

SEE ALSO

C Language Interfaces defines source-code interfaces for the C language as defined by the following references:

UNIX System V Programming Guide, Release 1.0, February 1982.

UNIX System V Programming Guide, Release 2.0, April 1984.

UNIX System V Programmer's Guide, Release 3.0, 1986.

Functions

NAME
intro — introduction to UNIX System V Functions

DESCRIPTION

(BA_OS) — Base System Routines

Base System Routines provide programs access to and control over basic system resources such as memory, files and process execution. The Base System defines a basic set of UNIX System V components needed to support a minimal, stand-alone run-time environment for executable programs originally written in a high-level language, such as C. An example of such a system would be a system dedicated to a single vertically-integrated application-package for office automation. In this environment, the end-user would not interact directly with the traditional UNIX System V shell and commands, and the Base System excludes end-user utilities (commands). Executable software designed for maximum portability should use Base Library Routines instead of any Commands and Utilities; thus, programs should use the *function* chown [see CHOWN(BA_OS)] to change the owner of a file instead of the *command* chown [see CHOWN(AU_CMD)]. This does not mean that programs using the Base System alone cannot execute other programs; using the function system, one program can execute another program [see SYSTEM(BA_OS)].

Computer systems supporting only components of the Base System need not provide the source-code libraries themselves. The Base System supports only the *execution* of programs; the Software Development Extension supports the *compilation* of those programs. A computer system that supports only the Base System provides only a run-time environment; it is assumed that software targeted to *execute* on such a system would be *compiled* on a computer system that supports the Software Development Extension.

The table on the following page shows the Base System Routines in three (3) groupings to reflect recommended usage by programs:

- The first set of functions (from abort to wait) should meet the needs of most programs.

- The second set of functions (from close to write) should be used by programs only when some special need requires it. For example, when possible, programs should use the function system rather than the functions fork and exec because it is easier to use and has more functionality. The corresponding Standard Input/Output, "*stdio*" routines [see VOCAB(BA_DEF)], should be used instead of the system calls close, creat, lseek, open, read and write (e.g., the *stdio* routine fopen should be used rather than the system call open).

- The third set of functions (_exit and sync), although defined as part of the basic set of UNIX System V components, should *not* be used by programs, but are used by other Base System components.

The Base System excludes some system service (OS) components; thus, programs using any of those require an *extended* environment [see (KE_OS) — Kernel Extension Routines].

The components marked with † first appeared in UNIX System V Release 2.0, and those marked with †† appeared in UNIX System V Release 3.0.

TABLE (BA_OS) — Base System Routines

abort	ABORT(BA_OS)	lockf	LOCKF(BA_OS)†
access	ACCESS(BA_OS)	mallinfo	MALLOC(BA_OS)†
alarm	ALARM(BA_OS)	malloc	MALLOC(BA_OS)
calloc	MALLOC(BA_OS)	mallopt	MALLOC(BA_OS)†
chdir	CHDIR(BA_OS)	mkdir	MKDIR(BA_OS)††
chmod	CHMOD(BA_OS)	mknod	MKNOD(BA_OS)
chown	CHOWN(BA_OS)	opendir	DIRECTORY(BA_OS)††
clearerr	FERROR(BA_OS)	pause	PAUSE(BA_OS)
closedir	DIRECTORY(BA_OS††	pclose	POPEN(BA_OS)
dup2	DUP2(BA_OS)††	pipe	PIPE(BA_OS)
dup	DUP(BA_OS)	popen	POPEN(BA_OS)
exit	EXIT(BA_OS)	readdir	DIRECTORY(BA_OS)††
fclose	FCLOSE(BA_OS)	realloc	MALLOC(BA_OS)
fcntl	FCNTL(BA_OS)	rewind	FSEEK(BA_OS)
fdopen	FOPEN(BA_OS)	rewinddir	DIRECTORY(BA_OS)††
feof	FERROR(BA_OS)	rmdir	RMDIR(BA_OS)††
ferror	FERROR(BA_OS)	setgid	SETGID(BA_OS)
fflush	FCLOSE(BA_OS)	setpgrp	SETPGRP(BA_OS)
fileno	FERROR(BA_OS)	setuid	SETUID(BA_OS)
fopen	FOPEN(BA_OS)	sighold	SIGSET(BA_OS)††
fread	FREAD(BA_OS)	sigignore	SIGSET(BA_OS)††
free	MALLOC(BA_OS)	signal	SIGNAL(BA_OS)
freopen	FOPEN(BA_OS)	sigrelse	SIGSET(BA_OS)††
fseek	FSEEK(BA_OS)	sigset	SIGSET(BA_OS)††
fstat	STAT(BA_OS)	sleep	SLEEP(BA_OS)
ftell	FSEEK(BA_OS)	stat	STAT(BA_OS)
fwrite	FWRITE(BA_OS)	stime	STIME(BA_OS)
getcwd	GETCWD(BA_OS)	system	SYSTEM(BA_OS)
getegid	GETGID(BA_OS)	time	TIME(BA_OS)
geteuid	GETUID(BA_OS)	times	TIMES(BA_OS)
getgid	GETGID(BA_OS)	ulimit	ULIMIT(BA_OS)
getpgrp	GETPID(BA_OS)	umask	UMASK(BA_OS)
getpid	GETPID(BA_OS)	uname	UNAME(BA_OS)
getppid	GETPID(BA_OS)	unlink	UNLINK(BA_OS)
getuid	GETUID(BA_OS)	ustat	USTAT(BA_OS)
ioctl	IOCTL(BA_OS)	utime	UTIME(BA_OS)
kill	KILL(BA_OS)	wait	WAIT(BA_OS)
link	LINK(BA_OS)		
close	CLOSE(BA_OS)	fork	FORK(BA_OS)
creat	CREAT(BA_OS)	lseek	LSEEK(BA_OS)
execl	EXEC(BA_OS)	mount	MOUNT(BA_OS)
execle	EXEC(BA_OS)	open	OPEN(BA_OS)
execlp	EXEC(BA_OS)	read	READ(BA_OS)
execv	EXEC(BA_OS)	umount	UMOUNT(BA_OS)
execve	EXEC(BA_OS)	write	WRITE(BA_OS)
execvp	EXEC(BA_OS)		
_exit	EXIT(BA_OS)	sync	SYNC(BA_OS)

(KE_OS) — Kernel Extension Routines

Kernel Extension Routines define operating system components that support process-accounting tools, software-development tools and programs requiring more sophisticated inter-process communication than Base System Routines provides. While the Base System supports a minimal run-time environment for executable software, the Kernel Extension provides additional operating system services which many applications can do without but which some applications must have. Programs using any of these components need the target run-time environment to support the Kernel Extension, and the Kernel Extension depends on the Base System.

In the following table, the components marked with # are optional and appear only on machines with the appropriate hardware.

TABLE (KE_OS) — Kernel Extension Routines

acct	ACCT(KE_OS)	ptrace	PTRACE(KE_OS)
chroot	CHROOT(KE_OS)	semctl	SEMCTL(KE_OS)
msgctl	MSGCTL(KE_OS)	semget	SEMGET(KE_OS)
msgget	MSGGET(KE_OS)	semop	SEMOP(KE_OS)
msgrcv	MSGRCV(KE_OS)	shmctl	SHMCTL(KE_OS)#
msgsnd	MSGSND(KE_OS)	shmget	SHMGET(KE_OS)#
nice	NICE(KE_OS)	shmat	SHMOP(KE_OS)#
plock	PLOCK(KE_OS)	shmdt	SHMOP(KE_OS)#
profil	PROFIL(KE_OS)		

(NS_OS) — Network Services Routines

The Network Services Routines of the Network Services Extension define the interfaces for directly accessing I/O processing-modules implemented in the kernel using the STREAMS I/O framework. STREAMS I/O provides a uniform mechanism for implementing network services in the kernel by defining standard programming interfaces for device-drivers and protocol-modules. STREAMS I/O and the Network Services Routines first appeared in UNIX System V Release 3.0 and depend on the Base System Routines.

TABLE (NS_OS) — Network Services Routines

getmsg	GETMSG(NS_OS)	poll	POLL(NS_OS)	putmsg	PUTMSG(NS_OS)

(BA_LIB) — Base Library Routines

Base Library Routines define general-purpose library routines that perform a wide range of useful functions including:

- standard I/O routines.
- string and character-handling routines.
- sorting and searching routines.
- mathematical functions.

All the components in the following table, except those marked with † are in both UNIX System V Release 1.0 and UNIX System V Release 2.0. Those marked with * are Level-2 in the *System V Interface Definition*; those marked with # are optional.

TABLE (BA_LIB) — Base Library Routines

Standard I/O Routines			
ctermid	CTERMID(BA_LIB)	puts	PUTS(BA_LIB)
fgetc	GETC(BA_LIB)	putw	PUTC(BA_LIB)
fgets	GETS(BA_LIB)	scanf	SCANF(BA_LIB)
fprintf	PRINTF(BA_LIB)	setbuf	SETBUF(BA_LIB)
fputc	PUTC(BA_LIB)	setvbuf	SETVBUF(BA_LIB)†
fputs	PUTS(BA_LIB)	sprintf	PRINTF(BA_LIB)
fscanf	SCANF(BA_LIB)	sscanf	SCANF(BA_LIB)
getc	GETC(BA_LIB)	tempnam	TMPNAM(BA_LIB)
getchar	GETC(BA_LIB)	tmpfile	TMPFILE(BA_LIB)
gets	GETS(BA_LIB)	tmpnam	TMPNAM(BA_LIB)
getw	GETC(BA_LIB)	ttyname	TTYNAME(BA_LIB)
isatty	TTYNAME(BA_LIB)	ungetc	UNGETC(BA_LIB)
perror	PERROR(BA_LIB)*	vfprintf	VPRINTF(BA_LIB)†
printf	PRINTF(BA_LIB)	vprintf	VPRINTF(BA_LIB)†
putc	PUTC(BA_LIB)	vsprintf	VPRINTF(BA_LIB)†
putchar	PUTC(BA_LIB)		

String and Character Handling Routines			
_toupper	CONV(BA_LIB)	memchr	MEMORY(BA_LIB)
_tolower	CONV(BA_LIB)	memcmp	MEMORY(BA_LIB)
advance	REGEXP(BA_LIB)	memcpy	MEMORY(BA_LIB)
asctime	CTIME(BA_LIB)	memset	MEMORY(BA_LIB)
atof	STRTOD(BA_LIB)	setkey	CRYPT(BA_LIB)#
atoi	STRTOL(BA_LIB)	step	REGEXP(BA_LIB)
atol	STRTOL(BA_LIB)	strcat	STRING(BA_LIB)
compile	REGEXP(BA_LIB)	strchr	STRING(BA_LIB)
crypt	CRYPT(BA_LIB)#	strcmp	STRING(BA_LIB)
ctime	CTIME(BA_LIB)	strcpy	STRING(BA_LIB)
encrypt	CRYPT(BA_LIB)#	strcspn	STRING(BA_LIB)
gmtime	CTIME(BA_LIB)	strlen	STRING(BA_LIB)
isalnum	CTYPE(BA_LIB)	strncat	STRING(BA_LIB)
isalpha	CTYPE(BA_LIB)	strncmp	STRING(BA_LIB)
isascii	CTYPE(BA_LIB)	strncpy	STRING(BA_LIB)
iscntrl	CTYPE(BA_LIB)	strpbrk	STRING(BA_LIB)
isdigit	CTYPE(BA_LIB)	strrchr	STRING(BA_LIB)
isgraph	CTYPE(BA_LIB)	strspn	STRING(BA_LIB)
islower	CTYPE(BA_LIB)	strtod	STRTOD(BA_LIB)†
isprint	CTYPE(BA_LIB)	strtok	STRING(BA_LIB)
ispunct	CTYPE(BA_LIB)	strtol	STRTOL(BA_LIB)
isspace	CTYPE(BA_LIB)	swab	SWAB(BA_LIB)
isupper	CTYPE(BA_LIB)	toascii	CONV(BA_LIB)
isxdigit	CTYPE(BA_LIB)	tolower	CONV(BA_LIB)
localtime	CTIME(BA_LIB)	toupper	CONV(BA_LIB)
memccpy	MEMORY(BA_LIB)	tzset	CTIME(BA_LIB)

TABLE (BA_LIB) — Base Library Routines (cont'd)

Sorting and Searching Routines			
bsearch	BSEARCH(BA_LIB)	lsearch	LSEARCH(BA_LIB)
clock	CLOCK(BA_LIB)	mrand48	DRAND48(BA_LIB)
drand48	DRAND48(BA_LIB)	nrand48	DRAND48(BA_LIB)
erand48	DRAND48(BA_LIB)	putenv	PUTENV(BA_LIB)†
ftw	FTW(BA_LIB)	qsort	QSORT(BA_LIB)
getenv	GETENV(BA_LIB)	rand	RAND(BA_LIB)
getopt	GETOPT(BA_LIB)	seed48	DRAND48(BA_LIB)
gsignal	SSIGNAL(BA_LIB)*	setjmp	SETJMP(BA_LIB)
hcreate	HSEARCH(BA_LIB)	srand48	DRAND48(BA_LIB)
hdestroy	HSEARCH(BA_LIB)	srand	RAND(BA_LIB)
hsearch	HSEARCH(BA_LIB)	ssignal	SSIGNAL(BA_LIB)*
jrand48	DRAND48(BA_LIB)	tdelete	TSEARCH(BA_LIB)
lcong48	DRAND48(BA_LIB)	tfind	TSEARCH(BA_LIB)†
lfind	LSEARCH(BA_LIB)†	tsearch	TSEARCH(BA_LIB)
longjmp	SETJMP(BA_LIB)	twalk	TSEARCH(BA_LIB)
lrand48	DRAND48(BA_LIB)	mktemp	MKTEMP(BA_LIB)

Mathematical Functions			
abs	ABS(BA_LIB)	j0	BESSEL(BA_LIB)
acos	TRIG(BA_LIB)	j1	BESSEL(BA_LIB)
asin	TRIG(BA_LIB)	jn	BESSEL(BA_LIB)
atan2	TRIG(BA_LIB)	ldexp	FREXP(BA_LIB)
atan	TRIG(BA_LIB)	log10	EXP(BA_LIB)
ceil	FLOOR(BA_LIB)	log	EXP(BA_LIB)
cos	TRIG(BA_LIB)	matherr	MATHERR(BA_LIB)
cosh	SINH(BA_LIB)	modf	FREXP(BA_LIB)
erf	ERF(BA_LIB)	pow	EXP(BA_LIB)
erfc	ERF(BA_LIB)	sin	TRIG(BA_LIB)
exp	EXP(BA_LIB)	sinh	SINH(BA_LIB)
fabs	FLOOR(BA_LIB)	sqrt	EXP(BA_LIB)
floor	FLOOR(BA_LIB)	tan	TRIG(BA_LIB)
fmod	FLOOR(BA_LIB)	tanh	SINH(BA_LIB)
frexp	FREXP(BA_LIB)	y0	BESSEL(BA_LIB)
gamma	GAMMA(BA_LIB)	y1	BESSEL(BA_LIB)
hypot	HYPOT(BA_LIB)	yn	BESSEL.(BA_LIB)

(SD_LIB) — Software Development Library

The Software Development Library defines facilities for compiling and
maintaining C language software. To satisfy the Software Development
Library requires supporting compilation of programs using any Base System
Routines, Kernel Extension Routines or Base Library Routines listed above.

The standard C library is automatically included in the Software Development
Library (that is, searched to resolve undefined external references). To
include other libraries requires specific loader options on the C compiler cc
command line. For example, the mathematical library (**Mathematical
Functions** in Base Library Routines) is searched by using the option -lm on
the command line:

```
cc file.c -lm
```

Notes on other libraries:

- The `lex` library (`cc -ll`) is needed to compile programs generated by `lex` [see LEX(SD_CMD)].

- The object file library (`cc -lld`) contains routines used to manipulate object files. The only such routines the Software Development Library needs are `sputl` and `sgetl` [see SPUTL(SD_LIB)].

- The `yacc` library (`cc -ly`) supports `yacc` [see YACC(SD_CMD)].

TABLE (SD_LIB) — Software Development Library

a641	A64L(SD_LIB)	getutent	GETUT(SD_LIB)
assert	ASSERT(SD_LIB)	getutid	GETUT(SD_LIB)
endgrent	GETGRENT(SD_LIB)	getutline	GETUT(SD_LIB)
endpwent	GETPWENT(SD_LIB)	l64a	A64L(SD_LIB)
endutent	GETUT(SD_LIB)	MARK	MARK(SD_LIB)
fgetgrent	GETGRENT(SD_LIB)	monitor	MONITOR(SD_LIB)
fgetpwent	GETPWENT(SD_LIB)	nlist	NLIST(SD_LIB)
getgrent	GETGRENT(SD_LIB)	putpwent	PUTPWENT(SD_LIB)
getgrgid	GETGRENT(SD_LIB)	pututline	GETUT(SD_LIB)
getgrnam	GETGRENT(SD_LIB)	setgrent	GETGRENT(SD_LIB)
getlogin	GETLOGIN(SD_LIB)	setpwent	GETPWENT(SD_LIB)
getpass	GETPASS(SD_LIB)	setutent	GETUT(SD_LIB)
getpwent	GETPWENT(SD_LIB)	sgetl	SPUTL(SD_LIB)
getpwnam	GETPWENT(SD_LIB)	sputl	SPUTL(SD_LIB)
getpwuid	GETPWENT(SD_LIB)	utmpname	GETUT(SD_LIB)

(NS_LIB) — Network Services Library

The Network Services Library defines a protocol-independent interface to networking services based on layers of the Open Systems Interconnection (OSI) Reference Model. [1,2] The Network Services Library provides functions for both connection-mode and connectionless-mode transport-services of the OSI Transport Layer Service Definition. [3] The Network Services Extension will include interfaces to other layers of the OSI Reference Model when they are defined.

TABLE (NS_LIB) — Network Services Library

t_accept	T_ACCEPT(NS_LIB)	t_rcv	T_RCV(NS_LIB)
t_alloc	T_ALLOC(NS_LIB)	t_rcvconnect	T_RCVCON(NS_LIB)
t_bind	T_BIND(NS_LIB)	t_rcvdis	T_RCVDIS(NS_LIB)
t_close	T_CLOSE(NS_LIB)	t_rcvrel	T_RCVREL(NS_LIB)
t_connect	T_CONNECT(NS_LIB)	t_rcvudata	T_RCVUDATA(NS_LIB)
t_error	T_ERROR(NS_LIB)	t_rcvuderr	T_RCVUDERR(NS_LIB)
t_free	T_FREE(NS_LIB)	t_snd	T_SND(NS_LIB)
t_getinfo	T_GETINFO(NS_LIB)	t_snddis	T_SNDDIS(NS_LIB)
t_getstate	T_GETSTATE(NS_LIB)	t_sndrel	T_SNDREL(NS_LIB)
t_listen	T_LISTEN(NS_LIB)	t_sndudata	T_SNDUDATA(NS_LIB)
t_look	T_LOOK(NS_LIB)	t_sync	T_SYNC(NS_LIB)
t_open	T_OPEN(NS_LIB)	t_unbind	T_UNBIND(NS_LIB)
t_optmgmt	T_OPTMGMT(NS_LIB)		

The Network Services Library depends on the Base System Routines, Network Services Routines and Base Library Routines.

SEE ALSO

1. IS 7498, "Information Processing Systems — Open Systems Interconnection — Basic Reference Model", 1983.

2. CCITT Recommendation X.200, "Reference Model of Open Systems Interconnection for CCITT Applications", 1984.

3. IS 8072, "Information Processing Systems — Open Systems Interconnection — Transport Service Definition", 1984.

NAME

a64l, l64a — convert between long integer and base-64 ASCII string

SYNOPSIS

```
long  a64l(s)
char  *s;

char  *l64a(l)
long  l;
```

DESCRIPTION

These routines are used to maintain numbers stored in *base-64* ASCII characters. In this notation, up to six characters can represent a `long` integer; with each character being a radix-64 digit.

The characters used to represent radix-64 digits are . for 0, / for 1, 0 through 9 for 2 through 11, A through Z for 12 through 37, and a through z for 38 through 63.

The routine a64l takes a pointer to a null-terminated base-64 representation and returns a corresponding `long` value. If the string pointed to by s contains more than six characters, a64l uses only the first six.

The routine l64a takes a `long` argument and returns a pointer to the corresponding base-64 representation. If the argument is 0, l64a returns a pointer to a null-string.

USAGE

The value returned by l64a may be a pointer into a static buffer, which would therefore be overwritten by each call.

NAME

abort — generate an abnormal process termination

SYNOPSIS

```
int abort( )
```

DESCRIPTION

The function abort first closes all open files if possible, then sends the signal SIGABRT to the process. This invokes abnormal process termination routines, such as a core dump, which are implementation dependent.

USAGE

The signal sent by abort, SIGABRT, should not be caught or ignored by programs.

SEE ALSO

EXIT(BA_OS), SIGNAL(BA_OS), SIGSET(BA_OS).

NAME

abs — return integer absolute value

SYNOPSIS

```
int abs(i)
int i;
```

DESCRIPTION

The function abs returns the absolute value of its integer operand.

USAGE

In two-complement representation, the absolute value of the negative integer with largest magnitude {INT_MIN} is undefined. Some implementations may catch this as an error but others may ignore it.

SEE ALSO

FLOOR(BA_LIB).

NAME
access — determine accessibility of a file

SYNOPSIS
```
#include <unistd.h>

int access(path, amode)
char *path;
int amode;
```

DESCRIPTION
The function access checks the file named by the path-name pointed to by path either for existence or for accessibility according to the bit-pattern contained in amode. In either case, access uses the real-user-ID instead of the effective-user-ID and the real-group-ID or equivalent instead of the effective-group-ID. The <unistd.h> header file defines symbolic constants for amode as follows:

F_OK   test for existence of file.
R_OK   test for *read* permission.
W_OK   test for *write* permission.
X_OK   test for *execute (search)* permission.

Either amode equals F_OK or a logical-OR of R_OK, W_OK and X_OK.

When checking for accessibility, the owner of a file has permission checked against the *owner* read, write and execute mode-bits. Members of the file's group other than the owner have permissions checked against the *group* mode-bits, and all others have permissions checked against the *other* mode-bits.

RETURN VALUE
If the requested access is permitted, access returns 0; otherwise, it returns −1 and errno indicates the error.

ERRORS
The function access fails and errno equals:

EACCES   if a component of the path-prefix denies search permission, or if the permission-bits of the file-mode forbid the requested access.

EINVAL   if amode is invalid.

ENOENT   if the named file does not exist.

ENOENT   if the path-name is longer than {PATH_MAX} characters.

ENOTDIR   if a component of the path-prefix is not a directory.

EROFS   if write access is requested for a file on a read-only file-system.

ETXTBSY   if write access is requested for a pure procedure (shared text) file being executed.

SEE ALSO
CHMOD(BA_OS), STAT(BA_OS).

NAME

acct — enable or disable process accounting

SYNOPSIS

```
int acct(path)
char *path;
```

DESCRIPTION

The function acct enables or disables the system-process accounting-routine.
For each process that terminates, acct, if enabled, writes an accounting-
record on an accounting-file. One of two things can cause termination:

1. a call to the EXIT(BA_OS) routine, or
2. a signal [see SIGNAL(BA_OS)].

The effective-user-ID of the calling-process must be super-user to use acct.

The argument path points to a path-name naming the accounting-file. If no
errors occur during the call, the accounting routine is enabled if path is
non-zero and is disabled if path is zero.

The format of an accounting-file produced as a result of calling acct has
records in the format defined by the structure acct in <sys/acct.h>
which defines the following data-type:

```
comp_t /* floating point - 13-bit fraction, */
       /*                  3-bit exponent */
```

and defines the following members in the structure acct:

```
char    ac_flag;      /* accounting flag */
char    ac_stat;      /* exit status */
ushort  ac_uid;       /* accounting user-ID */
ushort  ac_gid;       /* accounting group-ID */
dev_t   ac_tty;       /* control typewriter */
time_t  ac_btime;     /* beginning time */
comp_t  ac_utime;     /* user-time in CLKTCKs */
comp_t  ac_stime;     /* system-time in CLKTCKs */
comp_t  ac_etime;     /* elapsed-time in CLKTCKs */
comp_t  ac_mem;       /* memory usage */
comp_t  ac_io;        /* chars transferred */
comp_t  ac_rw;        /* blocks read or written */
char    ac_comm[8];   /* command name */
```

and defines the following symbolic names:

```
AFORK  /* has executed fork, but no exec */
ASU    /* used super-user privileges */
ACCTF  /* record type: 00 = acct */
```

The AFORK flag is set in ac_flag when the FORK(BA_OS) routine is
executed and reset when an EXEC(BA_OS) routine is executed. The ac_comm
field is inherited from the parent-process when a child-process is created with
the FORK(BA_OS) routine and is reset when the EXEC(BA_OS) routine is
executed. The variable ac_mem is a cumulative record of memory usage and
is incremented each time the system charges the process with a clock tick.

RETURN VALUE

On success, `acct` returns 0; on failure, it returns -1 and `errno` indicates the error.

ERRORS

The function `acct` fails and `errno` equals:

`EPERM`	if the effective-user-ID of the calling-process is not super-user.
`EBUSY`	if an attempt is being made to enable accounting when it is already enabled.
`ENOTDIR`	if a component of the path-prefix is not a directory.
`ENOENT`	if one or more components of the accounting-file path-name do not exist.
`EACCES`	if the file named by `path` is not an ordinary-file.
`EROFS`	if the file named by `path` resides on a read-only file-system.

SEE ALSO

EXIT(BA_OS), SIGNAL(BA_OS).

NAME

alarm — set a process alarm clock

SYNOPSIS

```
unsigned alarm(sec)
unsigned sec;
```

DESCRIPTION

The function alarm instructs the alarm clock of the calling-process to send the signal SIGALRM to the calling-process after the number of real time seconds specified by sec have elapsed [see SIGNAL(BA_OS)].

Alarm requests are not stacked; successive calls reset the alarm clock of the calling-process.

If sec is 0, any previously made alarm request is canceled.

The FORK(BA_OS) routine sets the alarm clock of a new process to 0. A process created by the EXEC(BA_OS) family of routines inherits the time left on the old process's alarm clock.

RETURN VALUE

On success, alarm returns the amount of time previously remaining in the alarm clock of the calling-process.

SEE ALSO

EXEC(BA_OS), FORK(BA_OS), PAUSE(BA_OS), SIGNAL(BA_OS).

NAME

    `assert` — verify program assertion

SYNOPSIS

    `#include <assert.h>`

    `void assert(expression)`
    `int expression;`

DESCRIPTION

    The macro `assert` is useful for putting diagnostics into programs. When it is executed, if `expression` is false (zero), `assert` prints:

        `assertion failed: expression, file` *xyz*`, line` *nnn*

    on the standard error output and aborts. In the error message, *xyz* is the name of the source file and *nnn* the source line number of the `assert` statement.

SEE ALSO

    ABORT(BA_OS).

USAGE

    Compiling with the pre-processor option `-DNDEBUG` or with the pre-processor control statement `#define NDEBUG` ahead of the `#include <assert.h>` statement will stop assertions from being compiled into the program.

NAME

j0, j1, jn, y0, y1, yn — Bessel functions

SYNOPSIS

```
#include <math.h>

double j0(x)
double x;

double j1(x)
double x;

double jn(n, x)
int n;
double x;

double y0(x)
double x;

double y1(x)
double x;

double yn(n, x)
int n;
double x;
```

DESCRIPTION

The functions j0 and j1 return Bessel functions of x of the 1st kind of orders *0* and *1* respectively. The function jn returns the Bessel function of x of the 1st kind of order n.

The functions y0 and y1 return Bessel functions of x of the 2nd kind of orders *0* and *1* respectively. The function yn returns the Bessel function of x of the 2nd kind of order n. For the functions y0, y1 and yn, the argument x must be positive.

RETURN VALUE

Non-positive arguments cause y0, y1 and yn to return the value −HUGE and to set errno to EDOM. In addition, a message for a DOMAIN error is printed on the standard error output.

Arguments too large in magnitude cause the functions j0, j1, y0 and y1 to return zero and to set errno to ERANGE. In addition, a message for a TLOSS error is printed on the standard error output [see MATHERR(BA_LIB)].

USAGE

The MATHERR(BA_LIB) routine can change these error-handling procedures.

SEE ALSO

MATHERR(BA_LIB).

NAME

bsearch — binary search on a sorted table

SYNOPSIS

```
char *bsearch(key, base, nel, width,  compar)
char *key;
char *base;
unsigned nel, width;
int (*compar)();
```

DESCRIPTION

The function bsearch is a binary search routine. It returns a pointer into a table indicating where a datum may be found. The table must be previously sorted in increasing order according to a user-provided comparison function, compar [see QSORT(BA_LIB)].

The argument key points to a datum instance to be sought in the table.

The argument base points to the element at the base of the table.

The argument nel is the number of elements in the table.

The argument width is the size of an element in bytes.

The argument compar is the name of the comparison function, which is called with two arguments of type char that point to the elements being compared. The compar function must return an integer less than, equal to or greater than zero, as the first argument is to be considered less than, equal to or greater than the second.

RETURN VALUE

A NULL pointer is returned if the key cannot be found in the table.

USAGE

The pointers to the key and the element at the base of the table, key and base, should be of type pointer-to-element and cast to type pointer-to-character.

The comparison function need not compare every byte, so arbitrary data may be contained in the elements in addition to the values being compared.

Although declared as type pointer-to-character, the value returned should be cast into type pointer-to-element.

EXAMPLES

The following example searches a table containing pointers to nodes consisting of a string and its length. The table is ordered alphabetically on the string in the node pointed to by each entry.

This code fragment reads in strings; it either finds the corresponding node and prints out the string and its length or it prints an error message.

```
#include <stdio.h>
#include <search.h>

#define TABSIZE 1000

struct node {                       /* these are in the table */
    char *string;
    int length;
};
struct node table[TABSIZE]; /* table to be searched */
    . . .
{
    struct node *node_ptr, node;
    int node_compare( );        /* routine to compare 2 nodes */
    char str_space[20];         /* space to read string into */
    . . .
    node.string = str_space;
    while (scanf("%s", node.string) != EOF) {
        node_ptr = (struct node *)bsearch((char *)(&node),
            (char *)table, TABSIZE,
            sizeof(struct node), node_compare);
        if (node_ptr != NULL) {
            (void)printf("string = %20s, length = %d\n",
                node_ptr->string, node_ptr->length);
        } else {
            (void) printf("not found: %s\n", node.string);
        }
    }
}
/*
 * This routine compares two nodes based on an
 * alphabetical ordering of the string field.
 */
int node_compare(node1, node2)
    struct node *node1, *node2;
{
    return strcmp(node1->string, node2->string);
}
```

SEE ALSO

HSEARCH(BA_LIB), LSEARCH(BA_LIB), QSORT(BA_LIB), TSEARCH(BA_LIB).

NAME

chdir — change working directory

SYNOPSIS

```
int chdir(path)
char *path;
```

DESCRIPTION

The function chdir causes the named directory to become the current working directory and the starting point for path-searches for path-names not beginning with /.

The argument path points to the path-name of a directory.

RETURN VALUE

On success, chdir returns 0; on failure, it returns −1, it does *not* change the current-working-directory, and errno indicates the error.

ERRORS

The function chdir fails and errno equals:

ENOTDIR   if a component of the path-name is not a directory.

ENOENT   if the named directory does not exist.

EACCES   if any component of the path-name denies search permission.

NAME

chmod — change mode of file

SYNOPSIS

```
#include <sys/types.h>
#include <sys/stat.h>

int chmod(path, mode)
char *path;
int mode;
```

DESCRIPTION

The function `chmod` sets the access-permission-bits of the mode of the named file according to the bit-pattern contained in `mode`.

The argument `path` points to a path-name naming a file.

The `<sys/stat.h>` header file defines symbolic constants for the access-permission-bits used to construct `mode`. The value of `mode` should be the logical-OR of the values of the desired permissions:

S_ISUID	Set user-ID on execution.
S_ISGID	Set group-ID on execution.
S_ISVTX	Reserved.
S_IRUSR	Read by owner.
S_IWUSR	Write by owner.
S_IXUSR	Execute (search) by owner.
S_IRGRP	Read by group.
S_IWGRP	Write by group.
S_IXGRP	Execute (search) by group.
S_IROTH	Read by others (i.e., anyone else).
S_IWOTH	Write by others.
S_IXOTH	Execute (search) by others.
S_ENFMT	Record locking enforced.

The effective-user-ID of the process must match the owner of the file or be super-user to change the mode of a file.

If the effective-user-ID of the process is not super-user and the effective-group-ID of the process does not match the group-ID of the file, `chmod` clears the access-permission-bit S_ISGID (set group-ID on execution). This prevents an ordinary user from making itself an effective member of a group to which it does not belong. Similarly, CHOWN(BA_OS) clears the set-user-ID-bit and set-group-ID-bit when invoked by other than the super-user.

For ordinary-files, if the mode-bit S_ENFMT (record-locking enforced) is set and the mode-bit S_IXGRP (execute or search by group) is clear, enforced record-locking is enabled. This will affect future calls on the file for functions defined in OPEN(BA_OS), CREAT(BA_OS), READ(BA_OS) and WRITE(BA_OS).

RETURN VALUE

On success, chmod returns 0; on failure, it returns – 1, it does *not* change the file-mode, and errno indicates the error.

ERRORS

The function chmod fails and errno equals:

ENOTDIR   if a component of the path-prefix is not a directory.

ENOENT   if the named file does not exist.

ENOENT   if the path-name is longer than {PATH_MAX} characters.

EACCES   if a component of the path-prefix denies search permission.

EPERM   if the effective-user-ID does not match the owner of the file and the effective-user-ID is not super-user.

EROFS   if the named file resides on a read-only file-system.

SEE ALSO

CHOWN(BA_OS), MKNOD(BA_OS).

NAME

chown — change owner and group of a file

SYNOPSIS

```
int chown(path, owner, group)
char *path;
int owner, group;
```

DESCRIPTION

The function chown sets the owner-ID and group-ID of the named file to the numeric values contained in owner and group, respectively.

The argument path points to a path-name naming a file.

Only processes with effective-user-ID equal to the file-owner or super-user may change the ownership of a file.

If chown is invoked successfully by other than the super-user, it clears the set-user-ID and set-group-ID-bits of the file-mode, 04000 and 02000 respectively. (This prevents ordinary users from making themselves effectively other users or members of a group to which they don't belong.)

RETURN VALUE

On success, chown returns 0; on failure, it returns − 1, it does *not* change the owner and group of the named file, and errno indicates the error.

ERRORS

The function chown fails and errno equals:

ENOTDIR   if a component of the path-prefix is not a directory.

ENOENT   if the named file does not exist.

EACCES   if a component of the path-prefix denies search permission.

EPERM   if the effective-user-ID does not match the owner of the file and the effective-user-ID is not super-user.

EROFS   if the named file resides on a read-only file-system.

SEE ALSO

CHMOD(BA_OS).

NAME

chroot — change root directory

SYNOPSIS

```
int chroot(path)
char *path;
```

DESCRIPTION

The function chroot causes the named-directory to become the root-directory, the starting point for path searches for path-names beginning with the character /. The user's working directory is unaffected by chroot.

The argument path points to a path-name naming a directory.

The effective-user-ID of the process must be super-user to change the root directory.

The .. entry in the root-directory is interpreted to mean the root-directory itself. Thus, .. cannot be used to access files outside the sub-tree rooted at the root-directory.

RETURN VALUE

On success, chroot returns 0; on failure, it returns −1 and errno indicates the error.

ERRORS

The function chroot fails, it does *not* change the root-directory, and errno equals:

ENOTDIR　　if any component of the path-name is not a directory.

ENOENT　　if the named directory does not exist.

EPERM　　if the effective-user-ID is not super-user.

SEE ALSO

CHDIR(BA_OS).

NAME

`clock` — report CPU time used

SYNOPSIS

`long clock()`

DESCRIPTION

The function `clock` returns the amount of CPU time (in microseconds) used since the first call to `clock`. The time reported is the sum of the user and system times of the calling-process and its terminated child-processes for which it has executed the WAIT(BA_OS), PCLOSE(BA_OS) or SYSTEM(BA_OS) routine.

USAGE

The value returned by `clock` is defined in microseconds for compatibility with systems that have CPU clocks with much higher resolution.

SEE ALSO

TIMES(BA_OS), WAIT(BA_OS), POPEN(BA_OS), SYSTEM(BA_OS).

NAME

close — close a file-descriptor

SYNOPSIS

```
int close(fildes)
int fildes;
```

DESCRIPTION

The function close closes the file-descriptor indicated by fildes.

The argument fildes is an open file-descriptor [see VOCAB(BA_DEF)].

All outstanding record-locks on the file indicated by fildes that are owned by the calling-process are removed.

RETURN VALUE

On success, close returns 0; on failure, it returns −1 and errno indicates the error.

ERRORS

The function close fails and errno equals:

EBADF   if fildes is not a valid open file-descriptor.

USAGE

Normally, programs should use the *stdio* routines to open, close, read and write files. Thus, programs that use the FOPEN(BA_OS) *stdio* routine to open a file should use the corresponding FCLOSE(BA_OS) *stdio* routine instead of close.

The record-locking features are an update that followed UNIX System V Release 1.0 and UNIX System V Release 2.0.

SEE ALSO

CREAT(BA_OS), DUP(BA_OS), EXEC(BA_OS), FCNTL(BA_OS), OPEN(BA_OS), PIPE(BA_OS).

NAME

`toupper`, `tolower`, `_toupper`, `_tolower`, `toascii` — translate characters

SYNOPSIS

```
#include <ctype.h>

int toupper(c)
int c;

int tolower(c)
int c;

int _toupper(c)
int c;

int _tolower(c)
int c;

int toascii(c)
int c;
```

DESCRIPTION

The functions `toupper` and `tolower` have as domain the range of the GETC(BA_LIB) routine: the integers from -1 through 255. If the argument of `toupper` represents a lower-case letter, the result is the corresponding upper-case letter. If the argument of `tolower` represents an upper-case letter, the result is the corresponding lower-case letter. All other arguments in the domain are returned unchanged.

The macros `_toupper`, `_tolower`, and `_toascii` are defined by the `<ctype.h>` header file. The macros `_toupper` and `_tolower` accomplish the same thing as `toupper` and `tolower` but have restricted domains and are faster. The macro `_toupper` requires a lower-case letter as its argument; its result is the corresponding upper-case letter. The macro `_tolower` requires an upper-case letter as its argument; its result is the corresponding lower-case letter. Arguments outside the domain cause undefined results.

The macro `toascii` yields its argument with all bits turned off that are not part of a standard ASCII character; it is intended for compatibility with other systems.

SEE ALSO

CTYPE(BA_LIB), GETC(BA_LIB).

NAME

creat — create a new file or rewrite an existing one

SYNOPSIS

```
#include <sys/types.h>
#include <sys/stat.h>

int creat(path, mode)
char *path;
int mode;
```

DESCRIPTION

The function creat creates a new ordinary-file or prepares to rewrite an existing file named by the path-name pointed to by path.

If the file exists, the length is truncated to zero, the mode and owner are unchanged, and the file is open for writing [see O_WRONLY in OPEN(BA_OS)]. If the file does not exist, the file's owner-ID is set to the effective-user-ID of the process; the group-ID of the file is set to the effective-group-ID of the process; and the access-permission-bits [see CHMOD(BA_OS)] of the file-mode are set to the value of mode modified as follows:

> The file-mode-bits are AND-ed with the complement of the process's file-mode-creation-mask. Thus, creat clears each bit in the file-mode whose counterpart in the file-mode-creation-mask is set [see UMASK(BA_OS)].

If successful, creat returns the file-descriptor and the file is open for writing. A new file may be created with a mode that forbids writing, but creat leaves the file open for writing even if mode forbids writing.

The <sys/stat.h> header file defines symbolic constants for the access-permission-bits used to construct mode [see CHMOD(BA_OS)].

The call creat(path, mode) equals the following [see OPEN(BA_OS)]:

```
open(path, O_WRONLY | O_CREAT | O_TRUNC, mode)
```

This call sets the file-pointer to the beginning of the file, and sets the file-descriptor to remain open across calls to any EXEC(BA_OS) routine [see FCNTL(BA_OS)].

No process may have more than {OPEN_MAX} files open simultaneously.

RETURN VALUE

On success, creat returns the file-descriptor (a non-negative integer); on failure, it returns −1 and errno indicates the error.

ERRORS

The function creat fails and errno equals:

ENOTDIR   if a component of the path-prefix is not a directory.

ENOENT   if a component of the path-name should exist but does not.

ENOENT   if the path-name is longer than {PATH_MAX} characters.

EACCES   if a component of the path-prefix denies search permission.

EACCES	if the file does not exist and the directory in which to create the file forbids writing.
EACCES	if the file exists and write permission is denied.
EROFS	if the named file resides or would reside on a read-only file-system.
ETXTBSY	if the file is a pure procedure (shared text) file being executed.
EISDIR	if the named file is an existing directory.
EMFILE	if the calling-process already has {OPEN_MAX} file-descriptors open.
ENOSPC	if the directory to contain the file cannot be extended.
ENFILE	if the system file table is full.
EAGAIN	if the file exists with enforced record-locking enabled and there are record-locks on the file [see CHMOD(BA_OS)].

USAGE

Normally, programs should use the *stdio* routines to open, close, read and write files. In this case, the FOPEN(BA_OS) *stdio* routine should be used instead of `creat`.

SEE ALSO

CHMOD(BA_OS), CLOSE(BA_OS), DUP(BA_OS), FCNTL(BA_OS), LSEEK(BA_OS), OPEN(BA_OS), READ(BA_OS), UMASK(BA_OS), WRITE(BA_OS).

NAME
crypt, setkey, encrypt — generate string encoding

SYNOPSIS
```
char *crypt(key, salt)
char *key, *salt;

void setkey(key)
char *key;

void encrypt(block, edflag)
char *block;
int edflag;
```

DESCRIPTION
The function crypt is a string-encoding function.

The argument key is a string to be encoded. The argument salt is a two-character string chosen from the set [a-zA-Z0-9 .]; this string is used to perturb the encoding algorithm, after which the string that key points to is used as the key to repeatedly encode a constant string. The returned value points to the encoded string. The first two characters are the salt itself.

The functions setkey and encrypt provide (rather primitive) access to the encoding algorithm. The argument to the entry setkey is a character array of length 64 containing only the characters with numerical value 0 and 1. If this string is divided into groups of 8, the low-order bit in each group is ignored; this gives a 56-bit key. This is the key that will be used with the above mentioned algorithm to encode the string block with the function encrypt.

The argument to the entry encrypt is a character array of length 64 containing only the characters with numerical value 0 and 1. The argument array is modified in place to a similar array representing the bits of the argument after having been subjected to the encoding algorithm using the key set by setkey.

If the argument edflag is zero, the argument is encoded.

USAGE
The return value of the function crypt points to static data that are overwritten by each call.

NAME
ctermid — generate file-name for terminal

SYNOPSIS
```
#include <stdio.h>

char *ctermid(s)
char *s;
```

DESCRIPTION
The function ctermid generates the path-name of the controlling terminal for the current process and stores it in a string.

If the argument s is a NULL pointer, the string is stored in an internal static area which will be overwritten at the next call to ctermid. The address of the static area is returned. Otherwise, s is assumed to point to a character array of at least L_ctermid elements; the path name is placed in this array and the value of s is returned. The constant L_ctermid is defined by the <stdio.h> header file.

USAGE
The difference between the TTYNAME(BA_LIB) routine and the function ctermid is that the TTYNAME(BA_LIB) routine must be passed a file-descriptor and returns the name of the terminal associated with that file-descriptor, while the function ctermid returns a string (e.g., /dev/tty) that will refer to the terminal if used as a file-name. Thus the TTYNAME(BA_LIB) routine is useful only if the process already has at least one file open to a terminal.

SEE ALSO
TTYNAME(BA_LIB).

NAME

ctime, localtime, gmtime, asctime, tzset — convert date and time to string

SYNOPSIS

```
#include <sys/types.h>
#include <time.h>

char *ctime(clock)
time_t *clock;

struct tm *localtime(clock)
time_t *clock;

struct tm *gmtime(clock)
time_t *clock;

char *asctime(tm)
struct tm *tm;

extern long timezone;

extern int daylight;

extern char *tzname[2];

void tzset()
```

DESCRIPTION

The function ctime converts a value of type time_t, pointed to by clock, representing the time in seconds since 00:00:00 GMT 1 Jan. 1970 [see TIME(BA_OS)] and returns a pointer to a 26-character string in the following form:

```
Sun Sep 16 01:03:52 1973
```

All the fields have constant width.

The functions localtime and gmtime return pointers to the tm structure described below:

The function localtime corrects for the time-zone and possible Daylight Saving Time.

The function gmtime converts directly to Greenwich Mean Time (GMT), which is the time the system uses.

The function asctime converts a tm structure to a 26-character string, as shown in the above example, and returns a pointer to the string.

The external long variable timezone contains the difference, in seconds, between GMT and local standard time (in EST, timezone is $5*60*60$); the external variable daylight is non-zero only if the standard USA Daylight Saving Time conversion should be applied. The program compensates for the peculiarities of this conversion in 1974 and 1975; if necessary, a table for these years can be extended.

The `<time.h>` header file declares all the functions, the external variables and the `tm` structure.

The `tm` structure includes the following members:

```
int tm_sec;    /* number of seconds past */
               /* the minute (0-59) */
int tm_min;    /* number of minutes past */
               /* the hour (0-59) */
int tm_hour;   /* current hour (0-23) */
int tm_mday;   /* day of month (1-31) */
int tm_mon;    /* month of year (0-11) */
int tm_year;   /* current year -1900 */
int tm_wday;   /* day of week (Sunday=0) */
int tm_yday;   /* day of year (0-365) */
int tm_isdst;  /* Daylight Saving Time flag */
```

The value of `tm_isdst` is non-zero if Daylight Saving Time is in effect.

If an environment variable named `TZ` is present, `asctime` uses the contents of the variable to override the default time-zone. The value of `TZ` must be a three-letter time-zone name, followed by an optional minus sign (for zones east of Greenwich) and a series of digits representing the difference between local time and Greenwich Mean Time in hours; this is followed by an optional three-letter name for a daylight time-zone. For example, the setting for New Jersey would be `EST5EDT`. The effects of setting `TZ` are thus to change the values of the external variables `timezone` and `daylight`. In addition, the time-zone names contained in the external variable

```
char *tzname[2] = { "EST", "EDT" };
```

are set from the environment variable `TZ`. The function `tzset` sets these external variables from `TZ`; `tzset` is called by `asctime` and may also be called explicitly by the user.

USAGE
The return values point to static data that is overwritten by each call.

SEE ALSO
ENVVAR(BA_ENV), TIME(BA_OS), GETENV(BA_LIB).

CAVEATS
The number in `TZ` will be defined as an optional minus sign followed by two hour-digits and two minute-digits, hhmm, to represent fractional time-zones.

NAME

isalpha, isupper, islower, isdigit, isxdigit, isalnum,
isspace, ispunct, isprint, isgraph, iscntrl, isascii —
classify characters

SYNOPSIS

```
#include <ctype.h>

int isalpha(c)
int c;

int isupper(c)
int c;

int islower(c)
int c;

int isdigit(c)
int c;

int isxdigit(c)
int c;

int isalnum(c)
int c;

int isspace(c)
int c;

int ispunct(c)
int c;

int isprint(c)
int c;

int isgraph(c)
int c;

int iscntrl(c)
int c;

int isascii(c)
int c;
```

DESCRIPTION

These macros, which are defined by the <ctype.h> header file, classify
character-coded integer values. Each is a predicate returning non-zero for
true, zero for false. The function isascii is defined on all integer values;
the rest are defined only where isascii is true and on the single non-ASCII
value EOF, which is defined by the <stdio.h> header file and represents
end-of-file.

`isalpha(c)`	c is a letter.
`isupper(c)`	c is an upper-case letter.
`islower(c)`	c is a lower-case letter.
`isdigit(c)`	c is a digit [0-9].
`isxdigit(c)`	c is a hexadecimal digit [0-9], [A-F] or [a-f].
`isalnum(c)`	c is an alphanumeric (letter or digit).
`isspace(c)`	c is a space, tab, carriage-return, new-line, vertical-tab or form-feed.
`ispunct(c)`	c is a punctuation mark (neither control nor alphanumeric nor space).
`isprint(c)`	c is a printing character, ASCII code 040 (space) through 0176 (tilde).
`isgraph(c)`	c is a printing character, like `isprint` except false for space.
`iscntrl(c)`	c is a delete character (0177) or an ordinary control-character (less than 040).
`isascii(c)`	c is an ASCII character, code between 0 and 0177 inclusive.

RETURN VALUE

If the argument to any of these macros is not in the domain of the function, the result is undefined.

SEE ALSO

FOPEN(BA_OS), VOCAB(BA_DEF) [ASCII character set].

NAME

closedir, opendir, readdir, rewinddir — directory operations

SYNOPSIS

```
#include <sys/types.h>
#include <dirent.h>

int closedir(dirp)
DIR *dirp;

DIR *opendir(filename)
char *filename;

struct dirent *readdir(dirp)
DIR *dirp;

void rewinddir(dirp)
DIR *dirp;
```

DESCRIPTION

The function closedir closes the directory-descriptor indicated by the argument dirp and frees the DIR structure associated with the directory-descriptor.

The function opendir opens the directory named by the argument filename and returns a pointer to the DIR structure associated with the directory.

The function readdir returns a pointer to a directory structure dirent that contains the next non-empty directory entry in the directory specified by the argument dirp.

The <dirent.h> header file defines the structure dirent, which describes a directory entry. It includes the inode number (d_ino) and the filename (d_name), which is a null-terminated string of at most {NAME_MAX} characters:

```
long d_ino;     /* inode number of entry */
char d_name[1]; /* name of file */
```

The function rewinddir(dirp) resets the position of the directory pointer specified by the argument dirp to the beginning of the directory.

RETURN VALUE

The function opendir returns a NULL pointer if filename cannot be accessed, or if filename is not a directory, or if enough memory to hold a DIR structure or a buffer for the directory entries cannot be allocated and errno indicates the error.

On success, readdir returns a valid pointer. On reaching the end of the directory, readdir returns a NULL pointer. Otherwise, readdir returns a NULL pointer and errno indicates the error.

On success, closedir returns 0; on failure, it returns –1 and errno indicates the error.

ERRORS

The function `opendir` fails and `errno` equals:

ENOTDIR	if a component of the path-prefix is not a directory.
EACCES	if a component of the path-prefix denies search permission.
EACCES	if read permission is denied for the specified directory.
EMFILE	if the calling-process already has {OPEN_MAX} file-descriptors or directory-descriptors open
ENOENT	if the path-name is longer than {PATH_MAX} characters.

The function `readdir` fails and `errno` equals:

ENOENT	if the current directory-descriptor is not located at a valid entry.
EBADF	if `dirp` is not a valid open directory-descriptor.

The function `closedir` fails and `errno` equals:

EBADF	if `dirp` is not a valid open directory-descriptor.

USAGE

The functions `closedir`, `opendir`, `readdir` and `rewinddir` were added in UNIX System V Release 3.0.

EXAMPLES

The following sample code will search a directory for the entry *name*:

```
dirp = opendir(".");
while ((dp = readdir(dirp)) ! = NULL)
    if (strcmp(dp->d_name, name) == 0) {
        closedir(dirp);
        return(FOUND);
    }
closedir(dirp);
return(NOT_FOUND);
```

NAME

drand48, erand48, lrand48, nrand48, mrand48, jrand48, srand48, seed48, lcong48 — generate uniformly distributed pseudo-random numbers

SYNOPSIS

double drand48( )

double erand48(xsubi)
unsigned short xsubi[3];

long lrand48( )

long nrand48(xsubi)
unsigned short xsubi[3];

long mrand48( )

long jrand48(xsubi)
unsigned short xsubi[3];

void srand48(seedval)
long seedval;

unsigned short *seed48(seed16v)
unsigned short seed16v[3];

void lcong48(param)
unsigned short param[7];

DESCRIPTION

This family of functions generates pseudo-random numbers using the well-known linear congruential algorithm and 48-bit integer arithmetic.

Functions drand48 and erand48 return non-negative double-precision floating-point values uniformly distributed over the interval [0.0,1.0).

Functions lrand48 and nrand48 return non-negative long integers uniformly distributed over the interval $[0, 2^{31})$.

Functions mrand48 and jrand48 return signed long integers uniformly distributed over the interval $[-2^{31}, 2^{31})$.

Functions srand48, seed48 and lcong48 are initialization entry points, one of which should be called before calling drand48, lrand48 or mrand48. While not recommended, constant default initializer values are supplied automatically if drand48, lrand48 or mrand48 is called without first calling an initialization entry point. Functions erand48, nrand48 and jrand48 need *no* initialization entry point called first.

All the routines generate a sequence of 48-bit integer values, X_i, according to the linear congruential formula:

$$X_{n+1} = (aX_n + c)_{\bmod m} \quad n \geqslant 0$$

The parameter m = 2^{48}; hence 48-bit integer arithmetic is performed.

Unless lcong48 is called, the multiplier a and the addend c are:

$$a = 5DEECE66D_{16} = 273673163155_8$$
$$c = B_{16} = 13_8$$

The value returned by any of the functions drand48, erand48, lrand48, nrand48, mrand48 or jrand48 is computed by first generating the next 48-bit X_i in the sequence. Then the appropriate number of bits, according to the type of data item to be returned, are copied from the high-order (leftmost) bits of X_i and transformed into the returned value.

The functions drand48, lrand48 and mrand48 store the last 48-bit X_i generated in an internal buffer; that is why they must be initialized prior to being invoked. The functions erand48, nrand48 and jrand48 require the calling program to provide storage for the successive X_i values in the array specified as an argument when the functions are invoked. That is why these routines do not have to be initialized; the calling program merely has to place the desired initial value of X_i into the array and pass it as an argument. By using different arguments, functions erand48, nrand48 and jrand48 allow separate modules of a large program to generate several *independent* streams of pseudo-random numbers. In other words, the sequence of numbers in each stream will *not* depend upon how many times the routines have been called to generate numbers for the other streams.

The initializer function srand48 sets the high-order 32-bits of X_i to the {LONG_BIT} bits contained in its argument. The low-order 16-bits of X_i are set to the arbitrary value $330E_{16}$.

The initializer function seed48 sets the value of X_i to the 48-bit value specified in the argument array. In addition, the previous value of X_i is copied into a 48-bit internal buffer, used only by seed48, and a pointer to this buffer is the value returned by seed48.

The initialization function lcong48 allows the user to specify the initial X_i, the multiplier a and the addend c. Argument array elements param[0-2] specify X_i, param[3-5] specify the multiplier a, and param[6] specifies the 16-bit addend c. After lcong48 has been called, a subsequent call to either srand48 or seed48 will restore the *standard* multiplier and addend values, a and c, specified earlier.

USAGE

The pointer returned by seed48, which can just be ignored if not needed, is useful if a program is to be restarted from a given point at some future time. Use the pointer to get at and store the last X_i value and then use this value to reinitialize via seed48 when the program is restarted.

SEE ALSO

RAND(BA_LIB).

NAME

dup — duplicate an open file-descriptor

SYNOPSIS

```
int dup(fildes)
int fildes;
```

DESCRIPTION

The function dup returns a new file-descriptor having the following in common with the original:

Same open file (or pipe).

Same file-pointer (i.e., both file-descriptors share one file-pointer).

Same access-mode (read, write or read/write).

The argument fildes is an open file-descriptor [see VOCAB(BA_DEF)].

The new file-descriptor is set to remain open across calls to the EXEC(BA_OS) routines [see FCNTL(BA_OS)].

The file-descriptor returned is the lowest one available.

RETURN VALUE

On success, dup returns the file-descriptor (a non-negative integer); on failure, it returns − 1 and errno indicates the error.

ERRORS

The function dup fails and errno equals:

EBADF   if fildes is not a valid open file-descriptor.

EMFILE   if the calling-process already has {OPEN_MAX} file-descriptors open.

SEE ALSO

CREAT(BA_OS), CLOSE(BA_OS), EXEC(BA_OS), FCNTL(BA_OS), OPEN(BA_OS), PIPE(BA_OS).

NAME

dup2 — duplicate an open file-descriptor

SYNOPSIS

```
int dup2(fildes, fildes2)
int fildes, fildes2;
```

DESCRIPTION

The function dup2 duplicates an open file-descriptor.

The argument fildes is an open file-descriptor [see VOCAB(BA_DEF)].

The argument fildes2 is a non-negative integer less than {OPEN_MAX}.

The argument fildes2 is set to refer to the same file as the argument fildes. If fildes2 already refers to an open file, this file-descriptor is first closed.

RETURN VALUE

On success, dup2 returns the file-descriptor (a non-negative integer); on failure, it returns −1 and errno indicates the error.

ERRORS

The function dup2 fails and errno equals:

EBADF   if fildes is not a valid open file-descriptor.

EBADF   if fildes2 is negative, or it is greater than or equal to {OPEN_MAX}.

USAGE

The function dup2 was added in UNIX System V Release 3.0.

SEE ALSO

CREAT(BA_OS), CLOSE(BA_OS), DUP(BA_OS), EXEC(BA_OS), FCNTL(BA_OS), LOCKF(BA_OS), OPEN(BA_OS), PIPE(BA_OS).

NAME

erf, erfc − error function and complementary error function

SYNOPSIS

```
#include <math.h>

double erf(x)
double x;

double erfc(x)
double x;
```

DESCRIPTION

The function erf returns the error function of x, defined as follows:

$$\frac{2}{\sqrt{\pi}} \int_0^x e^{-t^2} \, dt$$

The function erfc returns 1.0-erf(x).

USAGE

The function erfc is provided because of the extreme loss of relative accuracy if erf(x) is called for large x and the result subtracted from 1.0.

SEE ALSO

EXP(BA_LIB).

NAME

execl, execv, execle, execve, execlp, execvp — execute a file

SYNOPSIS

```
int execl(path, arg0, arg1, ... argn, (char *)0)
char *path, *arg0, *arg1, ... *argn;

int execv(path, argv)
char *path, *argv[];

int execle(path, arg0, arg1, ... argn, (char *)0, envp)
char *path, *arg0, *arg1, ... *argn, *envp[];

int execve(path, argv, envp)
char *path, *argv[], *envp[];

int execlp(file, arg0, arg1, ... argn, (char *)0)
char *file, *arg0, *arg1, ... *argn;

int execvp(file, argv)
char *file, *argv[];
```

DESCRIPTION

All forms of the function `exec` transform the calling-process into a new process. The new process is constructed from an ordinary, executable file called the *new-process-file*. This file consists of a header, a text segment and a data segment. There can be no return from a successful `exec` because the calling-process image is overlaid by the new process image.

When a C program is executed, it is called as follows:

```
main(argc, argv, envp)
int argc;
char **argv, **envp;
```

where `argc` is the argument count, `argv` is an array of character pointers to the arguments themselves and `envp` is an array of character pointers to null-terminated strings that make up the environment for the new process.

The argument `argc` is conventionally at least one and the initial member of the array `argv` points to a string containing the name of the file.

The argument `path` points to a path-name that identifies the new-process-file. For `execlp` and `execvp`, the argument `file` points to the new-process-file; the path-prefix for which is obtained by searching the directories passed as the *environment* line PATH= [see ENVVAR(BA_ENV) and SYSTEM(BA_OS)].

The arguments `arg0`, `arg1`, ... `argn` are pointers to null-terminated character-strings, which make up the argument list available to the new process. By convention, at least `arg0` must be present and point to a string that is the same as `file` or `path` (or its last component).

The argument `argv` is an array of character pointers to null-terminated strings. These strings make up the argument list available to the new process. By convention, `argv[0]` must point to a string that is the same as `file` or `path` (or its last component), and `argv` ends with a null pointer.

The argument `envp` is an array of character pointers to null-terminated strings. These strings make up the environment for the new process, and `envp` ends with a null-pointer. For `execl` and `execv`, a pointer to the environment of the calling-process is made available in the global cell:

```
extern char **environ;
```

and is used to pass the environment of the calling-process to the new process.

The file-descriptors open in the calling-process remain open in the new process, except for those whose *close-on-exec* flag is set [see FCNTL(BA_OS)]. For those file-descriptors that remain open, the file-pointer is unchanged.

Signals set to the default action (`SIG_DFL`) in the calling-process will be set to the default action in the new process. Signals set to be ignored (`SIG_IGN`) by the calling-process will be ignored by the new process. Signals set to be held (`SIG_HOLD`) by the calling-process will be held by the new process. Signals set to be caught by the calling-process will be set to the default action in the new process [see SIGNAL(BA_OS) and SIGSET(BA_OS)].

If the set-user-ID-on-execution mode-bit of the new-process-file is set, the `exec` sets the effective-user-ID of the new process to the owner-ID of the new-process-file [see CHMOD(BA_OS)]. Similarly, if the set-group-ID mode-bit of the new-process-file is set, the effective-group-ID of the new process is set to the group-ID of the new-process-file. The real-user-ID and real-group-ID of the new process remain the same as those of the calling-process. The effective-user-ID and group-ID of the new process are saved for use by the SETUID(BA_OS) routine.

The new process also inherits at least the following attributes from the calling-process:

```
process-ID
parent-process-ID
process-group-ID
tty-group-ID [see EXIT(BA_OS), SIGNAL(BA_OS) and SIGSET(BA_OS)]
time left until an alarm clock signal [see ALARM(BA_OS)]
current-working-directory
root-directory
file-mode-creation-mask [see UMASK(BA_OS)]
file-size limit [see ULIMIT(BA_OS)]
utime, stime, cutime and cstime [see TIMES(BA_OS)]
record-locks [see FCNTL(BA_OS) and LOCKF(BA_OS)]
```

RETURN VALUE

If the `exec` returns to the calling-process, an error has occurred; the `exec` returns – 1 and `errno` indicates the error.

ERRORS

An `exec` returns to the calling-process and `errno` equals:

E2BIG   if the number of bytes in the new process image's argument list exceeds the system-imposed limit of {ARG_MAX} bytes.

EACCES   if a directory in the new-process-file's path-prefix denies search permission, or if the new-process-file is not an ordinary-file [see MKNOD(BA_OS)], or if the new-process-file's mode denies execution permission.

EFAULT   if the new-process-file image is corrupted.

ELIBACC   Reserved.

ELIBEXEC   Reserved.

ENOENT   if one or more components of the path-name of the new-process-file do not exist.

ENOENT   if the path-name is longer than {PATH_MAX} characters.

ENOEXEC   if the exec is not an execlp or execvp, and the new-process-file has the appropriate access permission but is not a valid executable object.

ENOMEM   if the new process image requires more memory than is allowed by the hardware or system-imposed maximum.

ENOTDIR   if a component of the path-prefix of the new-process-file is not a directory.

ETXTBSY   if the new-process-file is a pure procedure (shared text) file that is currently open for writing by some process.

USAGE

Two interfaces for these functions are available. The list (l) versions: execl, execle and execlp are useful when a known file with known arguments is being called. The arguments are the character-strings that are the file-name and the arguments. The variable (v) versions: execv, execve and execvp are useful when the number of arguments is unknown in advance. The arguments are a file-name and a vector of strings containing the arguments.

If possible, programs should use the SYSTEM(BA_OS) routine, which is easier to use and has more functionality than the FORK(BA_OS) and EXEC(BA_OS) routines.

SEE ALSO

ALARM(BA_OS), EXIT(BA_OS), FORK(BA_OS), SIGNAL(BA_OS), SIGSET(BA_OS), TIMES(BA_OS), ULIMIT(BA_OS), UMASK(BA_OS).

NAME

exit, _exit — terminate process

SYNOPSIS

```
void exit(status)
int status;

void _exit(status)
int status;
```

DESCRIPTION

The function `exit` may cause cleanup actions before the process exits [see FCLOSE(BA_OS)]. The function `_exit` does not.

The functions `exit` and `_exit` terminate the calling-process with the following consequences:

All of the file-descriptors open in the calling-process are closed.

If the parent-process of the calling-process is executing a WAIT(BA_OS) routine, it is notified of the calling-process's termination and the low-order eight bits (i.e., bits `0377`) of `status` are made available to it. If the parent is not waiting, the child's status will be made available to it when the parent subsequently executes the WAIT(BA_OS) routine.

If the parent-process of the calling-process is not executing a WAIT(BA_OS) routine, the calling-process is transformed into a zombie-process. A zombie-process is an inactive process that has no process space allocated to it, and it will be deleted at some later time when its parent executes the WAIT(BA_OS) routine.

Terminating a process by exiting does not terminate its children. The parent-process-ID of all of the calling-process's existing child-processes and zombie-processes is set to the process-ID of a special system-process. That is, these processes are inherited by a special system-process.

If the calling-process is a process-group-leader, and is associated with a controlling-terminal [see TERMIO(BA_ENV)], the `SIGHUP` signal is sent to each process that has a process-group-ID and tty-group-ID equal to that of the calling-process.

RETURN VALUE

Neither `exit` nor `_exit` return a value.

USAGE

Normally programs should use `exit` rather than `_exit`.

SEE ALSO

SIGNAL(BA_OS), WAIT(BA_OS).

NAME

exp, log, log10, pow, sqrt — exponential, logarithm, power, square root functions

SYNOPSIS

```
#include <math.h>

double exp(x)
double x;

double log(x)
double x;

double log10(x)
double x;

double pow(x, y)
double x, y;

double sqrt(x)
double x;
```

DESCRIPTION

The function exp returns e^x.

The function log returns the natural logarithm of x. The value of x must be positive.

The function log10 returns the logarithm base ten of x. The value of x must be positive.

The functions pow returns x^y. If x is zero, y must be positive. If x is negative, y must be an integer.

The function sqrt returns the non-negative square root of x. The value of x may not be negative.

RETURN VALUE

The function exp returns HUGE when the correct value would overflow or 0 when the correct value would underflow and sets errno to ERANGE.

The functions log and log10 return −HUGE and set errno to EDOM when x is non-positive. A message indicating DOMAIN error (or SING error when x is 0) is printed on the standard error output.

The function pow returns 0 and sets errno to EDOM when x is 0 and y is non-positive, or when x is negative and y is not an integer. In these cases a message indicating DOMAIN error is printed on the standard error output. When the correct value for pow would overflow or underflow, pow returns ±HUGE or 0 respectively and sets errno to ERANGE.

The function sqrt returns 0 and sets errno to EDOM when x is negative. A message indicating DOMAIN error is printed on the standard error output.

USAGE

The MATHERR(BA_LIB) routine can change these error-handling procedures.

SEE ALSO

HYPOT(BA_LIB), MATHERR(BA_LIB), SINH(BA_LIB).

CAVEATS

A macro HUGE_VAL will be defined by the <math.h> header file. This macro will call a function which returns either $+\infty$ on a system supporting the **IEEE 754** standard or +{MAXDOUBLE} on a system that does not support the **IEEE 754** standard.

The function exp will return HUGE_VAL when the correct value overflows.

The functions log and log10 will return $-$HUGE_VAL when x is not positive.

The function sqrt will return -0 when the value of x is -0.

The return value of pow will be negative HUGE_VAL when an illegal combination of input arguments is passed to pow.

NAME

fclose, fflush — close or flush a *stdio*-stream

SYNOPSIS

```
#include <stdio.h>

int fclose(stream)
FILE *stream;

int fflush(stream)
FILE *stream;
```

DESCRIPTION

The function fclose causes any buffered data for the named stream to be written out, and the stream to be closed.

The function fclose is performed automatically for all open files upon calling the EXIT(BA_OS) routine.

The function fflush causes any buffered data for the named stream to be written to that file. The stream remains open.

RETURN VALUE

On success, fclose and fflush return 0; they return EOF if any error (such as trying to write to a file not open for writing) is detected.

SEE ALSO

CLOSE(BA_OS), EXIT(BA_OS), FOPEN(BA_OS), SETBUF(BA_LIB).

NAME

  fcntl — file control

SYNOPSIS

  ```
  #include <fcntl.h>

  int fcntl(fildes, cmd, arg)
  int fildes, cmd;
  ```

DESCRIPTION

  The function fcntl provides for control over open files.

  The argument fildes is an open file-descriptor [see VOCAB(BA_DEF)].

  The data type and value of arg are specific to the type of command specified by the argument cmd.

  The <fcntl.h> header file defines the symbolic names for commands and file-status flags.

  The commands available are:

  F_DUPFD   Return a new file-descriptor as follows:

             Lowest numbered available file-descriptor greater than or equal to arg.

             Same open file (or pipe) as the original file.

             Same file-pointer as the original file (i.e., both file-descriptors share one file-pointer).

             Same access-mode (*read*, *write* or *read/write*) [see ACCESS(BA_OS)].

             Same file-status flags [see OPEN(BA_OS)].

             Set the close-on-exec flag associated with the new file-descriptor to remain open across calls to any EXEC(BA_OS) routine.

  F_GETFD   Get the close-on-exec flag associated with the file-descriptor fildes. If the low-order bit is 0, the file remains open across calls to any EXEC(BA_OS) routine; otherwise, the file closes upon execution of any EXEC(BA_OS) routine.

  F_SETFD   Set the close-on-exec flag associated with fildes to the low-order bit of arg (0 or 1 as above).

  F_GETFL   Get file-status flags [see OPEN(BA_OS)]:

             O_RDONLY, O_WRONLY, O_RDWR, O_NDELAY, O_APPEND, O_SYNC.

  F_SETFL   Set file-status flags to arg. Only the flags O_NDELAY, O_APPEND and O_SYNC may be set with fcntl.

The following commands are used for record-locking [see also USAGE below]. Locks may be set on an entire file or segments of a file.

F_GETLK   Get the first lock which blocks the lock description given by the variable of type `struct flock` [see below] pointed to by `arg`. The information retrieved overwrites the information passed to `fcntl` in the structure `flock`. If no lock is found that would prevent this lock from being created, then the structure is passed back unchanged except for the lock type which is set to `F_UNLCK`.

> NOTE: This command was added to `fcntl` following UNIX System V Release 1.0 and UNIX System V Release 2.0, and cannot be expected to be available in those releases.

F_SETLK   Set or clear a file segment lock according to the variable of type `struct flock` [see below] pointed to by `arg`. `F_SETLK` can set read-locks (`F_RDLCK`) and write-locks (`F_WRLCK`), as well as remove either type of lock (`F_UNLCK`).

> The `<fcntl.h>` header file defines `F_RDLCK`, `F_WRLCK` and `F_UNLCK`. If a read-lock or write-lock cannot be set, `fcntl` returns immediately with an error value of – 1.

> NOTE: This command was added to `fcntl` following UNIX System V Release 1.0 and UNIX System V Release 2.0, and cannot be expected to be available in those releases.

F_SETLKW   This command is the same as `F_SETLK` except that if a read-lock or write-lock is blocked by other locks, the process sleeps until the segment is free to be locked.

> NOTE: This command was added to `fcntl` following UNIX System V Release 1.0 and UNIX System V Release 2.0, and cannot be expected to be available in those releases.

The `<fcntl.h>` header file defines the structure `flock`, which describes a lock. It describes the type (`l_type`), starting offset (`l_whence`), relative offset (`l_start`), size (`l_len`) and process-ID (`l_pid`):

```
short l_type;    /* F_RDLCK, F_WRLCK, F_UNLCK */
short l_whence;  /* flag for starting offset */
long  l_start;   /* relative offset in bytes */
long  l_len;     /* if 0 then until EOF */
short l_pid;     /* returned with F_GETLK */
```

When a read-lock has been set on a segment of a file, other processes may also set read-locks on that segment or a portion of it. A read-lock prevents any other process from setting a write-lock on any portion of the protected area. The file-descriptor on which to set a read-lock must be open with read-access.

A write-lock prevents any other process from setting a read-lock or a write-lock on any portion of the protected area. Only one write-lock and no read-locks may be set on a given segment of a file at a given time. The file-descriptor on which to set a write-lock must be open with write-access.

The value of l_whence is 0, 1 or 2 to indicate that the relative offset, l_start bytes, is measured from the start of the file, current position or end of the file, respectively. The value of l_len is the number of consecutive bytes to be locked. The process-ID field l_pid is only used with F_GETLK to return the value for a blocking-lock.

Locks may start and extend beyond the current end of a file, but may not be negative relative to the beginning of the file. A lock may be set to always extend to the end of file by setting l_len to zero (0). If such a lock also has l_start set to zero (0), the whole file is locked.

Changing or unlocking a segment from the middle of a larger locked segment leaves two smaller segments locked at each end of the originally locked segment. Locking a segment already locked by the calling-process causes the old lock type to be removed and the new lock type to take effect. All locks set by a process on a file are removed when the process closes the file-descriptor for the file or the process holding the file-descriptor terminates. Child-processes do not inherit locks after the FORK(BA_OS) operation.

If an ordinary-file has enforced record-locking enabled, then record-locks on the file will affect calls to CREAT(BA_OS), OPEN(BA_OS), READ(BA_OS) and WRITE(BA_OS).

RETURN VALUE

On success, fcntl returns a value greater than or equal to zero that depends on cmd as follows:

F_DUPFD	a new file-descriptor.
F_GETFD	a value of flag (only the low-order bit is defined).
F_SETFD	a value other than -1.
F_GETFL	a value of file flags.
F_SETFL	a value other than -1.
F_GETLK	a value other than -1.
F_SETLK	a value other than -1.
F_SETLKW	a value other than -1.

On failure, fcntl returns -1 and errno indicates the error.

ERRORS

The function fcntl fails and errno equals:

EACCES   if cmd is F_SETLK, the type of lock (l_type) is a read-lock (F_RDLCK) or write-lock (F_WRLCK), and the segment of a file to be locked is already write-locked by another process, or the type is a write-lock and the segment of a file to be locked is already read-locked or write-locked by another process.

EBADF　　　　if fildes is not a valid open file-descriptor.

EBADF　　　　if cmd is F_SETLK or F_SETLKW, the type of lock
　　　　　　　　(l_type) is a read-lock (F_RDLCK), and fildes is not a
　　　　　　　　valid file-descriptor open for reading.

EBADF　　　　if cmd is F_SETLK or F_SETLKW, the type of lock
　　　　　　　　(l_type) is a write-lock (F_WRLCK), and fildes is not a
　　　　　　　　valid file-descriptor open for writing.

EDEADLK　　if cmd is F_SETLKW and a deadlock condition is detected.

EINVAL　　　if cmd is F_DUPFD and arg is negative or greater than or
　　　　　　　　equal to {OPEN_MAX}.

EINVAL　　　if cmd is F_GETLK, F_SETLK or F_SETLKW and arg
　　　　　　　　points to invalid data.

EMFILE　　　if cmd is F_DUPFD and the calling-process already has
　　　　　　　　{OPEN_MAX} file-descriptors open.

ENOLCK　　　if cmd is F_SETLK or F_SETLKW, the type of lock is a read-
　　　　　　　　lock or write-lock, and {LOCK_MAX} regions are already locked
　　　　　　　　system-wide.

USAGE

In the future, errno will equal EAGAIN rather than EACCES when a
section of a file is already locked by another process; portable programs should
expect and test for either value, for example:

```
...
flk->l_type = F_RDLCK;
if (fcntl(fd, F_SETLK, flk) == -1)
    if ((errno == EACCES) || (errno == EAGAIN))
        /*
         * section locked by another process,
         * check for either EAGAIN or EACCES
         * due to different implementations
         */
    else if ...
        /*
         * check for other errors
         */
```

The features of fcntl that deal with record-locking are an update that
followed UNIX System V Release 1.0 and UNIX System V Release 2.0.

SEE ALSO

CLOSE(BA_OS), EXEC(BA_OS), OPEN(BA_OS), LOCKF(BA_OS), READ(BA_OS),
WRITE(BA_OS).

CAVEATS

The error condition which currently sets errno to EACCES will instead set
errno to EAGAIN [see also USAGE above].

NAME

`ferror, feof, clearerr, fileno` — *stdio*-stream status inquiries

SYNOPSIS

```
#include <stdio.h>

int ferror(stream)
FILE *stream;

int feof(stream)
FILE *stream;

void clearerr(stream)
FILE *stream;

int fileno(stream)
FILE *stream;
```

DESCRIPTION

The function `ferror` determines if an I/O error (e.g., `EINTR`, `ENOSPC`) occurred when reading from or writing onto the *stdio*-stream named by `stream`.

The function `feof` determines if `EOF` occurred when reading from the *stdio*-stream named by `stream`.

The function `clearerr` resets both the error and `EOF` indicator to false for the *stdio*-stream named by `stream`. The `EOF` indicator is reset when the file-pointer associated with `stream` is repositioned (e.g., by the FSEEK(BA_OS) or REWIND(BA_OS) routines) or can be reset with `clearerr`.

The function `fileno` gets the integer file-descriptor associated with the *stdio*-stream named by `stream` [see OPEN(BA_OS)].

RETURN VALUE

The function `ferror` returns non-zero when an I/O error occurred reading from or writing onto the *stdio*-stream named by `stream`; otherwise, it returns zero.

The function `feof` returns non-zero when `EOF` occurred reading from the *stdio*-stream named by `stream`; otherwise, it returns zero.

The function `fileno` returns the integer file-descriptor number associated with the *stdio*-stream named by `stream`.

USAGE

All of these functions are macros; thus, they cannot be declared or redeclared.

The function `fileno` returns a file-descriptor that non-*stdio* routines, such as WRITE(BA_OS) and LSEEK(BA_OS), can use to manipulate the associated file, but these routines are not recommended for use by programs.

SEE ALSO

OPEN(BA_OS), FOPEN(BA_OS).

NAME

`floor, ceil, fmod, fabs` — floor, ceiling, remainder, absolute value functions

SYNOPSIS

```
#include <math.h>

double floor(x)
double x;

double ceil(x)
double x;

double fmod(x, y)
double x, y;

double fabs(x)
double x;
```

DESCRIPTION

The function `floor` returns the largest integer (as a double-precision number) not greater than `x`.

The function `ceil` returns the smallest integer not less than `x`.

The function `fmod` returns the floating-point remainder of the division of `x` by `y`, `x` if `y` is zero or if `x/y` would overflow. Otherwise the number is f with the same sign as `x`, such that $x = iy + f$ for some integer i, and $|f| < |y|$.

The function `fabs` returns the absolute value of `x`, i.e., $|x|$.

SEE ALSO

ABS(BA_LIB).

NAME

    fopen, freopen, fdopen — open a *stdio*-stream

SYNOPSIS

```
#include <stdio.h>

FILE *fopen(path, type)
char *path, *type;

FILE *freopen(path, type, stream)
char *path, *type;
FILE *stream;

FILE *fdopen(fildes, type)
int fildes;
char *type;
```

DESCRIPTION

The function fopen opens the file named by path and associates it with a stream [see VOCAB(BA_DEF)]. The function fopen returns a pointer to the FILE structure associated with the stream.

The function freopen substitutes the named file in place of the open stream. The original stream is closed, regardless of whether the open ultimately succeeds. The function freopen returns a pointer to the FILE structure associated with stream.

The function freopen is typically used to attach the preopened streams associated with stdin, stdout and stderr to other files. The standard error output stream, stderr, is by default unbuffered but use of freopen causes it to be buffered or line-buffered.

The argument path points to a character-string that names the file to be opened.

The argument type is a character-string having one of the following values:

    r   open for reading.

    w   truncate or create for writing.

    a   append; open for writing at the end of the file, or create for writing.

    r+   open for update (reading and writing).

    w+   truncate or create for update.

    a+   append; open or create for update (appending) to the end of the file.

When a file is opened for update, both input and output may be done on the resulting stream. However, output may not be directly followed by input without an intervening call to the FSEEK(BA_OS) or REWIND(BA_OS) routine, and input may not be directly followed by output without an intervening call to the FSEEK(BA_OS) or REWIND(BA_OS) routine or an input operation which encounters end-of-file.

When a file is opened for append (i.e., when `type` is a or a+) it is impossible to overwrite information already in the file. The FSEEK(BA_OS) routine may be used to reposition the file-pointer to any position in the file, but when output is written to the file, the current file-pointer is disregarded. All output is written at the end of the file. For example, if two separate processes open the same file for append, each process may write to the file without overwriting output being written by the other, and the output from the two processes would be interleaved in the file.

The function `fdopen` associates a `stream` with a file-descriptor, `fildes`. The `type` of `stream` given to `fdopen` must agree with the mode of the already open file. File-descriptors are obtained from the routines which open files but do not return pointers to a `FILE` structure `stream`. Streams are necessary input for many of the *stdio* routines.

RETURN VALUE

The functions `fopen` and `freopen` return a `NULL` pointer if `path` cannot be accessed or if `type` is invalid or if the file cannot be opened.

The function `fdopen` returns a `NULL` pointer if `fildes` is not an open file-descriptor or if `type` is invalid or if the file cannot be opened.

The function `fopen` or `fdopen` may also fail without setting `errno` if no *stdio*-streams are free.

ERRORS

When the file cannot be opened, `fopen` or `freopen` fails and `errno` equals:

ENOTDIR   if a component of the path-prefix in `path` is not a directory.

ENOENT   if the named file does not exist or a component of the path-name should exist but does not.

EACCES   if *search* permission is denied for a component of the path-prefix or `type` permission is denied for the named file.

EISDIR   if the named file is a directory and `type` permission is *write* or *read/write*.

EROFS   if the named file resides on a read-only file-system and `type` permission is *write* or *read/write*.

ETXTBSY   if the file is a pure procedure (shared text) file being executed and `type` permission is *write* or *read/write*.

EINTR   if a signal is caught during `fopen`, `freopen` or `fdopen`.

SEE ALSO

CREAT(BA_OS), DUP(BA_OS), OPEN(BA_OS), PIPE(BA_OS), FCLOSE(BA_OS), FSEEK(BA_OS).

NAME

fork — create a new process

SYNOPSIS

int fork ( )

DESCRIPTION

The function fork creates a new process (child-process) that is a copy of the calling-process (parent-process). The child-process inherits the following attributes from the parent-process:

real-user-id, real-group-id, effective-user-id, effective-group-id
environment
close-on-exec flag [see EXEC(BA_OS)]
signal-handling settings (SIG_DFL, SIG_IGN, SIG_HOLD, *address*)
set-user-ID mode-bit
set-group-ID mode-bit
process-group-ID
tty-group-ID [see EXIT(BA_OS), SIGNAL(BA_OS) and SIGSET(BA_OS)]
current-working-directory
root-directory
file-mode-creation-mask [see UMASK(BA_OS)]
file-size limit [see ULIMIT(BA_OS)]

Additional attributes associated with an Extension to the Base System may be inherited from the parent-process [see, for example, EFFECTS(KE_ENV)].

The child-process differs from the parent-process as follows:

The child-process has a unique process-ID

The child-process has a different parent-process-ID (i.e., the process-ID of the parent-process).

The child-process has its own copy of the parent's file-descriptors. Each of the child-process's file-descriptors shares a common file-pointer with the corresponding file-descriptor of the parent-process.

The child-process's utime, stime, cutime and cstime are set to 0 [see TIMES(BA_OS)].

The time left until an alarm clock signal is reset to 0.

The child-process does not inherit record-locks set by the parent-process [see FCNTL(BA_OS) or LOCKF(BA_OS)].

RETURN VALUE

On success, fork returns 0 to the child-process and returns the process-ID of the child-process to the parent-process; on failure, it returns − 1 to the parent-process, it does *not* create a child-process, and errno indicates the error.

ERRORS

The function `fork` fails and `errno` equals:

EAGAIN   if the system-imposed limit on the total number of processes
            under execution system-wide {PROC_MAX} or by a single user-ID
            {CHILD_MAX} would be exceeded.

ENOMEM   if the process requires more space than the system can supply.

USAGE

The function `fork` creates a new process that is a copy of the calling-process
and both processes will run as system resources become available. Because the
goal is typically to create a new process that is *different* from the parent-
process (i.e., the goal is to start a new program running), often the child-
process immediately calls an EXEC(BA_OS) routine to transform itself and start
the new program.

If possible, programs should use the SYSTEM(BA_OS) routine, which is easier to
use and has more functionality than the FORK(BA_OS) and EXEC(BA_OS)
routines.

SEE ALSO

ALARM(BA_OS), EXEC(BA_OS), FCNTL(BA_OS), LOCKF(BA_OS), SIGNAL(BA_OS),
SIGSET(BA_OS), TIMES(BA_OS), ULIMIT(BA_OS), UMASK(BA_OS), WAIT(BA_OS).

NAME

fread — buffered input

SYNOPSIS

```
#include <sys/types.h>
#include <stdio.h>

int fread(ptr, size, nitems, stream)
char *ptr;
size_t size;
int nitems;
FILE *stream;
```

DESCRIPTION

The function `fread` reads into an array pointed to by `ptr` up to `nitems` items of data from the named input `stream`, where an item of data is a sequence of bytes (not necessarily terminated by a null byte) of length `size`. The function `fread` stops appending bytes if an end-of-file or error condition is encountered while reading `stream`, or if `nitems` items have been read. The function `fread` increments the data-pointer in `stream` to point to the byte following the last byte read if there is one [see FSEEK(BA_OS)]. The function `fread` does not change the contents of `stream`.

RETURN VALUE

On success, `fread` returns the number of items read. If `size` or `nitems` is non-positive, `fread` returns 0 and does *not* read any items.

USAGE

The FERROR(BA_OS) or FEOF(BA_OS) routines must be used to distinguish between an error condition and an end-of-file condition.

SEE ALSO

FERROR(BA_OS), FOPEN(BA_OS), FSEEK(BA_OS), FWRITE(BA_OS), GETC(BA_LIB), GETS(BA_LIB), PRINTF(BA_LIB), PUTC(BA_LIB), PUTS(BA_LIB), READ(BA_OS), SCANF(BA_LIB), WRITE(BA_OS).

NAME

frexp, ldexp, modf — manipulate parts of floating-point numbers

SYNOPSIS

```
double frexp(value, eptr)
double value;
int *eptr;

double ldexp(value, exp)
double value;
int exp;

double modf(value, iptr)
double value, *iptr;
```

DESCRIPTION

Every non-zero number can be written uniquely as $x*2^n$, where the *mantissa* (fraction) x is in the range $0.5 \leqslant |x| < 1.0$ and the *exponent* n is an integer. The function frexp returns the mantissa of a double value and stores the exponent indirectly in the location pointed to by eptr. If value is 0, both results returned by frexp are 0.

The function ldexp returns the quantity value*2^{exp}.

The function modf returns the fractional part of value and stores the integral part indirectly in the location pointed to by iptr. Both the fractional and integer parts have the same sign as value.

RETURN VALUE

If ldexp would cause overflow, ±HUGE is returned (according to the sign of value) and errno is set to ERANGE.

If ldexp would cause underflow, 0 is returned and errno is set to ERANGE.

CAVEATS

A macro HUGE_VAL will be defined by the <math.h> header file. This macro will call a function which returns either +∞ on a system supporting the IEEE 754 standard or +{MAXDOUBLE} on a system that does not support the IEEE 754 standard.

The return value of ldexp will be ±HUGE_VAL (according to the sign of value) in case of overflow.

NAME

`fseek, rewind, ftell` — reposition a file-pointer in a *stdio*-stream

SYNOPSIS

```
#include <stdio.h>
#include <unistd.h>

int fseek(stream, offset, whence)
FILE *stream;
long offset;
int whence;

void rewind(stream)
FILE *stream;

long ftell(stream)
FILE *stream;
```

DESCRIPTION

The function `fseek` sets the position of the next input or output operation on the `stream`. The new position is at the signed distance `offset` bytes from the beginning, from the current position or from the end of the file, according to the value of `whence`, which the `<unistd.h>` header file defines as follows:

Name	Description
SEEK_SET	set position equal to `offset` bytes.
SEEK_CUR	set position to current location plus `offset`.
SEEK_END	set position to EOF plus `offset`.

The call `rewind(stream)` equals the following:

```
fseek(stream,0L,SEEK_SET)
```

except that `rewind` returns no value.

The functions `fseek` and `rewind` undo any effects of the UNGETC(BA_LIB) routine. After `fseek` or `rewind`, the next operation on a file opened for update may be either input or output.

The function `ftell` returns the offset of the current byte relative to the beginning of the file associated with the named `stream`. The offset is always measured in bytes.

RETURN VALUE

The function `fseek` returns non-zero for improper seeks; otherwise, it returns zero. An improper seek is, for example, an `fseek` on a file that has not been opened via the FOPEN(BA_OS) routine; on a device incapable of seeking, such as a terminal; or on a stream opened via the POPEN(BA_OS) routine.

SEE ALSO

FOPEN(BA_OS), POPEN(BA_OS), UNGETC(BA_LIB).

NAME

ftw — walk a file tree

SYNOPSIS

```
#include <ftw.h>

int ftw(path, fn, param)
char *path;
int (*fn)();
int param;
```

DESCRIPTION

The function ftw recursively descends the directory hierarchy rooted in path visiting each directory before visiting any of its descendants. For each object in the hierarchy, ftw calls a user-defined function fn passing it three arguments. The first argument passed is a character pointer to a null-terminated string containing the name of the object. The second argument passed to fn is a pointer to a stat structure [see STAT(BA_OS)] containing information about the object, and the third argument passed is an integer flag. Possible values of the flag, defined by the <ftw.h> header file, are FTW_F for a file, FTW_D for a directory, FTW_DNR for a directory that cannot be read and FTW_NS for an object for which stat could not successfully be executed. If the integer is FTW_DNR, descendants of that directory will not be processed. If the integer is FTW_NS, the contents of the stat structure are undefined.

The function ftw uses one file-descriptor for each level in the tree. The argument param limits the number of file-descriptors to be in the range of 1 to {OPEN_MAX}. The function ftw will run more quickly if param is at least as large as the number of levels in the tree.

RETURN VALUE

The tree traversal continues until the tree is exhausted or fn returns a non-zero value or ftw detects some error (such as an I/O error). If the tree is exhausted, ftw returns 0. If fn returns a non-zero value, ftw stops its tree traversal and returns whatever value fn returned.

If ftw detects an error other than EACCES (see FTW_DNR and FTW_NS above), it returns – 1 and errno equals the type of error. The external variable errno may contain the error values that are possible when a directory is opened [see OPEN(BA_OS)] or when the STAT(BA_OS) routine is executed on a directory or file.

USAGE

Because ftw is recursive, it is possible for it to terminate with a memory fault when applied to very deep file structures.

SEE ALSO

STAT(BA_OS), MALLOC(BA_OS).

NAME

fwrite — buffered output

SYNOPSIS

```
#include <sys/types.h>
#include <stdio.h>

int fwrite(ptr, size, nitems, stream)
char *ptr;
size_t size;
int nitems;
FILE *stream;
```

DESCRIPTION

The function fwrite appends to the named output stream at most nitems items of data from the array pointed to by ptr. The function fwrite stops appending when it has appended nitems items of data or if an error condition is encountered on stream. The function fwrite does not change the contents of the array pointed to by ptr. The function fwrite increments the data-pointer in stream by the number of bytes written.

RETURN VALUE

On success, fwrite returns the number of items written. If size or nitems is non-positive, fwrite returns 0 and does *not* write any items.

USAGE

The FERROR(BA_OS) or FEOF(BA_OS) routines must be used to distinguish between an error condition and an end-of-file condition.

SEE ALSO

FERROR(BA_OS), FOPEN(BA_OS), FREAD(BA_OS), FSEEK(BA_OS), GETC(BA_LIB), GETS(BA_LIB), PRINTF(BA_LIB), PUTC(BA_LIB), PUTS(BA_LIB), READ(BA_OS), SCANF(BA_LIB), WRITE(BA_OS).

NAME

gamma — log gamma function

SYNOPSIS

```
#include <math.h>

double gamma(x)
double x;

extern int signgam;
```

DESCRIPTION

The function gamma returns $\ln(|\Gamma(x)|)$, where $\Gamma(x)$ is defined as:

$$\int_0^\infty e^{-t} t^{x-1} dt$$

The sign of $\Gamma(x)$ is returned in the external integer signgam. The argument x may not be a non-positive integer.

The following C program fragment might be used to calculate Γ:

```
if ((y = gamma(x)) > LN_MAXDOUBLE)
    error();
y = signgam * exp(y);
```

RETURN VALUE

For non-positive integer arguments, gamma returns HUGE and errno equals EDOM. A message indicating SING error is printed on the standard error output [see MATHERR(BA_LIB)].

If the correct value overflows, gamma returns HUGE and errno equals ERANGE.

USAGE

The MATHERR(BA_LIB) routine can change these error-handling procedures.

SEE ALSO

EXP(BA_LIB), MATHERR(BA_LIB).

CAVEATS

A macro HUGE_VAL will be defined by the <math.h> header file. This macro will call a function which returns either $+\infty$ on a system supporting the IEEE 754 standard or +{MAXDOUBLE} on a system that does not support the IEEE 754 standard.

If the correct value overflows, gamma returns HUGE_VAL.

NAME

getc, getchar, fgetc, getw — get character or word from *stdio*

SYNOPSIS

```
#include <stdio.h>

int getc(stream)
FILE *stream;

int getchar()

int fgetc(stream)
FILE *stream;

int getw(stream)
FILE *stream;
```

DESCRIPTION

The macro getc returns as an integer the next character (i.e., byte) from the named input stream stream and sets the file-pointer, if defined, ahead one character in stream. The macro getchar is defined as getc(stdin). Both getc and getchar are macros.

The function fgetc behaves like getc, but is a function instead of a macro. The function fgetc runs more slowly than getc but it takes less space per invocation and its name can be passed as an argument to a function.

The function getw reads the next word (i.e., integer) from the named input stream, stream and sets the file-pointer, if defined, to point to the next word. The size of a word is the size of an integer and varies from machine to machine. The function getw needs no special alignment in the file.

RETURN VALUE

These functions return EOF at end-of-file or on an error. Because EOF is an integer constant, use the FERROR(BA_OS) routines to detect these errors

USAGE

If the integer value returned by getc, getchar or fgetc is assigned to a character variable and then compared against the integer constant EOF, the comparison may never succeed because sign-extension of a character on widening to integer is machine-dependent.

Because word-length and byte-ordering are machine-dependent, files written using putw may not be read using getw on a different processor.

Because it is implemented as a macro, getc incorrectly treats stream when it has side-effects. In particular, getc(*f++) does not work sensibly, and fgetc should be used instead.

SEE ALSO

FCLOSE(BA_OS), FERROR(BA_OS), FOPEN(BA_OS), FREAD(BA_OS), GETS(BA_LIB), PUTC(BA_LIB), SCANF(BA_LIB).

NAME

getcwd — get path-name of current working directory

SYNOPSIS

```
char *getcwd(buf, size)
char *buf;
int size;
```

DESCRIPTION

The function getcwd returns a pointer to the current directory path-name. The value of size must be at least two greater than the length of the path-name to be returned.

RETURN VALUE

If size is not large enough or if an error occurs in a lower-level function, getcwd returns NULL and errno indicates the error.

ERRORS

The function getcwd fails and errno equals:

EINVAL   if size is zero

ERANGE   if size not large enough to hold the path-name.

NAME

getenv — return value for environment name

SYNOPSIS

```
char *getenv(name)
char *name;
```

DESCRIPTION

The function getenv searches the environment list for a string of the form:

```
name = value
```

and returns a pointer to value in the current environment if such a string is present. Otherwise, it returns a NULL pointer.

SEE ALSO

EXEC(BA_OS), SYSTEM(BA_OS), PUTENV(BA_LIB).

NAME

getgid, getegid — get real-group-ID and effective-group-ID.

SYNOPSIS

```
unsigned short getgid( )

unsigned short getegid( )
```

DESCRIPTION

The function getgid returns the real-group-ID of the calling-process.

The function getegid returns the effective-group-ID of the calling-process.

SEE ALSO

GETGID(BA_OS), SETGID(BA_OS), SETUID(BA_OS).

NAME

getgrent, getgrgid, getgrnam, setgrent, endgrent,
fgetgrent — get group file entry

SYNOPSIS

```
#include <grp.h>
#include <stdio.h>

struct group *getgrent()

struct group *getgrgid(gid)
int gid;

struct group *getgrnam(name)
char *name;

void setgrent()

void endgrent()

struct group *fgetgrent(f)
FILE *f;
```

DESCRIPTION

The routines getgrent, getgrgid and getgrnam each return pointers
to a group structure that breaks out the fields of a /etc/group file entry.
The <grp.h> header file defines the group structure with these members:

```
char *gr_name; /* the name of the group */
int  gr_gid;   /* the numerical group-ID */
char **gr_mem; /* pointer array to member names */
```

The first call to getgrent returns a pointer to the first group structure in
the file; each successive call returns the successive group structure in the file.

The routine getgrgid searches the file for a group-ID matching gid and
returns a pointer to the particular structure in which to find it.

The routine getgrnam searches the file for a group-name matching *name*
and returns a pointer to the particular structure in which to find it.

The routine setgrent rewinds the group-file to allow repeated searches.

The routine endgrent closes the group-file when processing is done.

The routine fgetgrent returns a pointer to the next group structure in
the file f; this file must have the format of /etc/group.

RETURN VALUE

Each function returns a NULL pointer if end-of-file or an error occurs.

FILES

/etc/group

USAGE

All data may be stored in a static area, so it should be copied to save it.

SEE ALSO

GETLOGIN(SD_LIB), GETPWENT(SD_LIB).

NAME

    `getlogin` — get login-name

SYNOPSIS

    `char *getlogin( );`

DESCRIPTION

    The routine `getlogin` returns a pointer to the login-name as found in the file `/etc/utmp`. It may be used in conjunction with the routine `getpwnam` [see GETPWENT(SD_LIB)] to locate the correct password-file entry when the same user-ID is shared by several login-names.

    If `getlogin` is called within a process that is not attached to a terminal, it returns a NULL pointer. The correct procedure for determining the login-name is to call `getlogin` and if it fails to call `getpwuid`.

RETURN VALUE

    The function `getlogin` returns a NULL pointer if `name` is not found.

FILES

    `/etc/utmp`

SEE ALSO

    GETGRENT(SD_LIB), GETPWENT(SD_LIB).

USAGE

    The return value may point to static data that is overwritten by each call.

NAME

`getmsg` — receive next STREAMS I/O message

SYNOPSIS

```
#include <stropts.h>

int getmsg(fd, ctlptr, dataptr, flags)
int fd;
struct strbuf *ctlptr;
struct strbuf *dataptr;
int *flags;
```

DESCRIPTION

The function `getmsg` retrieves the contents of a message located at the stream-head read-queue from a STREAMS-device, and places the contents into user specified buffer(s). The message must contain either a data part, a control part or both. The data and control parts of the message are placed into separate buffers, as described below. The semantics of each part is defined by the STREAMS module that generated the message.

The argument `fd` is a file-descriptor that denotes an open stream.

The arguments `ctlptr` and `dataptr` each point to a `strbuf` structure which contains the following members:

```
int  maxlen; /* maximum buffer length */
int  len;    /* length of data */
char *buf;   /* ptr to buffer */
```

where `buf` points to a buffer in which the data or control information is to be placed, and `maxlen` indicates the maximum number of bytes this buffer can hold. On return, `len` equals the number of bytes of data or control information actually received; or equals 0 if there is a zero-length control or data part; or equals − 1 if no data or control information is present in the message.

The argument `ctlptr` holds the control part of the message, and `dataptr` holds the data part of the message. If `ctlptr` (or `dataptr`) equals NULL or `maxlen` equals − 1, the control (or data) part of the message is not processed and is left on the stream-head read-queue, and `len` equals − 1.

If `maxlen` equals 0 and there is a zero-length control (or data) part, that zero-length part is removed from the read-queue and `len` equals 0.

If `maxlen` equals 0 and there are more than zero bytes of control (or data) information, that information is left on the read-queue and `len` equals 0.

If `maxlen` in `ctlptr` (or `dataptr`) is less than the control (or data) part of the message, `maxlen` bytes are retrieved. In this case, the remainder of the message is left on the stream-head read-queue and `getmsg` returns a non-zero value, as described below under RETURN VALUE.

The argument `flags` can equal 0 or RS_HIPRI and is used as described below. If information is retrieved from a priority message, `flags` equals RS_HIPRI on return.

By default, getmsg processes the first priority or non-priority message available on the stream-head read-queue. However, a user may choose to retrieve only priority messages by setting flags to RS_HIPRI. In this case, getmsg only processes the next message if it is a priority message.

If O_NDELAY is clear, getmsg blocks until a message of the type(s) specified by flags (priority or either) is available on the stream-head read-queue.

If O_NDELAY is set and a message of the specified type(s) is not present on the read-queue, getmsg fails and errno equals EAGAIN.

If a hangup occurs on the stream from which messages are to be retrieved, getmsg continues to operate normally, as described above, until the stream-head read-queue is empty. Thereafter, it returns 0 in the len fields of ctlptr and dataptr.

RETURN VALUE

On success, getmsg returns a non-negative value:

A value of 0 indicates that a full message was read successfully.

A value of MORECTL indicates that more control information is waiting for retrieval.

A value of MOREDATA indicates that more data is waiting for retrieval.

A value of MORECTL ┆ MOREDATA indicates that both types of information remain.

Subsequent getmsg calls will retrieve the remainder of the message.

ERRORS

The function getmsg fails and errno equals:

EAGAIN   if O_NDELAY is set, and no messages are available.

EBADF   if fd is not a valid file-descriptor open for reading.

EBADMSG   if the queued message to be read is not valid for getmsg.

EFAULT   if ctlptr, dataptr or flags points to a location outside the allocated address space.

EINTR   if a signal is caught during the getmsg operation.

EINVAL   if flags specifies an illegal value, or the stream denoted by fd is linked under a multiplexer.

ENOSTR   if fd fails to denote a stream.

The function getmsg can also fail if a STREAMS error message is received at the stream-head before the call to getmsg. The error returned is the value contained in the STREAMS error message.

SEE ALSO

READ(BA_OS), POLL(NS_OS), PUTMSG(NS_OS), STREAMIO(NS_ENV), WRITE(BA_OS).

NAME

getopt — get option letter from argument vector

SYNOPSIS

```
int getopt(argc, argv, optstring)
int argc;
char *argv[ ], *optstring;

extern char *optarg;
extern int optind, opterr;
```

DESCRIPTION

The function getopt is a command-line parser. It returns the next option letter in argv that matches a letter in optstring.

The argument optstring is a string of recognized option letters; if a letter is followed by a colon, the option is expected to have an argument that must be separated from it by white space.

The function getopt stores the argv index of the next argument to be processed in the external variable optind, which is initialized to 1 before the first call to getopt.

The function getopt sets optarg to point to the start of the option argument.

The following rules form the UNIX System V standard for command syntax:

RULE 1: Command names must be between two and nine characters.

RULE 2: Command names must include lower-case letters and digits only.

RULE 3: Option names must be a single character in length.

RULE 4: All options must be delimited by the – character.

RULE 5: Options with no arguments may be grouped behind one delimiter.

RULE 6: The first option-argument following an option must be preceded by white space.

RULE 7: Option arguments cannot be optional.

RULE 8: Groups of option arguments following an option must be separated by commas or separated by white space and quoted.

RULE 9: All options must precede operands on the command line.

RULE 10: The characters – – may be used to delimit the end of the options.

RULE 11: The order of options relative to one another should not matter.

RULE 12: The order of operands may matter and position-related interpretations should be determined on a command-specific basis.

RULE 13: The – character preceded and followed by white space should be used only to mean standard input.

The function getopt is the command-line parser that will enforce the rules of this command syntax standard.

When all options are processed (i.e., up to the first non-option argument), getopt returns EOF. The special option -- may be used to delimit the end of the options; EOF will be returned and -- will be skipped.

RETURN VALUE

The function getopt prints an error message on stderr and returns a question-mark (?) when it gets an option letter not in optstring. Setting opterr to 0 disables this error message.

EXAMPLES

The following code fragment shows how one can process the arguments for a command that takes the mutually exclusive options a and b and the options f and o, both of which require arguments:

```
main( argc, argv )
    int argc;
    char *argv[ ];
{
    int c;
    int bflg, aflg, errflg;
    char *ifile;
    char *ofile;
    extern char *optarg;
    extern int optind;
    . . .
    while ((c = getopt(argc, argv, "abf:o:")) != EOF)
        switch (c) {
        case 'a': if (bflg)
                    errflg++;
                else
                    aflg++;
                break;
        case 'b': if (aflg)
                    errflg++;
                else
                    bproc( );
                break;
        case 'f': ifile = optarg;
                break;
        case 'o': ofile = optarg;
                break;
        case '?': errflg++;
        }
    if (errflg) {
        fprintf(stderr, "usage: . . . ");
        exit(2);
    }
    for ( ; optind < argc; optind++) {
        if (access(argv[optind], 4)) {
    . . .
}
```

NAME

getpass — read a password

SYNOPSIS

```
char *getpass(prompt)
char *prompt;
```

DESCRIPTION

The routine getpass reads up to a new-line or an EOF from the file /dev/tty, after prompting on the standard error output with the null-terminated string prompt and disabling echoing. A pointer is returned to a null-terminated string of at most 8 characters. If /dev/tty cannot be opened, a NULL pointer is returned. An interrupt will terminate input and send an interrupt signal to the calling program before returning.

FILES

/dev/tty

USAGE

The return value points to static data that is overwritten by each call.

NAME

getpid, getpgrp, getppid — get process-ID, process-group-ID and parent-process-ID

SYNOPSIS

```
int getpid( )
```

```
int getpgrp( )
```

```
int getppid( )
```

DESCRIPTION

The function getpid returns the process-ID of the calling-process.

The function getpgrp returns the process-group-ID of the calling-process.

The function getppid returns the parent-process-ID of the calling-process.

SEE ALSO

EXEC(BA_OS), FORK(BA_OS), SETPGRP(BA_OS), SIGNAL(BA_OS).

NAME

getpwent, getpwuid, getpwnam, setpwent, endpwent, fgetpwent — get password file entry

SYNOPSIS

```
#include <pwd.h>
#include <stdio.h>

struct passwd *getpwent()

struct passwd *getpwuid(uid)
int uid;

struct passwd *getpwnam(name)
char *name;

void setpwent()

void endpwent()

struct passwd *fgetpwent(f)
FILE *f;
```

DESCRIPTION

Each of the functions getpwent, getpwuid and getpwnam returns a pointer to a structure containing the broken-out fields of a line in the /etc/passwd file. Each line in the file contains a passwd structure, declared in the <pwd.h> header file. The structure contains at least the following members:

```
char *pw_name;      /* login-name */
char *pw_passwd;    /* encrypted-password */
int  pw_uid;        /* numerical user-ID */
int  pw_gid;        /* numerical group-ID */
char *pw_dir;       /* initial-working-directory */
char *pw_shell;     /* command-interpreter */
```

The function getpwent when first called returns a pointer to the first passwd structure in the file; thereafter, it returns a pointer to the next passwd structure in the file; so successive calls can be used to search the entire file.

The function getpwuid searches the file for a user-ID matching uid and returns a pointer to the particular structure in which to find it.

The function getpwnam searches the file for a login-name matching name and returns a pointer to the particular structure in which to find it.

The function setpwent rewinds the password-file to allow repeated searches.

The function endpwent closes the password-file when processing is done.

The function fgetpwent returns a pointer to the next passwd structure in the file f, which must have the format of /etc/passwd.

RETURN VALUE

Each function returns a NULL pointer if end-of-file or an error occurs.

FILES

`/etc/passwd`

SEE ALSO

GETLOGIN(SD_LIB), GETGRENT(SD_LIB).

USAGE

All information may be contained in a static area, so it should be copied if it is to be saved.

NAME

gets, fgets — get a string from *stdio*

SYNOPSIS

```
#include <stdio.h>

char *gets(s)
char *s;

char *fgets(s, n, stream)
char *s;
int n;
FILE *stream;
```

DESCRIPTION

The function gets reads characters from the standard input stream, stdin, into the array pointed to by s until a new-line character is read or an end-of-file occurs. The new-line character is discarded and the string is terminated with a null-character.

The function fgets reads characters from stream into the array pointed to by s until n-1 characters are read or a new-line character is read and transferred to s or an end-of-file occurs. The string is then terminated with a null-character.

RETURN VALUE

If end-of-file occurs and no characters were read, neither gets nor fgets transfer characters to s and they return a NULL pointer; if a read error occurs (such as trying to use these functions on a file that is not open for reading), they return a NULL pointer; otherwise, they return s.

USAGE

Reading too long a line through gets may cause gets to fail. The use of fgets is recommended.

SEE ALSO

FERROR(BA_OS), FOPEN(BA_OS), FREAD(BA_OS), GETC(BA_LIB), SCANF(BA_LIB).

NAME

getuid, geteuid — get real-user-ID and effective-user-ID.

SYNOPSIS

unsigned short getuid( )

unsigned short geteuid( )

DESCRIPTION

The function getuid returns the real-user-ID of the calling-process.

The function geteuid returns the effective-user-ID of the calling-process.

SEE ALSO

GETGID(BA_OS), SETGID(BA_OS), SETUID(BA_OS).

NAME

getutent, getutid, getutline, pututline, setutent,
endutent, utmpname — access utmp file entry

SYNOPSIS

```
#include <utmp.h>

struct utmp *getutent( )

struct utmp *getutid(id)
struct utmp *id;

struct utmp *getutline(line)
struct utmp *line;

void pututline(utmp)
struct utmp *utmp;

void setutent( )

void endutent( )

void utmpname(file)
char *file;
```

DESCRIPTION

Each of the routines getutent, getutid and getutline returns a
pointer to a structure, which is defined in the header file <utmp.h>. The
structure contains at least the following members:

```
char   ut_user[ ]; /* user login-name */
char   ut_id[ ];   /* /etc/inittab-ID */
char   ut_line[ ]; /* device-name */
short  ut_pid;     /* process-ID */
short  ut_type;    /* type of entry */
```

In addition, (at least) the following type values for ut_type are defined:

EMPTY, RUN_LVL, BOOT_TIME, OLD_TIME, NEW_TIME,
INIT_PROCESS, LOGIN_PROCESS, USER_PROCESS,
DEAD_PROCESS, ACCOUNTING.

The routine getutent reads in the next entry from the /etc/utmp file.
It opens the file if not already open, and fails on reaching the end of the file.

The routine getutid searches forward from the current point in the
/etc/utmp file; if the ut_type value of the structure id is RUN_LVL,
BOOT_TIME, OLD_TIME or NEW_TIME, then it stops when it finds an
entry with a ut_type matching the ut_type of the structure id. If the
ut_type value is INIT_PROCESS, LOGIN_PROCESS,
USER_PROCESS or DEAD_PROCESS, then it stops when it finds an entry
whose type is one of these four and whose ut_id field matches the ut_id
field of id. If the end-of-file is reached without a match, getutid fails.

The routine getutline searches forward from the current point in the /etc/utmp file until it finds an entry of the type LOGIN_PROCESS or USER_PROCESS which also has a ut_line value matching that of line. If the end-of-file is reached without a match, getutline fails.

The routine pututline writes out the supplied /etc/utmp structure into the /etc/utmp file. It uses getutid to search forward for the proper place if it finds that it is not already at the proper place. It is expected that normally the user of pututline will have searched for the proper entry using one of the above routines. If so, pututline will not search. If pututline does not find a matching slot for the new entry, it will add a new entry to the end of the file.

The routine setutent resets the input stream to the beginning of the file. To examine the entire file, it must be reset before each search for a new entry.

The routine endutent closes the currently open file.

The routine utmpname allows the user to change the name of the file examined by these routines, from /etc/utmp to any other file, usually this other file is /etc/wtmp. If the file does not exist, this will not show up until the first attempt to reference the file because utmpname does not open the file; it just closes the old file if it is currently open and saves the new file-name.

RETURN VALUE

A NULL pointer is returned upon failure to read, whether for permissions or having reached the end of file, or upon failure to write.

FILES

```
/etc/utmp
/etc/wtmp
```

USAGE

The most current entry is saved in a static structure that must be copied before making further accesses.

Each call to either getutid or getutline sees the routine examine the static structure before performing more I/O. If the contents of the static structure match what it is searching for, it looks no further. For this reason, to use getutline to search for multiple occurrences, it is necessary to zero out the static after each success, or getutline will just return the same pointer over and over again.

There is one exception to the rule about removing the structure before doing further reads. If the user modifies the contents of the static structure returned by getutent, getutid or getutline, and passes the pointer back to pututline, the implicit read done by pututline (if it finds that it is not already at the correct place in the file) does not hurt the contents.

The sizeof operator finds the sizes of the arrays in the structure.

NAME

hsearch, hcreate, hdestroy — manage hash search tables

SYNOPSIS

```
#include <search.h>

ENTRY *hsearch(item, action)
ENTRY item;
ACTION action;

int hcreate(nel)
unsigned nel;

void hdestroy( )
```

DESCRIPTION

The function hsearch is a hash-table search routine. It returns a pointer into a hash table indicating the location at which an entry can be found. The comparison function used by hsearch is strcmp [see STRING(BA_LIB)].

The argument item is a structure of type ENTRY (defined by the <search.h> header file) containing two character pointers:

item.key   points to the comparison key,

item.data   points to any other data to be associated with that key.

(Pointers to types other than char should be cast to pointer-to-character.)

The argument action is a member of an enumeration type ACTION, defined by the <search.h> header file, indicating the disposition of the entry if it cannot be found in the table.

ENTER indicates that the item should be inserted in the table at an appropriate point. Given a duplicate of an existing item, the new item is not entered, and hsearch returns a pointer to the existing item.

FIND indicates that no entry should be made. Unsuccessful resolution is indicated by the return of a NULL pointer.

The function hcreate allocates sufficient space for the table and must be called before hsearch is used. The value of nel is an estimate of the maximum number of entries that the table will contain. This number may be adjusted upward by the algorithm in order to obtain certain mathematically favorable circumstances.

The function hdestroy destroys the search table and may be followed by another call to hcreate.

RETURN VALUE

Either if the action is FIND and the item can not be found or if the action is ENTER and the table is full, hsearch returns a NULL pointer.

If sufficient space for the table cannot be allocated, hcreate returns 0.

USAGE

Both `hsearch` and `hcreate` use the MALLOC(BA_OS) routines to allocate space.

EXAMPLES

The example reads in strings followed by two numbers and stores them in a hash table, then reads in strings and finds the entry in the table and prints it.

```
#include <stdio.h>
#include <search.h>

struct info {       /* these are in the table */
    int age, room;      /* apart from the key. */
};
#define NUM_EMPL 5000  /* # of elements in the table */

main()
{
    /* space for strings */
    char string_space[NUM_EMPL*20];
    /* space for employee info */
    struct info info_space[NUM_EMPL];
    /* next avail space for strings */
    char *str_ptr = string_space;
    /* next avail space for info */
    struct info *info_ptr = info_space;
    ENTRY item, *found_item, *hsearch();
    char name_to_find[30];  /* name to look for in table */
    int i = 0;
    /* create table */
    (void) hcreate(NUM_EMPL);
    while (scanf("%s%d%d", str_ptr, &info_ptr->age,
        &info_ptr->room) != EOF && i++ < NUM_EMPL) {
        /* put info in structure, and structure in item */
        item.key = str_ptr;
        item.data = (char *)info_ptr;
        str_ptr += strlen(str_ptr) + 1;
        info_ptr++;
        /* put item into table */
        (void) hsearch(item, ENTER);
    }
    /* access table */
    item.key = name_to_find;
    while (scanf("%s", item.key) != EOF) {
        if ((found_item = hsearch(item, FIND)) != NULL) {
        /* if item is in the table */
        (void) printf("found %s, age = %d, room = %d\n",
            found_item->key,
            ((struct info *)found_item->data)->age,
            ((struct info *)found_item->data)->room);
        } else {
        (void) printf("no such employee %s\n",
            name_to_find)
        }
    }
}
```

SEE ALSO

MALLOC(BA_OS), BSEARCH(BA_LIB), LSEARCH(BA_LIB), STRING(BA_LIB), TSEARCH(BA_LIB).

CAVEATS

The restriction of having only one hash search table active at any given time will be removed.

NAME

`hypot` — Euclidean distance function

SYNOPSIS

```
#include <math.h>

double hypot(x, y)
double x, y;
```

DESCRIPTION

The function `hypot` returns `sqrt(x * x + y * y)`, taking precautions against unwarranted overflows.

RETURN VALUE

If the correct value overflows, `hypot` returns HUGE and `errno` equals ERANGE.

The MATHERR(BA_LIB) routine can change these error-handling procedures.

SEE ALSO

MATHERR(BA_LIB).

CAVEATS

A macro `HUGE_VAL` will be defined by the `<math.h>` header file. This macro will call a function which returns either $+\infty$ on a system supporting the **IEEE 754** standard or +{MAXDOUBLE} on a system that does not support the **IEEE 754** standard.

If the correct value overflows, `hypot` returns `HUGE_VAL`.

NAME

`ioctl` − control device

SYNOPSIS

```
int ioctl(fildes, request, arg)
int fildes, request;
```

DESCRIPTION

The function `ioctl` performs a variety of device control-functions by passing the request to a device-driver to perform *device-specific* control-functions.

> NOTE: This control is not frequently used and the basic input/output operations are performed by the READ(BA_OS) and WRITE(BA_OS) routines.

The argument `fildes` is an open file-descriptor that refers to a device.

The argument `request` selects the device control-function and depends on the device being addressed.

The argument `arg` represents additional information needed by the specific device to perform the requested function. The data-type of `arg` depends upon the particular control-function, but it is either an integer or a pointer to a device-specific data-structure. In addition to device-specific functions, many device-drivers provide generic functions, (e.g., the general terminal interface [see TERMIO(BA_ENV)] and STREAMS I/O interface [see STREAMIO(NS_ENV)]).

RETURN VALUE

On success, `ioctl` returns a value that depends upon the device control-function, but must be an integer value; on failure, it returns − 1 and `errno` indicates the error.

ERRORS

The function `ioctl` fails and `errno` equals:

EBADF if `fildes` is not a valid open file-descriptor.

ENOTTY if `fildes` is not associated with a device-driver that accepts control-functions.

EINTR if a signal is caught during the `ioctl` operation.

The function `ioctl` also fails if the device-driver detects an error. In this case, the error is passed through `ioctl` without change to the caller. A particular device-driver might not have all of the following error cases. Requests to standard device-drivers fail and `errno` equals:

EINVAL if `request` or `arg` are not valid for this device.

EIO if a physical I/O error occurs.

ENXIO if `request` and `arg` are valid for this device-driver, but the particular sub-device can not perform the service requested.

SEE ALSO

The specific device reference documents and generic devices such as the general terminal interface [see TERMIO(BA_ENV)] and STREAMS I/O interface [see STREAMIO(NS_ENV)].

NAME

kill — send a signal to a process or a group of processes

SYNOPSIS

```
#include <signal.h>
int kill(pid, sig)
int pid, sig;
```

DESCRIPTION

The function kill sends a signal to a process or a group of processes.

The signal sent is specified by sig, and is either 0 or from the list in SIGNAL(BA_OS). If sig is 0 (the null-signal), error checking is done but no signal is sent. This checks the validity of pid. The process or group of processes to receive sig is specified by pid as follows:

If pid < 0 , send sig to the process whose process-ID equals pid.

If pid = 0 , send sig to all processes, except special system-processes, whose process-group-ID equals the process-group-ID of the sending-process.

If pid < 0 , but not −1, send sig to all processes whose process-group-ID equals the absolute value of pid.

If pid = −1 , send sig to all processes, except special system-processes.

Of the processes specified by pid, only those where the real-user-ID or effective-user-ID of the sending-process matches the real-user-ID or effective-user-ID of the receiving-process are sent the signal, unless the effective-user-ID of the sending-process is super-user.

RETURN VALUE

On success, kill returns 0; on failure, it returns −1, it does *not* send any signal, and errno indicates the error.

ERRORS

The function kill fails and errno equals:

EINVAL   if sig is not a valid signal number.

EINVAL   if sig is SIGKILL and pid is a special system-process.

ESRCH   if no process corresponding to pid can be found.

EPERM   if the user-ID of the sending-process is not super-user, and its real-user-ID (or effective-user-ID) does not match either the real-user-ID or effective-user-ID of the receiving-process.

EPERM   if sig is SIGKILL and pid is a special system-process.

SEE ALSO

GETPID(BA_OS), SETPGRP(BA_OS), SIGNAL(BA_OS).

NAME

link — link to a file

SYNOPSIS

```
int link(path1, path2)
char *path1, *path2;
```

DESCRIPTION

The function link creates a new link (directory entry) for the existing file.

The argument path1 points to a path-name naming an existing file.

The argument path2 points to a path-name naming the new directory entry to be created.

RETURN VALUE

On success, link returns 0; on failure, it returns −1, it does *not* create any link, and errno indicates the error.

ERRORS

The function link fails and errno equals:

ENOTDIR　if a component of either path-prefix is not a directory.

ENOENT　if a component of either path-name should exist but does not.

EACCES　if a component of either path-prefix denies search permission, or if the requested link requires writing in a directory with a mode that denies write permission.

EEXIST　if the link named by path2 exists.

EPERM　if the file named by path1 is a directory and the effective-user-ID is not super-user.

EXDEV　if the link named by path2 and the file named by path1 are on different logical devices (file-systems) and the implementation does not permit cross-device links.

EROFS　if the requested link requires writing in a directory on a read-only file-system.

EMLINK　if the maximum number of links to a single file, {LINK_MAX}, would be exceeded.

ENOSPC　if the directory to contain the link cannot be extended.

SEE ALSO

UNLINK(BA_OS).

NAME

lockf — record-locking on files

SYNOPSIS

```
#include <unistd.h>

int lockf(fildes, function, size)
int fildes, function;
long size;
```

DESCRIPTION

The function lockf can lock sections of a file with advisory-mode or enforcement-mode locks depending on the mode of the file [see CHMOD(BA_OS)].

> NOTE: The function lockf first became available following UNIX System V Release 1.0 and UNIX System V Release 2.0.

Calls to lockf from other processes which try to lock the locked file section either return an error value or go to sleep until the resource becomes unlocked. All the locks for a process are removed when the process terminates [see FCNTL(BA_OS) for more information about record-locking].

The argument fildes is an open file-descriptor. The file-descriptor must have been opened with write-only permission (O_WRONLY) or with read/write permission (O_RDWR) in order to establish a lock with this function call [see OPEN(BA_OS)].

The argument function is a control value which specifies the action to be taken. The <unistd.h> header file defines the permissible values for function as follows:

```
#define F_ULOCK 0 /* unlock locked sections */
#define F_LOCK  1 /* lock a section */
                  /* for exclusive use */
#define F_TLOCK 2 /* test and lock a section */
                  /* for exclusive use */
#define F_TEST  3 /* test section for locks */
                  /* by other processes */
```

F_TEST detects if a lock by another process is present on the specified section; F_LOCK and F_TLOCK both lock a section of a file if the section is available; F_ULOCK removes locks from a section of the file. All other values of function are reserved for future extensions and result in an error return if they are not implemented.

The argument size is the number of contiguous bytes to be locked or unlocked. The resource to be locked or unlocked starts at the current offset in the file and extends forward for a positive size or backward for a negative size (the preceding bytes up to but not including the current offset). If size is 0, the section from the current offset through the largest file offset {FCHR_MAX} is locked (i.e., from the current offset through the present or any future end-of-file). An area need not be allocated to the file in order to be locked as such locks may exist past the end-of-file.

The sections locked with F_LOCK or F_TLOCK may, in whole or in part, contain or be contained by a previously locked section for the same process. When this occurs, or if adjacent locked sections would occur, the sections are combined into a single locked section. If the request requires that a new element be added to the table of active locks and this table is already full, an error is returned, and the new section is not locked.

F_LOCK and F_TLOCK requests differ only in the action taken if the resource is unavailable. F_LOCK causes the calling-process to sleep until the resource is available; F_TLOCK causes lockf to return −1 and errno to equal EACCES if the section is already locked by another process.

F_ULOCK requests may release (wholly or in part) one or more locked sections controlled by the process. Locked sections are unlocked starting at the point of the file offset through size bytes or to the end of file if size is 0. When all of a locked section is not released (i.e., the beginning or end of the area to be unlocked falls within a locked section), the remaining portions of that section are still locked by the process. For example, releasing a center portion of a locked section leaves the portions of the section before and after it locked and requires an additional element in the table of active locks. If this table is full, an EDEADLK error is returned in errno and the requested section is not released.

A potential for deadlock occurs if a process controlling a locked resource is put to sleep by accessing another process's locked resource. Thus, calls to lockf or the FCNTL(BA_OS) routine scan for a deadlock prior to sleeping on a locked resource. An error return is made if sleeping on the locked resource would cause a deadlock.

Sleeping on a resource is interrupted with any signal. The ALARM(BA_OS) routine may be used to provide a timeout facility in programs requiring it.

RETURN VALUE

On success, lockf returns 0; on failure, it returns −1 and errno indicates the error.

ERRORS

The function lockf fails and errno equals:

EACCES   if function is F_TLOCK or F_TEST, and the section is already locked by another process.

EBADF   if fildes is not a valid open file-descriptor.

EBADF   if function is F_LOCK or F_TLOCK, and fildes is not a valid file-descriptor open for writing.

EDEADLK   if function is F_LOCK and a deadlock would occur; also if function is F_LOCK, F_TLOCK or F_ULOCK, and {LOCK_MAX} regions are already locked system-wide.

USAGE

In the future, `errno` will equal `EAGAIN` rather than `EACCES` when a section of a file is already locked by another process; portable programs should expect and test for either value, for example:

```
...
if (lockf(fd, F_TLOCK, siz) == -1)
    if ((errno == EAGAIN) || (errno == EACCES))
        /*
         * section locked by another process
         * check for either EAGAIN or EACCES
         * due to different implementations
         */
    else if ...
        /*
         * check for other errors
         */
```

Record-locking should not be used in combination with the FOPEN(BA_OS), FREAD(BA_OS), FWRITE(BA_OS), etc. *stdio* routines. Instead, the more primitive, non-buffered routines (e.g., the OPEN(BA_OS) routine) should be used. Unexpected results may occur in processes that do buffering in the user address space. The process may later read/write data which is/was locked. The *stdio* routines are the most common source of unexpected buffering.

SEE ALSO

CHMOD(BA_OS), CLOSE(BA_OS), CREAT(BA_OS), FCNTL(BA_OS), OPEN(BA_OS), READ(BA_OS), WRITE(BA_OS).

CAVEATS

The error condition which currently sets `errno` to `EACCES` will instead set `errno` to `EAGAIN` [see also USAGE above].

NAME

    lsearch, lfind — linear search and update

SYNOPSIS

    #include <search.h>

    char *lsearch(key, base, nelp, width, compar)
    char *key;
    char *base;
    unsigned *nelp;
    unsigned width;
    int (*compar)();

    char *lfind(key, base, nelp, width, compar)
    char *key;
    char *base;
    unsigned *nelp;
    unsigned width;
    int (*compar)();

DESCRIPTION

    The function lsearch is a linear search routine. It returns a pointer into a table indicating where a datum may be found. If the datum does not occur, it is added at the end of the table.

    The function lfind is the same as lsearch except that if the datum is not found, it is not added to the table. Instead, a NULL pointer is returned.

    The argument key points to the datum to be sought in the table.

    The argument base points to the first element in the table.

    The argument nelp points to an integer variable containing the current number of elements in the table. The variable pointed to by nelp is incremented if the datum is added to the table.

    The argument width is the size of an element in bytes.

    The argument compar is the name of the comparison function that the user must supply (strcmp, for example). It is called with two arguments that point to the elements being compared. The function must return zero if the elements are equal and non-zero otherwise.

RETURN VALUE

    If the searched for datum is found, both lsearch and lfind return a pointer to it; otherwise, lfind returns NULL and lsearch returns a pointer to the newly added element.

USAGE

    The function lfind was added in UNIX System V Release 2.0.

    The pointers to the key and the element at the base of the table should be of type pointer-to-element and cast to type pointer-to-character.

    The comparison function need not compare every byte, so arbitrary data may be contained in the elements in addition to the values being compared.

Although declared as type pointer-to-character, the value returned should be cast into type pointer-to-element.

Space for the table must be managed by the program. Undefined results can occur if there is not enough room in the table to add a new item.

EXAMPLES

This fragment will read in ≤ TABSIZE strings of length ≤ ELSIZE and store them in a table, eliminating duplicates.

```
#include <stdio.h>
#include <search.h>

#define TABSIZE 50
#define ELSIZE 120

char line[ELSIZE], tab[TABSIZE][ELSIZE], *lsearch();
unsigned nel = 0;
int strcmp();
while (fgets(line,ELSIZE,stdin)!=NULL && nel<TABSIZE)
    (void) lsearch(line, (char *)tab, &nel, ELSIZE, strcmp);
```

SEE ALSO

BSEARCH(BA_LIB), HSEARCH(BA_LIB), TSEARCH(BA_LIB).

CAVEATS

A NULL pointer will be returned by the function lsearch with errno set appropriately, if there is not enough room in the table to add a new item.

NAME

lseek — move read/write file-pointer

SYNOPSIS

```
#include <unistd.h>

long lseek(fildes, offset, whence)
int fildes;
long offset;
int whence;
```

DESCRIPTION

The function lseek sets the file-pointer associated with fildes as specified by whence. The <unistd.h> header file defines the symbolic constants for whence as follows:

Name	Description
SEEK_SET	set file-pointer equal to offset bytes.
SEEK_CUR	set file-pointer to current location plus offset bytes.
SEEK_END	set file-pointer to EOF plus offset bytes.

The argument fildes is an open file-descriptor [see VOCAB(BA_DEF)].

If successful, lseek returns the resulting pointer location, as measured in bytes from the beginning of the file; lseek modifies the file-pointer without affecting the physical device. The significance of the file-pointer associated with a device incapable of seeking, such as a terminal, is undefined.

The function lseek allows the file-pointer to be set beyond the existing data in the file. If data are later written at this point, subsequent reads in the gap between the previous end of data and the newly written data will return bytes of value 0 until data are written into the gap.

RETURN VALUE

On success, lseek returns a file-pointer value; on failure, it returns − 1, it does *not* change the file-pointer, and errno indicates the error.

ERRORS

The function lseek fails and errno equals:

EBADF   if fildes is not an open file-descriptor.

ESPIPE   if fildes is associated with a pipe or FIFO.

EINVAL   if whence is not SEEK_SET, SEEK_CUR or SEEK_END.

USAGE

Normally, programs should use the *stdio* routines to open, close, read, write and manipulate files. Thus, programs that use the FOPEN(BA_OS) *stdio* routine to open a file should use the FSEEK(BA_OS) *stdio* routine instead of lseek.

SEE ALSO

CREAT(BA_OS), DUP(BA_OS), FCNTL(BA_OS), OPEN(BA_OS).

NAME

malloc, free, realloc, calloc, mallopt, mallinfo — fast main
memory allocator

SYNOPSIS

```
#include <malloc.h>

char *malloc(size)
unsigned size;

void free(ptr)
char *ptr;

char *realloc(ptr, size)
char *ptr;
unsigned size;

char *calloc(nelem, elsize)
unsigned nelem, elsize;

int mallopt(cmd, value)
int cmd, value;

struct mallinfo mallinfo()
```

DESCRIPTION

The functions malloc and free provide a simple general-purpose memory
allocation package.

The function malloc returns a pointer to a block of at least size bytes
suitably aligned for any use.

The argument to free is a pointer to a block that malloc previously
allocated; after the free operation completes, this space is made available for
further allocation.

Undefined results will occur if the space assigned by malloc is overrun or if
an invalid value for ptr is passed to free.

The function realloc changes the size of the block pointed to by ptr to
size bytes and returns a pointer to the (possibly moved) block. The contents
will be unchanged up to the lesser of the new and old sizes.

The function calloc allocates space for an array of nelem elements of size
elsize. The space is initialized to zeros.

Available in UNIX System V Release 2.0, mallopt plus mallinfo allow
tuning the allocation algorithm at execution time.

The function mallopt initiates a mechanism that can be used to allocate
small blocks of memory quickly. Using this scheme, a large-group (called a
holding-block) of these small-blocks is allocated at one time. Then, each time
a program requests a small amount of memory from malloc a pointer to one
of the *pre-allocated* small-blocks is returned. Different holding-blocks are
created for different sizes of small-blocks and are created when needed.

The function `mallopt` allows the programmer to set three parameters to maximize efficient small-block allocation for a particular application. The three parameters are:

The value of `size` below which requests to `malloc` will be filled using the special small-block algorithm. Initially, this value, which will be called *maxfast*, is zero, which means that the small-block option is not normally in use by `malloc`.

The number of small-blocks in a holding-block. If holding-blocks have many more small-blocks than the program is using, space will be wasted. If holding-blocks are too small, have too few small-blocks in each, performance gain is lost.

The *grain* of small-block sizes. This value determines what range of small-block sizes will be considered to be the same size. This influences the number of separate holding-blocks allocated. For example, if *grain* were 16-bytes, all small-blocks of 16-bytes or less would belong to one holding-block and blocks from 17-bytes to 32-bytes would belong to another holding-block. Thus, if *grain* is too small space may be wasted because many holding-blocks may be created.

The values for the argument `cmd` to `mallopt` are:

M_MXFAST
: Set *maxfast* to `value`. The algorithm allocates all blocks below the size of *maxfast* in large-groups and then doles them out very quickly. The default value for *maxfast* is 0.

M_NLBLKS
: Set *numlblks* to `value`. The above mentioned large-groups each contain *numlblks* blocks. The value for *numlblks* must be greater than 1. The default value for *numlblks* is 100.

M_GRAIN
: Set *grain* to `value`. The sizes of all blocks smaller than *maxfast* are considered to be rounded up to the nearest multiple of *grain*. The value for *grain* must be greater than 0. The default value for *grain* is the smallest number of bytes which will allow alignment of any data type. The `value` will be rounded up to a multiple of the default when *grain* is set.

M_KEEP
: Preserve data in a freed-block until the next call to `malloc`, `realloc` or `calloc`. This option is provided only for compatibility with the older version of `malloc` and is not recommended.

These `cmd` values are defined by the `<malloc.h>` header file.

The function `mallopt` may be called repeatedly, but the parameters may not be changed after the first small-block is allocated from a holding-block. If `mallopt` is called again after the first small-block is allocated using the small-block algorithm, it returns an error.

The function `mallinfo` can be used during a program development to determine the best settings of these parameters for a particular application. The function `mallinfo` must not be called until after some storage has been allocated using `malloc`. The function `mallinfo` provides information describing space usage. It returns the structure `mallinfo`, which includes the following members:

```
int arena;     /* total space in arena */
int ordblks;   /* number of ordinary-blocks */
int smblks;    /* number of small-blocks */
int hblkhd;    /* space in holding-block overhead */
int hblks;     /* number of holding-blocks */
int usmblks;   /* space in small-blocks in use */
int fsmblks;   /* space in free small-blocks */
int uordblks;  /* space in ordinary-blocks in use */
int fordblks;  /* space in free ordinary-blocks */
int keepcost;  /* space penalty for keep option */
```

The structure `mallinfo` is defined by the `<malloc.h>` header file.

RETURN VALUE

Each of the allocation functions `malloc`, `realloc`, and `calloc` returns a pointer to space suitably aligned (after possible pointer coercion) for storage of any type of object.

The functions `malloc`, `realloc`, and `calloc` return a NULL pointer if `nbytes` is 0 or if there is not enough available memory. When `realloc` returns NULL, the block pointed to by `ptr` is left intact.

If `mallopt` is called after any allocation from a holding-block or if the arguments `cmd` or `value` are invalid, `mallopt` returns a non-zero value; otherwise, it returns 0.

USAGE

The functions `mallopt` and `mallinfo` and the `<malloc.h>` header file first appeared in UNIX System V Release 2.0. To get the newer functions, a developer must use the following:

```
cc -lmalloc
```

Without this, the older functions remain as the default.

In UNIX System V Release 2.0, the developer can control whether the contents of the freed space are destroyed or left undisturbed (see `mallopt` above). In UNIX System V Release 1.0, the contents are left undisturbed.

Allocation time increases when many objects have been allocated and not freed. The additional UNIX System V Release 2.0 routines provide some flexibility in dealing with this.

NAME

MARK — profile within a function

SYNOPSIS

```
#define MARK
#include <prof.h>

void MARK(name)
```

DESCRIPTION

The macro MARK will introduce a mark called name that will be treated the same as a function entry point. Execution of the mark will add to a counter for that mark, and program-counter time spent will be accounted to the immediately preceding mark or to the function if there are no preceding marks within the active function.

The identifier name may be any combination of letters, numbers or underscores. Each name in a single compilation must be unique, but may be the same as any ordinary program symbol.

For marks to be effective, the symbol MARK must be defined before the header file <prof.h> is included. This may be defined by a preprocessor directive as in the synopsis, or by a command line argument, i.e.:

```
cc -p -DMARK foo.c
```

If MARK is not defined, the MARK(name) statements may be left in the source files containing them and will be ignored.

EXAMPLES

In this example, marks can be used to determine how much time is spent in each loop. Unless this example is compiled with MARK defined on the command line, the marks are ignored.

```
#include <prof.h>
foo()
{
    int i, j;
    ...
    MARK(loop1);
    for (i = 0; i < 2000; i++) {
        ...
    }
    MARK(loop2);
    for (j = 0; j < 2000; j++) {
        ...
    }
}
```

SEE ALSO

PROFIL(KE_OS), MONITOR(SD_LIB), PROF(SD_CMD).

NAME

`matherr` — error-handling function

SYNOPSIS

```
#include <math.h>

int matherr(x)
struct exception *x;
```

DESCRIPTION

The function `matherr` is invoked by math library routines when errors are detected. Users may define their own procedures for handling errors, by including a function named `matherr` in their programs. The function `matherr` must be of the form described above. When an error occurs, a pointer to the `exception` structure `x` will be passed to the user-supplied `matherr` function. This structure, which is defined by the `<math.h>` header file, includes the following members:

```
int type;
char *name;
double arg1, arg2, retval;
```

The element `type` is an integer describing the type of error that has occurred from the following list defined by the `<math.h>` header file:

DOMAIN	argument domain error.
SING	argument singularity.
OVERFLOW	overflow range error.
UNDERFLOW	underflow range error.
TLOSS	total loss of significance.
PLOSS	partial loss of significance.

The element `name` points to a string containing the name of the routine that incurred the error. The elements `arg1` and `arg2` are the first and second arguments with which the routine was invoked.

The element `retval` is set to the default value that will be returned by the routine unless the user's `matherr` function sets it to a different value.

If the user's `matherr` function returns non-zero, no error message will be printed, and `errno` will not be set.

If the function `matherr` is not supplied by the user, the default error-handling procedures, described with the math library routines involved, will be invoked upon error. If the user does not supply the function `matherr`, the default error-handling procedures, described with the math library routines involved, will be invoked upon error. These procedures are also summarized in the table below. In every case, `errno` is set to EDOM or ERANGE and the program continues.

ERRORS

DEFAULT ERROR HANDLING PROCEDURES						
Types of Errors						
type	DOMAIN	SING	OVERFLOW	UNDERFLOW	TLOSS	PLOSS
errno	EDOM	EDOM	ERANGE	ERANGE	ERANGE	ERANGE
BESSEL:	—	—	—	—	M, 0	•
y0, y1, yn	M, −H	—	—	—	—	—
EXP:	—	—	H	0	—	—
LOG, LOG10:						
(arg < 0)	M, −H	—	—	—	—	—
(arg = 0)	—	M, −H	—	—	—	—
POW:	—	—	±H	0	—	—
neg ** non-int	M, 0	—	—	—	—	—
0 ** non-pos						
SQRT:	M, 0	—	—	—	—	—
GAMMA:	—	M, H	H	—	—	—
HYPOT:	—	—	H	—	—	—
SINH:	—	—	±H	—	—	—
COSH:	—	—	H	—	—	—
SIN, COS, TAN:	—	—	—	—	M, 0	•
ASIN, ACOS, ATAN2:	M, 0	—	—	—	—	—

ABBREVIATIONS	
•	As much as possible of the value is returned.
M	Message is printed (EDOM error).
H	HUGE is returned.
−H	−HUGE is returned.
±H	+HUGE or −HUGE is returned.
0	0 is returned.

EXAMPLES

```
#include <math.h>

int matherr(x)
    register struct exception *x;
{
    switch (x->type) {
    case DOMAIN: /* change sqrt to return sqrt(-arg1), not 0 */
        if (!strcmp(x->name, "sqrt")) {
            x->retval = sqrt(-x->arg1);
            return (0);  /* print message and set errno */
        }
    case SING:   /* print message and abort */
        fprintf(stderr, "domain error in %s\n", x->name);
        abort();
    case PLOSS:  /* print detailed error message */
        fprintf(stderr, "loss of significance in %s(%g) = %g\n",
            x->name, x->arg1, x->retval);
        return (1);   /* take no other action */
    }
    /* all other errors, execute default procedure */
    return (0);
}
```

CAVEATS

The math functions which return HUGE or ±HUGE on overflow will return
HUGE_VAL or ±HUGE_VAL respectively.

NAME

    memccpy, memchr, memcmp, memcpy, memset — memory operations

SYNOPSIS

    #include <memory.h>

    char *memccpy(s1, s2, c, n)
    char *s1, *s2;
    int c, n;

    char *memchr(s, c, n)
    char *s;
    int c, n;

    int memcmp(s1, s2, n)
    char *s1, *s2;
    int n;

    char *memcpy(s1, s2, n)
    char *s1, *s2;
    int n;

    char *memset(s, c, n)
    char *s;
    int c, n;

DESCRIPTION

These functions operate as efficiently as possible on memory areas (arrays of characters bounded by a count, not terminated by a null-character). They do not check for the overflow of any receiving memory area.

The function memccpy copies characters from memory area s2 into s1, stopping after the first occurrence of character c has been copied or after n characters have been copied, whichever comes first. It returns a pointer to the character after the copy of c in s1, or a NULL pointer if c was not found in the first n characters of s2.

The function memchr returns a pointer to the first occurrence of character c in the first n characters of memory area s, or a NULL pointer if c does not occur.

The function memcmp compares its arguments, looking at the first n characters only. It returns an integer less than, equal to or greater than 0, according as s1 is lexicographically less than, equal to or greater than s2.

The function memcpy copies n characters from memory area s2 to s1. It returns s1.

The function memset sets the first n characters in memory area s to the value of character c. It returns s.

USAGE

All these functions are defined by the `<memory.h>` header file.

The function `memcmp` uses native character comparison. The sign of the value returned when one of the characters has its high-order bit set is implementation-dependent.

Character movement is performed differently in different implementations. Thus overlapping moves may be unpredictable.

SEE ALSO

STRING(BA_LIB).

CAVEATS

The declarations in the `<memory.h>` header file will be moved to the `<string.h>` header file.

NAME
    mkdir — make a directory

SYNOPSIS
    #include <sys/types.h>
    #include <sys/stat.h>

    int mkdir(path, mode)
    char *path
    int mode;

DESCRIPTION
    The function mkdir creates a new directory.

    The argument path specifies the name of the new directory.

    The argument mode specifies the initial mode of the new directory. The
    protection bits of mode are modified by the process's file-mode-creation-mask
    [see UMASK(BA_OS)]. The value of the argument mode should be the logical
    OR of the values of the desired permissions:

Name	Description
S_IREAD	Read by owner.
S_IWRITE	Write by owner.
S_IEXEC	Execute (search) by owner.
S_IRGRP	Read by group.
S_IWGRP	Write by group.
S_IXGRP	Execute (search) by group.
S_IROTH	Read by others (i.e., anyone else).
S_IWOTH	Write by others.
S_IXOTH	Execute (search) by others.

    The directory's owner-ID is set to the process's effective-user-ID. The
    directory's group-ID is set to the process's effective-group-ID. The newly
    created directory is empty, except for possible directory entries for . (the
    directory itself) and .. (the parent-directory) [see directory in
    VOCAB(BA_DEF)].

RETURN VALUE
    On success, mkdir returns 0; on failure, it returns −1, it does *not* create
    directory, and errno indicates the error.

ERRORS
    The function mkdir fails and errno equals:

    ENOTDIR   if a component of the path-prefix is not a directory.

    ENOENT   if a component of the path-prefix does not exist.

    ENOENT   if the path-name is longer than {PATH_MAX} characters.

    EACCES   if a component of the path-prefix denies search permission, or if
               the parent-directory of the directory to be created denies write
               permission.

EEXIST   if the named path-name exists.

EROFS   if the directory to be created resides on a read-only file-system.

EMLINK   if the maximum number of links to the parent-directory,
            {LINK_MAX}, would be exceeded.

EIO   if a physical I/O error occurs.

ENOSPC   if no free space is available on the device containing the
            directory.

USAGE

The function mkdir was added in UNIX System V Release 3.0.

SEE ALSO

CHMOD(BA_OS), UMASK(BA_OS).

NAME

mknod — make a directory, special or ordinary-file, or a FIFO

SYNOPSIS

```
#include <sys/types.h>
#include <sys/stat.h>

int mknod(path, mode, dev)
char *path;
int mode, dev;
```

DESCRIPTION

The function mknod creates a new file named by the path-name pointed to by path.

The mode of the new file is initialized from mode. The <sys/stat.h> header file defines symbolic constants for the access-permission-bits used to construct mode. The value of mode should be the logical-OR of the values of the desired permissions:

Name	Description
S_IFMT	file type; one of the following:

	S_IFIFO	FIFO-special
	S_IFCHR	character-special
	S_IFDIR	directory node
	S_IFBLK	block-special
	S_IFREG	ordinary-file

Name	Description
S_ISUID	set user-ID on execution
S_ISGID	set group-ID on execution
S_ISVTX	(reserved)
S_ENFMT	record-locking enforced
S_IRUSR	read by owner
S_IWUSR	write by owner
S_IXUSR	execute (search) by owner
S_IRGRP	read by group
S_IWGRP	write by group
S_IXGRP	execute (search) by group
S_IROTH	read by others (i.e., anyone else)
S_IWOTH	write by others
S_IXOTH	execute (search) by others

Values of mode other than those above are undefined and should not be used.

The *owner*, *group* and *other* permission-bits of mode are modified by the process's file-mode-creation-mask:

The function mknod clears each bit whose corresponding bit in the process's file-mode-creation-mask is set [see UMASK(BA_OS)].

If mode indicates a block-special or character-special file, dev is a configuration-dependent specification of a character or block I/O device. If mode does not indicate a block-special or character-special device, dev is ignored. The value of dev comes from the st_rdev field of the stat structure [see STAT(BA_OS)].

The owner-ID of the file is set to the effective-user-ID of the process. The group-ID of the file is set to the effective-group-ID of the process.

The function mknod may be invoked only by the super-user for file types other than FIFO-special.

RETURN VALUE

On success, mknod returns 0; on failure, it returns −1, it does *not* create a new file, and errno indicates the error.

ERRORS

The function mknod fails and errno equals:

EPERM   if the effective-user-ID of the process is not super-user and the file type is not FIFO-special.

ENOTDIR   if a component of the path-prefix is not a directory.

ENOENT   if a component of the path-prefix does not exist.

ENOENT   if the path-name is longer than {PATH_MAX} characters.

EACCES   if a component of the path-prefix denies search permission and the effective-user-ID of the process is not super-user.

EROFS   if the directory in which the file is to be created resides on a read-only file-system.

EEXIST   if the named file exists.

ENOSPC   if the directory to contain the new file cannot be extended.

USAGE

Normally, programs should use the MKDIR(BA_OS) routine to make a directory, since the function mknod may not establish directory entries for . (the directory itself) and .. (the parent-directory) [see directory in VOCAB(BA_DEF)] and super-user privilege is not required.

SEE ALSO

CHMOD(BA_OS), EXEC(BA_OS), STAT(BA_OS), UMASK(BA_OS).

NAME

mktemp — make a unique file-name

SYNOPSIS

```
char *mktemp(template)
char *template;
```

DESCRIPTION

The function `mktemp` replaces the contents of the string pointed to by `template` by a unique file-name and returns `template`. The string in `template` should look like a file-name with six trailing `X`s; `mktemp` replaces the `X`s with a letter and the current process-ID. The letter is chosen so that the resulting name does not duplicate an existing file.

RETURN VALUE

The function `mktemp` returns the pointer `template`. If a unique name cannot be created, `template` points to a null-string.

SEE ALSO

GETPID(BA_OS), TMPFILE(BA_LIB), TMPNAM(BA_LIB).

CAVEATS

The function `mktemp` returns a `NULL` pointer if a unique name cannot be created.

NAME

monitor — prepare execution profile

SYNOPSIS

```
#include <mon.h>

void monitor(lowpc, highpc, buffer, bufsize, nfunc)
int (*lowpc)(), (*highpc)();
WORD *buffer;
int bufsize, nfunc;
```

DESCRIPTION

The routine monitor is an interface to the profil system service routine [see PROFIL(KE_OS)]; lowpc and highpc are the addresses of two functions; buffer is the address of a (user supplied) array of bufsize WORDs (WORD is defined in the <mon.h> header file). The monitor routine arranges to record a histogram of periodically sampled values of the program-counter, and of counts of calls of certain functions, in the buffer. The lowest address sampled is that of lowpc and the highest is just below highpc; lowpc may not equal 0 for this use of monitor. At most nfunc call counts can be kept; only calls of functions compiled with the profiling option -p of cc are recorded.

An executable program created using cc with the -p option automatically includes calls for monitor with default parameters; therefore monitor need not be called explicitly except to gain fine control over profiling.

For the results to be significant, especially where there are small, heavily used routines, it is suggested that the buffer be no more than a few times smaller than the range of locations sampled.

To profile the entire program, it is sufficient to use the following:

```
extern int etext();
...
monitor((int (*)())2, etext, buf, bufsize, nfunc);
```

The routine etext lies just above all the program text.

To stop execution monitoring and write the results, use the following:

```
monitor((int(*)())0,(int(*)())0,0,0,0);
```

then use prof [see PROF(SD_CMD)] to examine the results.

The environmental variable PROFDIR names the output file for monitor:

If no PROFDIR exists, file mon.out is created in the current directory.

If PROFDIR is a null-string, no profiling is done and no output file created.

Otherwise, the value of PROFDIR names the directory in which to create the output file.

If PROFDIR equals `dirname`, the output file is named:

    dirname/*pid*.mon.out

where *pid* is the program's process-ID.

When `monitor` is called automatically using `cc` with the `-p` option, the output file created is named:

    dirname/*pid*.*progname*

where *progname* is the name of the program.

FILES
    dirname/*pid*.mon.out
    dirname/*pid*.*progname*

SEE ALSO
    PROFIL(KE_OS), CC(SD_CMD), PROF(SD_CMD).

NAME

mount — mount a file-system

SYNOPSIS

```
int mount(spec, dir, rwflag)
char *spec, *dir;
int rwflag;
```

DESCRIPTION

The function mount requests that a removable file-system contained on the block-special file identified by the argument spec be mounted on the directory identified by the argument dir.

The arguments spec and dir are pointers to path-names.

When mount succeeds, references to the file named by dir will refer to the root-directory on the mounted file-system.

The low-order bit of the argument rwflag is used to control write permission on the mounted file-system; if the bit is set to 1, writing is forbidden; otherwise, writing is permitted according to individual file accessibility.

The function mount may be invoked only by the super-user.

RETURN VALUE

On success, mount returns 0; on failure, it returns −1 and errno indicates the error.

ERRORS

The function mount fails and errno equals:

EPERM   if the effective-user-ID is not super-user.

ENOENT   if any of the named files does not exist.

ENOTDIR   if a component of a path-prefix is not a directory.

ENOTBLK   if the device identified by spec is not block-special.

ENXIO   if the device identified by spec does not exist.

ENOTDIR   if dir is not a directory.

EBUSY   if dir is currently mounted on, is someone's current working directory, or is otherwise busy.

EBUSY   if the device identified by spec is currently mounted.

EBUSY   if there are no more mount-table entries.

USAGE

The function mount is not recommended for use by programs.

SEE ALSO

UMOUNT(BA_OS).

CAVEATS

The external variable `errno` will be set to `EAGAIN` rather than `EBUSY` when the system mount-table is full.

Additional optional arguments will be added to the `mount` function. New bit-patterns will be added to the set of possible values of the argument `rwflag`. Some of these patterns will be used to indicate if an optional argument is present.

NAME

`msgctl` — message-control-operations

SYNOPSIS

```
#include <sys/types.h>
#include <sys/ipc.h>
#include <sys/msg.h>

int msgctl(msqid, cmd, buf)
int msqid, cmd;
struct msqid_ds *buf;
```

DESCRIPTION

The function `msgctl` provides a variety of message-control-operations as specified by `cmd`. The following values for `cmd` and the message-control-operations they specify are available:

IPC_STAT   Put the current value of each member of the `msqid_ds` structure in the structure pointed to by `buf`.

IPC_SET   Set the following members of the `msqid_ds` structure to the corresponding value found in the structure pointed to by `buf`:

```
msg_perm.uid
msg_perm.gid
msg_perm.mode /* only low 9-bits */
msg_qbytes
```

Only a process with an effective-user-ID equal to either super-user or to either `msg_perm.cuid` or `msg_perm.uid` in the `msqid_ds` structure can execute this `cmd`, and only super-user can raise the value of `msg_qbytes`.

IPC_RMID   Remove the message-queue-identifier specified by `msqid` from the system and destroy the message-queue and `msqid_ds` structure. Only a process whose effective-user-ID equals either super-user or either `msg_perm.cuid` or `msg_perm.uid` in the `msqid_ds` structure can execute this `cmd`.

RETURN VALUE

On success, `msgctl` returns 0; on failure, it returns – 1 and `errno` indicates the error.

ERRORS

The function `msgctl` fails and `errno` equals:

EINVAL   if `msqid` is not a valid message-queue-identifier; or `cmd` is not a valid command.

EACCES   if `cmd` is `IPC_STAT` and the calling-process does not have read permission.

EPERM   if cmd is `IPC_RMID` or `IPC_SET` and the effective-user-ID of the calling-process does not equal either super-user or either `msg_perm.cuid` or `msg_perm.uid` in the `msqid_ds` structure.

EPERM   if cmd is `IPC_SET`, an attempt is being made to increase the value of `msg_qbytes`, and the effective-user-ID of the calling-process does not equal super-user.

SEE ALSO

MSGGET(KE_OS), MSGRCV(KE_OS), MSGSND(KE_OS).

NAME

`msgget` — get message-queue

SYNOPSIS

```
#include <sys/types.h>
#include <sys/ipc.h>
#include <sys/msg.h>

int msgget(key, msgflg)
key_t key;
int msgflg;
```

DESCRIPTION

The function `msgget` returns the message-queue-identifier associated with the argument `key`.

A message-queue-identifier with its associated `msqid_ds` structure and message-queue are created for the argument `key` if one of the following are true:

if the argument `key` equals `IPC_PRIVATE`.

if the argument `key` does not already have a message-queue-identifier associated with it, and (`msgflg & IPC_CREAT`) is true.

Upon creation, the data structure associated with the new message-queue-identifier is initialized as follows:

Set `msg_perm.cuid` and `msg_perm.uid` to the effective-user-ID of the calling-process.

Set `msg_perm.cgid` and `msg_perm.gid` to the effective-group-ID of the calling-process.

Set the low-order 9-bits of `msg_perm.mode` to the low-order 9-bits of `msgflg`.

Set `msg_qnum` to 0.

Set `msg_lspid` and `msg_lrpid` to 0.

Set `msg_stime` and `msg_rtime` to 0.

Set `msg_ctime` to the current-time.

Set `msg_qbytes` to the system-limit.

RETURN VALUE

On success, `msgget` returns a message-queue-identifier (a non-negative integer); on failure, it returns – 1 and `errno` indicates the error.

ERRORS

The function `msgget` fails and `errno` equals:

EACCES   if a message-queue-identifier exists for the argument `key`, but operation-permission as set by the low-order 9-bits of `msgflg` is denied.

ENOENT   if a message-queue-identifier does not exist for the argument
           `key` and (`msgflg & IPC_CREAT`) is "false".

ENOSPC   if a message-queue-identifier is to be created but the system-
           imposed limit on the maximum number of allowed message-
           queue-identifiers system-wide would be exceeded.

EEXIST   if a message-queue-identifier exists for the argument `key` but
           ((`msgflg & IPC_CREAT`) `&&` (`msgflg & IPC_EXCL`))
           is "true".

SEE ALSO

MSGCTL(KE_OS), MSGRCV(KE_OS), MSGSND(KE_OS).

NAME

msgrcv — receive message

SYNOPSIS

```
#include <sys/types.h>
#include <sys/ipc.h>
#include <sys/msg.h>

int msgrcv(msqid, msgp, msgsz, msgtyp, msgflg)
int msqid;
struct mymsg *msgp;
int msgsz;
long msgtyp;
int msgflg;
```

DESCRIPTION

The function msgrcv reads a message from the queue associated with the message-queue-identifier specified by msqid and places it in the user-defined structure pointed to by msgp. The structure must contain the message type field along with the message text buffer. In the structure mymsg, the member mtype is the received message's type as specified by the sending-process and the member mtext is the message text [see MSGSND(KE_OS)].

The argument msgsz specifies the size in bytes of mtext. The received message is truncated to msgsz bytes if it is larger than msgsz and (msgflg & MSG_NOERROR) is "true". The truncated part of the message is lost and no indication of the truncation is given to the calling-process.

The <sys/msg.h> header file defines the symbolic name MSG_NOERROR.

The argument msgtyp specifies the type of message requested as follows:

If msgtyp = 0, the first message on the queue is received.

If msgtyp > 0, the first message of type msgtyp is received.

If msgtyp < 0, the first message of the lowest type that is less than or equal to the absolute value of msgtyp is received.

The argument msgflg specifies the action to be taken if a message of the desired type is not on the queue. These actions are as follows:

If (msgflg & IPC_NOWAIT) is "false", the calling-process suspends execution until one of the following occurs:

- A message of the desired type is placed on the queue.

- The message-queue-identifier msqid is removed from the system. When this occurs, errno equals EIDRM and − 1 is returned.

- The calling-process receives a signal that is to be caught. In this case a message is not received and the calling-process resumes execution in the manner prescribed in SIGNAL(BA_OS).

If (msgflg & IPC_NOWAIT) is "true", the calling-process immediately returns with − 1 and errno equals ENOMSG.

On success, the following actions take place on the `msqid_ds` structure:

`msg_qnum` is decremented by 1.

`msg_lrpid` is set to the process-ID of the calling-process.

`msg_rtime` is set to the current time.

RETURN VALUE

On success, `msgrcv` returns the number of bytes put in the buffer `mtext`; on failure, it returns − 1 and `errno` indicates the error.

ERRORS

The function `msgrcv` fails, it does *not* receive any messages, and `errno` equals:

EINVAL	if `msqid` is not a valid message-queue-identifier; or if the value of `msgsz` is less than 0.
EACCES	if the calling-process is denied operation-permission.
EINTR	if a signal interrupts `msgrcv`.
EIDRM	if the message-queue-identifier `msqid` has been removed from the system.
E2BIG	if the length of `mtext` exceeds the value of `msgsz` and (`msgflg` & `MSG_NOERROR`) is "false".
ENOMSG	if the queue does not contain a message of the desired type and (`msgtyp` & `IPC_NOWAIT`) is "true".

SEE ALSO

MSGCTL(KE_OS), MSGGET(KE_OS), MSGSND(KE_OS), SIGNAL(BA_OS).

NAME

msgsnd — send message

SYNOPSIS

```
#include <sys/types.h>
#include <sys/ipc.h>
#include <sys/msg.h>

int msgsnd(msqid, msgp, msgsz, msgflg)
int msqid;
struct mymsg *msgp;
int msgsz, msgflg;
```

DESCRIPTION

The function msgsnd sends a message to the queue associated with the message-queue-identifier specified by msqid.

The argument msgp points to a user-defined buffer that must contain first a field of type long integer to specify the type of the message, and then a data portion to hold the text of the message as follows:

```
struct mymsg {
    long mtype;     /* message type */
    char mtext[];   /* message text */
}
```

The structure member mtype is a positive integer the receiving-process can use for message selection [see MSGRCV(KE_OS)]. The structure member mtext is any text of length msgsz bytes.

The argument msgsz can range from 0 to a system-imposed maximum.

The argument msgflg specifies the action to take if any or all of the following are true:

The number of bytes already on the queue equals msg_qbytes.

The total number of messages on all queues system-wide equals the system-imposed limit.

These actions are as follows:

If (msgflg & IPC_NOWAIT) is "false", the calling-process suspends execution until one of the following occurs:

- The condition responsible for the suspension no longer exists, in which case the message is sent.

- The message-queue-identifier msqid is removed from the system [see MSGCTL(KE_OS)]. When this occurs, errno equals EIDRM and −1 is returned.

- The calling-process receives a signal that is to be caught. In this case the message is not sent and the calling-process resumes execution in the manner prescribed in the SIGNAL(BA_OS) routine.

If (msgflg & IPC_NOWAIT) is "true", the message is *not* sent and the calling-process returns immediately.

On success, the following actions take place on the `msqid_ds` structure:

`msg_qnum` is increased by 1.

`msg_lspid` is set to the process-ID of the calling-process.

`msg_stime` is set to the current time.

RETURN VALUE

On success, `msgsnd` returns 0; on failure, it returns − 1 and `errno` indicates the error.

ERRORS

The function `msgsnd` fails, it does *not* send any messages, and `errno` equals:

`EINVAL`	if `msqid` is not a valid message-queue-identifier; or if the value of `mtype` is less than 1; or if the value of `msgsz` is less than 0 or greater than the system-imposed limit.
`EACCES`	if the calling-process is denied operation-permission.
`EAGAIN`	if the message cannot be sent for one of the reasons cited above and (`msgflg & IPC_NOWAIT`) is "true".
`EINTR`	if a signal interrupts `msgsnd`.
`EIDRM`	if the message-queue-identifier `msgid` has been removed from the system.

SEE ALSO

MSGCTL(KE_OS), MSGGET(KE_OS), MSGRCV(KE_OS), SIGNAL(BA_OS).

NAME

`nice` — change priority of a process

SYNOPSIS

```
int nice(incr)
int incr;
```

DESCRIPTION

The function `nice` adds the value of `incr` to the nice-value of the calling-process. A process's *nice-value* is a positive number for which a more positive value results in lower CPU priority.

The system imposes an implementation-specific, maximum process-nice-value of $2*\{NZERO\}-1$ and a minimum process-nice-value of `0`. If adding `incr` to the process's current nice-value causes the result to be above or below these limits, the process's nice-value is set to the corresponding limit.

RETURN VALUE

On success, `nice` returns the process's new nice-value minus `{NZERO}`.

ERRORS

The function `nice` fails, it does *not* change the process's nice-value, and `errno` equals:

EPERM   if `incr` is negative or greater than $2*\{NZERO\}$ and the effective-user-ID of the calling-process is not super-user.

SEE ALSO

EXEC(BA_OS).

NAME

nlist — get entries from name list

SYNOPSIS

```
#include <nlist.h>

int nlist(filename, nl)
char *filename;
struct nlist *nl;
```

DESCRIPTION

The routine nlist examines the name list in the executable file whose name is pointed to by filename, and selectively extracts a list of values and puts them in the array of nlist structures pointed to by nl. The name-list nl consists of an array of structures containing names of variables, types and values. The list is terminated with a null-name; that is, a null-string is in the name position of the structure. Each variable-name is looked up in the name-list of the file. If the name is found, the type and value of the name are inserted in the next two fields. The type field will be set to 0 unless the file was compiled with the -g option of cc. If the name is not found, both entries are set to 0.

This function is useful for examining the system name-list kept in the namelist file. In this way programs can obtain system-addresses that are up to date.

RETURN VALUE

Returns -1 upon error; otherwise returns 0.

All value entries are set to 0 if the file cannot be read or if it does not contain a valid name-list.

NAME

open — open file for reading or writing

SYNOPSIS

```
#include <fcntl.h>

int open(path, oflag [, mode ])
char *path;
int oflag, mode;
```

DESCRIPTION

The function `open` opens a file-descriptor for the named file.

The argument `path` points to a path-name naming a file.

The function `open` sets the file-status flags according to `oflag`. The `<fcntl.h>` header file defines the symbolic names of flags. The values of `oflag` are constructed by OR-ing flags from the following list (only one of the first three flags below may be used):

`O_RDONLY`	Open for reading only.
`O_WRONLY`	Open for writing only.
`O_RDWR`	Open for reading and writing.
`O_APPEND`	Set the file-pointer to the end of the file prior to each write.
`O_NDELAY`	This flag will affect subsequent reads and writes [see READ(BA_OS) and WRITE(BA_OS)].

When opening a FIFO with `O_RDONLY` or `O_WRONLY` set:

If `O_NDELAY` is clear, `open` for reading-only blocks until a process opens the file for writing, but `open` for writing-only blocks until a process opens the file for reading.

If `O_NDELAY` is set, `open` for reading-only returns without delay, but `open` for writing-only returns an error if no process currently has the file open for reading.

When opening a file associated with a communication line:

If `O_NDELAY` is clear, `open` blocks until carrier is present.

If `O_NDELAY` is set, `open` returns without waiting for carrier.

`O_SYNC`	This flag will affect subsequent writes if opening an ordinary-file. Each write [see WRITE(BA_OS)] should wait for both the file-data and file-status to be physically updated.
`O_TRUNC`	If the file exists, its length is truncated to 0, and the mode, owner and group are unchanged.
`O_EXCL`	If the file exists and `O_CREAT` is set, `open` fails.

O_CREAT　　If the file does not exist, it is created, the owner-ID of the file is set to the effective-user-ID of the process, the group-ID of the file is set to the effective-group-ID of the process, and the access-permission-bits [see CHMOD(BA_OS)] of the file-mode are set to the value of `mode` modified as follows [see CREAT(BA_OS)]:

The file-mode bits are AND-ed with the complement of the process's file-mode-creation-mask. Thus, `open` clears each bit in the file-mode whose corresponding bit in the file-mode-creation-mask is set [see UMASK(BA_OS)].

Otherwise, if the file exists and O_EXCL is clear, this flag has no effect.

The file-pointer used to mark the current position within the file is set to the beginning of the file.

The new file-descriptor is the lowest-numbered file-descriptor available and is set to remain open across calls to any EXEC(BA_OS) routines [see FCNTL(BA_OS)].

RETURN VALUE

On success, `open` returns an open file-descriptor; on failure, it returns −1 and `errno` indicates the error.

ERRORS

The function `open` fails and `errno` equals:

ENOTDIR　　if a component of the path-prefix is not a directory.

ENOENT　　if O_CREAT is clear and the named file does not exist.

ENOENT　　if a component of the path-name should exist but does not.

ENOENT　　if the path-name is longer than {PATH_MAX} characters.

EACCES　　if a component of the path-prefix denies search permission.

EACCES　　if O_CREAT is set, the file does not exist, and the directory that would contain the file does not permit writing.

EACCES　　if the `oflag` permission is denied for the named file.

EISDIR　　if the named file is a directory and the `oflag` permission is write or read/write.

EROFS　　if the named file resides on a read-only file-system and the `oflag` permission is write or read/write.

EMFILE　　if the calling-process already has {OPEN_MAX} file-descriptors open.

ENXIO　　if the named file is a character-special or block-special file and the device associated with this special file does not exist; or if O_NDELAY is set, the named file is a FIFO, O_WRONLY is set and no process has the file open for reading.

ETXTBSY   if the file is a pure procedure (shared text) file being executed and `oflag` specifies write or read/write permission.

EEXIST   if `O_CREAT` and `O_EXCL` are set, and the named file exists.

EINTR   if a signal is caught during the `open` operation.

ENFILE   if the system-file-table is full, {SYS_OPEN} files are open system-wide.

ENOSPC   if the directory to contain the file cannot be extended, the file does not exist, and `O_CREAT` is set.

EAGAIN   if the file exists with enforced record-locking enabled, `O_TRUNC` is set and there are record-locks on the file [see CHMOD(BA_OS)].

USAGE

Normally, programs should use the *stdio* routines to open, close, read and write files. Thus, programs should use the FOPEN(BA_OS) *stdio* routine instead of `open`.

SEE ALSO

CLOSE(BA_OS), CREAT(BA_OS), DUP(BA_OS), FCNTL(BA_OS), LSEEK(BA_OS), READ(BA_OS), WRITE(BA_OS).

NAME

pause — suspend process until signal

SYNOPSIS

```
int pause()
```

DESCRIPTION

The function pause suspends the calling-process until it receives a signal. The signal must be one that is not currently set to be ignored by the calling-process.

RETURN VALUE

If the signal causes termination of the calling-process, pause will not return. In case of error, pause returns – 1 and errno equals EINTR.

ERRORS

The function pause fails and errno equals:

EINTR   if the signal is *caught* by the calling-process and control is returned from the signal-catching function, the calling-process resumes execution from the point of suspension.

SEE ALSO

ALARM(BA_OS), KILL(BA_OS), SIGNAL(BA_OS), WAIT(BA_OS).

NAME

perror — system error messages

SYNOPSIS

```
void perror(s)
char *s;

extern int errno;

extern char *sys_errlist[ ];

extern int sys_nerr;
```

DESCRIPTION

The function `perror` produces a message on the standard error output describing the last error encountered during a call to a function.

The string pointed to by the argument s is printed first, then a colon and a blank, then the message and a new-line. To be of most use, the argument string should include the name of the program that incurred the error.

The error number is taken from the external variable `errno`, which is set when errors occur but not cleared when successful calls are made.

If given a null-string, `perror` prints only the message and a new-line.

The array of message strings `sys_errlist` is provided to make messages consistent. The variable `errno` can be used as an index in this array to get the message string without the new-line.

The external variable `sys_nerr` is the largest message number provided for in the array; it should be checked because new error codes may be added to the system before they are added to the array.

CAVEATS

New error handling routines will be added to support the UNIX System V Error Message Standard as a tool for application-developers to use. The UNIX System V Error Message Standard is designed to apply to: firmware/diagnostics, the operating system, networks, commands, languages and, when appropriate, applications. All *new* UNIX System V error messages will follow the standard, and existing error messages will be modified over time. The standard UNIX System V error message as seen by the end-user may have up to five informational elements:

Element	Description
LABEL	source of the error.
SEVERITY	one of at least 4 severity codes.
PROBLEM	description of the problem.
ACTION	error-recovery action.
TAG	unique error message identifier.

Each element is described in more detail below.

The standard specifies the information important in error-recovery, but does not specify the format in which to deliver the information. For example, with a graphical user-interface, the LABEL might be presented as an icon. An operating system error message meeting the standard information requirements is shown below with, OS as the LABEL, HALT as the SEVERITY, Timeout Table Overflow as the PROBLEM, See Administration Manual as the ACTION, and OS-136 as the TAG.

```
OS:  HALT:  Timeout Table Overflow.
     TO FIX:  See Administration Manual.  OS-136
```

The standard allows systematic omission of one or more elements in specific environments that do not need them for successful error-recovery. For example, while operating system errors need all five elements, a firmware error message can omit the ACTION because an expert service person is typically the user of this message and the ACTION may be too long to store in firmware. Software that obviously puts the user in a special environment (e.g., a spread-sheet program) where the user sees only errors from that environment may omit the LABEL. Because a primary use of the TAG is for reporting or to point to on-line documentation, it may be omitted when appropriate (e.g., when there is no on-line documentation).

LABEL   This element of the message identifies the error source (e.g., OS, UUCP, application-name, etc.) and could double as a pointer to documentation.

SEVERITY   This element of the message indicates the consequences of the error for the user. Four levels of severity (which can be expanded by system builders who want additional distinctions) are outlined below.

HALT   indicates that the processor, OS, application or database is corrupted and that processing should be stopped immediately to rectify the problem. This severity indicates an emergency.

ERROR   indicates that a condition that may soon interfere with resource use has occurred. This severity indicates that corrective action is needed.

WARNING   indicates an aberrant condition (e.g., stray hardware interrupt, free file space is low) that should be monitored, but needs no immediate action.

INFO   gives information about a user request or about the state of the system (e.g., a printer taken off-line).

PROBLEM   This element of the message clearly describes the error condition. In much of today's software, this element is the only one provided in the message.

ACTION This element of the message describes the first step to be taken in the error-recovery process. For OS errors, this section of the message might be one of five standard strings:

1. `See Hardware Vendor`

2. `See Software Vendor`

3. `See Administrator Procedure`

4. `See Operator Procedure`

5. `See Manual`

These strings should be clearly identified as action to be taken (e.g., by preceding them with the prefix: `TO FIX:`).

TAG This is a unique identifier for the message, used both internally and to obtain online documentation for the message *on those systems that have capacity to store such information.*

NAME

`pipe` — create an interprocess channel

SYNOPSIS

```
int pipe(fildes)
int fildes[2];
```

DESCRIPTION

The function `pipe` creates an I/O mechanism called a *pipe* and returns two file-descriptors, `fildes[0]` and `fildes[1]`. The file associated with `fildes[0]` is opened for reading, the file associated with `fildes[1]` is opened for writing, and the `O_NDELAY` flag is cleared.

Up to {PIPE_MAX} bytes of data are buffered by the pipe before the writing-process is blocked. A read-only file-descriptor `fildes[0]` accesses the data written to `fildes[1]` on a first-in-first-out, FIFO, basis.

RETURN VALUE

On success, `pipe` returns 0; on failure, it returns − 1 and `errno` indicates the error.

ERRORS

The function `pipe` fails and `errno` equals:

EMFILE   if the calling-process already has {OPEN_MAX} − 1 or more file-descriptors open.

ENFILE   if more than {SYS_OPEN} files would be open in the system.

SEE ALSO

READ(BA_OS), WRITE(BA_OS).

NAME

plock — lock process, text or data in memory

SYNOPSIS

```
#include <sys/lock.h>

int plock(op)
int op;
```

DESCRIPTION

The function plock allows the calling-process to lock its text segment (text-lock), its data segment (data-lock), or both its text and data segments (process-lock) into memory. Locked segments are immune to all routine swapping. The function plock also allows these segments to be unlocked. The effective-user-ID of the calling-process must be super-user to use this call. The argument op specifies the following, which are defined by the <sys/lock.h> header file:

PROCLOCK	lock text and data segments into memory (process-lock).
TXTLOCK	lock text segment into memory (text-lock).
DATLOCK	lock data segment into memory (data-lock).
UNLOCK	remove locks.

RETURN VALUE

On success, plock returns 0 to the calling-process; on failure, it returns − 1 and errno indicates the error.

ERRORS

The function plock fails, it does *not* perform the requested operation, and errno equals:

EPERM	if the effective-user-ID of the calling-process is not super-user.
EINVAL	if op is PROCLOCK and a process-lock, a text-lock, or a data-lock already exists on the calling-process.
EINVAL	if op is TXTLOCK and a text-lock, or a process-lock already exists on the calling-process.
EINVAL	if op is DATLOCK and a data-lock, or a process-lock already exists on the calling-process.
EINVAL	if op is UNLOCK and the calling-process has no locks on it.

USAGE

The function plock should not be used by most programs. Only programs that must have the type of real-time control it provides should use it.

SEE ALSO

EXEC(BA_OS), EXIT(BA_OS), FORK(BA_OS).

NAME
poll — STREAMS I/O multiplexing

SYNOPSIS
```
#include <stropts.h>
#include <poll.h>

int poll(fds, nfds, timeout)
struct pollfd fds[];
unsigned long nfds;
int timeout;
```

DESCRIPTION
The function `poll` provides users with a mechanism for multiplexing input/output over a set of file-descriptors that reference open STREAMS. The function `poll` identifies those STREAMS on which a user can send or receive messages, or on which certain events occurred. A user can receive messages using READ(BA_OS) and GETMSG(NS_OS) and send messages using WRITE(BA_OS) and PUTMSG(NS_OS).

The argument `fds` specifies the file-descriptors to be examined and the events of interest for each file-descriptor. It is a pointer to an array with one element for each open file-descriptor of interest. The array's elements are `pollfd` structures which contain the following members:
```
int    fildes;     /* file-descriptor */
short  events;     /* requested events */
short  revents;    /* returned events */
```
where `fildes` specifies an open file-descriptor, and `events` and `revents` are bitmasks constructed by OR-ing any combination of the following event flags:

POLLERR   An error message arrived at the stream-head.
           This flag is only valid in `revents`; `events` does not use it.

POLLHUP   A hangup occurred on the stream.
           This flag is only valid in `revents`; `events` does not use it.
           This flag and `POLLOUT` are mutually exclusive because a
           stream can never be writable if a hangup occurred; however, this
           flag is not mutually exclusive with `POLLIN` or `POLLPRI`.

POLLIN   A non-priority message is on the stream-head read-queue.
           In `revents`, this flag and `POLLPRI` are mutually exclusive.
           This flag is set even if the message is of zero length.

POLLNVAL   The specified `fildes` value fails to denote an open stream.
           This flag is only valid in `revents`; `events` does not use it.

POLLOUT   The first downstream write-queue in the stream is not full.
           Priority messages can be sent any time [see PUTMSG(NS_OS)].

POLLPRI   A priority message is on the stream-head read-queue.
           In `revents`, this flag and `POLLIN` are mutually exclusive.
           This flag is set even if the message is of zero length.

For each element of the array pointed to by `fds`, `poll` examines the given file-descriptor for the event(s) specified in `events`. The number of file-descriptors to be examined is specified by `nfds`. If `nfds` exceeds `NOFILES`, which is the system limit of open files, `poll` fails.

If `fildes` is negative, `events` is ignored and `revents` is set to zero in that entry on return from `poll`.

The results of the `poll` query are stored in the `revents` field in the `pollfd` structure. Bits set in the `revents` bitmask indicate which of the requested events occur. If none occur, none of the specified bits are set in `revents` when `poll` returns. Even when clear in `events`, the event flags `POLLHUP`, `POLLERR` and `POLLNVAL` are set in `revents` whenever the conditions they denote occur.

If none of the defined events occurred on any selected file-descriptor, `poll` waits at least `timeout` msec for an event to occur on any of the selected file-descriptors. On a computer without millisecond timing accuracy, `timeout` rounds up to the nearest legal value available on that system.

If `timeout` is 0, `poll` returns immediately.

If `timeout` is -1, `poll` blocks until a requested event occurs or until the call is interrupted.

The `O_NDELAY` flag does *not* affect `poll`.

RETURN VALUE

On success, `poll` returns a non-negative value:

A positive value indicates the total number of file-descriptors selected (i.e., file-descriptors for which `revents` is non-zero).

A zero value means `poll` timed-out and no file-descriptors were selected.

On failure, `poll` returns -1 and `errno` indicates the error.

ERRORS

The function `poll` fails and `errno` equals:

`EAGAIN`	if allocation of internal data structures failed but should be attempted again.
`EFAULT`	if an argument points outside the allocated address space.
`EINTR`	if a signal is caught during the `poll` operation.
`EINVAL`	if `nfds` is negative, or if `nfds` is greater than `NOFILES`.

SEE ALSO

READ(BA_OS), GETMSG(NS_OS), PUTMSG(NS_OS), STREAMIO(NS_ENV), WRITE(BA_OS).

NAME

popen, pclose — initiate pipe to/from a process

SYNOPSIS

```
#include <stdio.h>

FILE *popen(command, type)
char *command, *type;

int pclose(stream)
FILE *stream;
```

DESCRIPTION

The function popen creates a pipe between the calling program and the command to be executed.

The arguments to popen are pointers to null-terminated strings containing, respectively, a command line [see SYSTEM(BA_OS)] and an I/O mode, either r for reading or w for writing.

The function popen returns a stream pointer such that one can write to the standard input of the command, if the I/O mode is w by writing to the file stream; and one can read from the standard output of the command, if the I/O mode is r by reading from the file stream.

A stream opened by popen should be closed by pclose, which waits for the associated process to terminate and returns the exit status of the command.

Because open files are shared, a type r command may be used as an input filter and a type w command as an output filter.

RETURN VALUE

The function popen returns a NULL pointer if files or processes cannot be created or if command cannot be executed.

The function pclose returns − 1 if stream is not associated with a command of popen.

USAGE

The FSEEK(BA_OS) routine should not be used with a stream opened by popen.

SEE ALSO

FCLOSE(BA_OS), FOPEN(BA_OS), PIPE(BA_OS), SYSTEM(BA_OS), WAIT(BA_OS).

NAME

printf, fprintf, sprintf — print formatted output

SYNOPSIS

```
#include <stdio.h>

int printf(format [ , arg ...] )
char *format;

int fprintf(stream, format [ , arg ...] )
FILE *stream;
char *format;

int sprintf(s, format [ , arg ...] )
char *s, *format;
```

DESCRIPTION

The function printf places output on the standard output stream stdout.

The function fprintf places output on the named output stream stream.

The function sprintf places output, followed by the null-character (\0) in consecutive bytes starting at *s. The user must ensure that enough storage is available. Each function returns the number of characters transmitted (not including the \0 in the case of sprintf) or a negative value if an output error occurred.

Each function converts, formats and prints its args under control of format, a character-string containing the following three types of objects:

1. plain-characters that are simply copied to the output stream;

2. escape-sequences that represent non-graphic characters; and

3. conversion-specifications.

The following escape-sequences produce the associated action on display devices capable of the action:

\b   Backspace moves the printing position to one character before the current position, unless the current position is the start of a line.

\f   Form Feed moves the printing position to the initial printing position of the next logical page.

\n   New line moves the printing position to the start of the next line.

\r   Carriage return moves the printing position to the start of the current line.

\t   Horizontal tab moves the printing position to the next implementation-defined horizontal tab position on the current line.

\v   Vertical tab moves the printing position to the start of the next implementation-defined vertical tab position.

The character % introduces each conversion-specification. After %, the following appear in sequence:

Zero or more *flags* to modify the result of the conversion-specification.

An optional string of decimal digits to specify a minimum *field-width*. If the converted value has fewer characters than the field-width, it is padded on the left (or right, if the left-adjustment flag (–), described below, has been given) to the field-width.

A *precision* to set the minimum number of digits to appear in d, i, o, u, x or X conversions (the field is padded with leading zeros), the number of digits to appear after the decimal-point in e, E and f conversions, the maximum number of significant digits in g and G conversions; or the maximum number of characters to print from a string in s conversions. The precision takes the form of a dot (.) followed by a decimal digit-string; a null digit-string is treated as zero. Padding set by the precision overrides padding set by the field-width.

An optional l (ell) to specify that a following d, i, o, u, x or X conversion-character applies to a long integer arg. An l before any other conversion-character is ignored.

A conversion-character to specify the conversion to apply (see below).

The *flag* characters and their meanings are:

–   Left-justify the result of the conversion within the field.

+   Begin the result of a signed conversion with a sign (+ or –).

blank Prepend a *blank* to the result if the first character of a signed conversion is not a sign (i.e., ignore the blank-flag if the +-flag also appears).

Convert the value to an *alternate form*; for c, d, i, s and u conversions, the flag has no effect; for o conversion, it increases the precision to force the first digit of the result to be a zero; for x or X conversion, a non-zero result has 0x or 0X prepended to it; for e, E, f, g and G conversions, the result always contains a decimal-point, even if no digits follow the point (normally, a decimal-point appears in the result of these conversions only if a digit follows it); for g and G conversions, trailing zeroes are *not* removed from the result as they normally are.

A *field-width* or *precision* may be indicated by an asterisk (*) instead of a digit-string. In this case, an integer arg supplies the field-width or precision. The arg actually converted is not fetched until the conversion letter is seen, so any args specifying field-width or precision must come *before* any arg to be converted. If the precision argument is negative, it is changed to zero.

Each conversion-character fetchs zero or more args. The results are undefined if there are insufficient args for the format. If the format is exhausted while args remain, the excess args are ignored.

If the character after % is not a valid conversion-character, the results of the conversion are undefined. The conversion-characters and their meanings are:

%   Print a %; no argument is converted.

c   Print the character `arg`.

d,i,o,u,x,X   Convert the integer `arg` to signed decimal (d or i), unsigned octal (o), unsigned decimal (u) or unsigned hexadecimal notation (x and X). The x conversion uses the letters `abcdef` and the X conversion uses the letters `ABCDEF`. The precision of `arg` specifies the minimum number of digits to appear. If the value being converted can be represented in fewer digits than the specified minimum, it is expanded with leading zeroes. The default precision is 1. The result of converting a zero value with a precision of 0 is a null-string.

e,E   Convert the float or double `arg` to the style $[-]d . ddd$ e $\pm dd$, where there is one digit before the decimal-point and the number of digits after it equals the precision. When the precision is missing, six digits are produced; if the precision is 0, no decimal-point appears. The E conversion-character produces a number with E instead of e introducing the exponent.

           The exponent always contains at least two digits. However, if the value to be printed is greater than or equal to 1E+100, additional exponent digits are printed as necessary.

f   Convert the float or double `arg` to decimal notation in the style $[-]ddd . ddd$, where the number of digits after the decimal-point equals the precision-specification. If the precision is omitted from `arg`, six digits are output; if the precision is explicitly 0, no decimal-point appears.

g,G   Print the float or double `arg` in style f or e (or in style E in the case of a G conversion-character), with the precision specifying the number of significant digits. The style used depends on the value converted: style e is used only if the exponent resulting from the conversion is less than –4 or greater than the precision. Trailing zeroes are removed from the result. A decimal-point appears only if it is followed by a digit.

s   Print characters from the string pointed to by `arg` until a null-character (\0) is found or the number of characters indicated by the precision-specification of `arg` is reached. If the precision is omitted from `arg`, it is taken to be infinite, so all characters up to the first null-character are printed. A NULL value for `arg` yields undefined results.

In no case does a non-existent or small field-width cause truncation of a field; if the result of a conversion is wider than the field-width, the field is simply expanded to contain the conversion result. Characters generated by `printf` and `fprintf` are printed as if the PUTC(BA_LIB) routine had been called.

RETURN VALUE

The functions `printf`, `fprintf` and `sprintf` return the number of characters transmitted, or return -1 if an error occurred.

EXAMPLES

To print a date and time in the following form:

```
Sunday, July 3, 10:02
```

where `weekday` and `month` are pointers to null-terminated strings, use:

```
printf("%s, %s %i, %d:%.2d",
       weekday, month, day, hour, min);
```

To print π to 5 decimal places, use:

```
printf("pi = %.5f", 4 * atan(1.0));
```

SEE ALSO

PUTC(BA_LIB), SCANF(BA_LIB), FOPEN(BA_OS).

CAVEATS

The function `printf` will make available character string representations for ∞ and "Not a Number" (NaN: a symbolic entity encoded in floating point format) to support the **IEEE 754** standard.

NAME

    profil — execution time profile

SYNOPSIS

    void profil(buff, bufsiz, offset, scale)
    char *buff;
    int bufsiz, offset, scale;

DESCRIPTION

The argument buff points to an area of memory whose length (in bytes) is given by bufsiz. After the call to profil, the user's program counter (pc) is examined each clock tick ({CLK_TCK} times per second); offset is subtracted from it, and the result multiplied by scale. If the resulting number corresponds to an entry inside buff, that entry is incremented. An "entry" is defined as a series of bytes with length sizeof(short).

The scale is interpreted as an unsigned, fixed-point fraction with binary point at the left: 0177777 (octal) gives a 1-1 mapping of pc's to words in buff; 077777 (octal) maps each pair of instruction words together. 02 (octal) maps all instructions onto the beginning of buff (producing a non-interrupting core clock).

Profiling is turned off by giving a scale of 0 or 1. It is rendered ineffective by giving a bufsiz of 0. Profiling is turned off when an EXEC(BA_OS) routine is executed, but remains on in both child and parent after a call to the FORK(BA_OS) routine. Profiling will be turned off if an update in buff would cause a memory fault.

RETURN VALUE

Not defined.

USAGE

The function profil would normally be used by a program only during development to analyze the program's performance.

NAME

ptrace — process trace

SYNOPSIS

```
int ptrace(request, pid, addr, data)
int request, pid, data;
```

DESCRIPTION

The function ptrace provides a means by which a parent-process may control the execution of a child-process. Its primary use is for the implementation of breakpoint debugging. The child-process behaves normally until it encounters a signal [see SIGNAL(BA_OS)] at which time it enters a stopped state and its parent is notified via the WAIT(BA_OS) routine. When the child is in the stopped state, its parent can examine and modify its *core-image* using ptrace. Also, the parent can cause the child either to terminate or continue, with the possibility of ignoring the signal that caused it to stop.

The data type of addr depends upon the request passed ptrace.

The argument request determines the precise action to be taken by ptrace and is one of the following:

0   This request must be issued by the child-process if it is to be traced by its parent. It turns on the child's trace flag that stipulates that the child should be left in a stopped state upon receipt of a signal rather than the state specified by func [see SIGNAL(BA_OS)]. The arguments pid, addr, and data are ignored, and a return value is not defined for this request. Peculiar results will ensue if the parent does not expect to trace the child.

The remainder of the requests can only be used by the parent-process. For each, pid is the process-ID of the child. The child must be in a stopped state before these requests are made.

1, 2   With these requests, the word at location addr in the address space of the child-process is returned to the parent-process. If instruction (I) and data (D) space are separated, request 1 returns a word from I-space, and request 2 returns a word from D-space. If I-space and D-space are not separated either request 1 or request 2 may be used with equal results. The argument data is ignored. These two requests fail if addr is not the start address of a word, in which case, the parent-process is returned − 1 and the parent's errno equals EIO.

3   With this request, the word at location addr in the child's *user-area* in the system's address space is returned to the parent-process.

The argument data is ignored. This request fails if addr is not the start address of a word or is outside the *user-area*, in which case, the parent-process is returned − 1 and the parent's errno equals EIO.

4, 5   With these requests, the value of `data` is written into the address
         space of the child at location `addr`. If I-space and D-space are
         separated, request 4 writes a word into I-space, and request 5 writes a
         word into D-space. If I-space and D-space are not separated, either
         request 4 or request 5 may be used with equal results. Upon
         successful completion, the value written into the address space of the
         child is returned to the parent.

         These two requests fail if `addr` is a location in a pure procedure space
         and another process is executing in that space, or `addr` is not the start
         address of a word. Upon failure the parent-process is returned − 1 and
         the parent's `errno` equals EIO.

6   With this request, a few entries in the child's *user-area* can be written.

         The value of `data` is written and `addr` is the location of the entry.
         Entries that can be written are implementation-specific but might
         include general registers portions of the *processor-status-word*.

7   This request causes the child to resume execution. If `data` is 0, all
         pending signals including the one that caused the child to stop are
         canceled before it resumes execution.

         If `data` is a valid signal number, the child resumes execution as if it
         had incurred that signal, and any other pending signals are canceled.
         The argument `addr` must equal 1 for this request. Upon successful
         completion, the value of `data` is returned to the parent. This request
         fails if `data` is not 0 or a valid signal number, in which case, the
         parent-process is returned − 1 and the parent's `errno` equals EIO.

8   This request causes the child to terminate with the same consequences
         as the EXIT(BA_OS) routine.

9   This request is implementation-dependent but if operative, it is used to
         request single-stepping through the instructions of the child.

To forestall possible fraud, `ptrace` inhibits the set-user-ID facility on
subsequent EXEC(BA_OS) routines. If a traced process calls and EXEC(BA_OS)
routine, it will stop before executing the first instruction of the new image
showing signal `SIGTRAP`.

RETURN VALUE

On success, `ptrace` returns a value specific to the request type (see above);
on failure, it returns − 1.

ERRORS

In general, `ptrace` fails and `errno` equals:

EIO   if `request` is an illegal number. See the summary for each
             request type above.

ESRCH   if `pid` identifies a child that does not exist or has not executed a
             `ptrace` with request 0.

USAGE

The function `ptrace` should not be used by programs. It is only used by software debugging programs and it is hardware-dependent.

When `ptrace` is used to read a word from the address space of the child-process, `request` 1, 2 or 3, the data read and value returned by `ptrace` could be – 1. In this case, a return value of – 1 would not indicate an error.

SEE ALSO

EXEC(BA_OS), SIGNAL(BA_OS), WAIT(BA_OS).

NAME

putc, putchar, fputc, putw — put character or word onto *stdio*

SYNOPSIS

```
#include <stdio.h>

int putc(c, stream)
int c;
FILE *stream;

int putchar(c)
int c;

int fputc(c, stream)
int c;
FILE *stream;

int putw(w, stream)
int w;
FILE *stream;
```

DESCRIPTION

The function putc writes character c onto named output stream, stream, where the file-pointer, if defined, points. Both putc and putchar are macros, and putchar is defined as putc(c, stdout).

The function fputc behaves like putc, but is a function instead of a macro. The function fputc runs more slowly than putc but it takes less space per invocation and its name can be passed as an argument to a function.

The function putw writes the word (i.e., integer w onto the named output stream, stream, where the file-pointer, if defined, points). The size of a word is the size of an integer and varies from machine to machine. The function putw neither assumes nor causes special alignment in the file.

RETURN VALUE

On success, putc, fputc and putchar each return the value they wrote. On failure, they return the constant EOF. This occurs if stream is not open for writing or if it cannot grow. The function putw returns non-zero if an error occurs; otherwise, it returns zero.

USAGE

Because it is implemented as a macro, putc incorrectly treats stream when it has side-effects. In particular, putc(c, *f++); may not work sensibly, and fputc should be used instead.

Because word-length and byte-ordering are machine-dependent, files written using putw may not be read using getw on a different processor.

SEE ALSO

FCLOSE(BA_OS), FERROR(BA_OS), FOPEN(BA_OS), FREAD(BA_OS), PRINTF(BA_LIB), PUTS(BA_LIB), SETBUF(BA_LIB).

NAME

putenv — change or add value to environment

SYNOPSIS

```
int putenv(string)
char *string;
```

DESCRIPTION

The argument string points to a string of the the following form:

```
name = value
```

The function putenv makes the value of the environment variable name equal to value by altering an existing variable or creating a new one. In either case, the string pointed to by string becomes part of the environment, so altering the string will change the environment. The space used by string is no longer used once a new string-defining name is passed to the function putenv.

RETURN VALUE

The function putenv returns non-zero if it can not obtain enough space for an expanded environment, otherwise zero.

USAGE

The function putenv was added in UNIX System V Release 2.0.

The function putenv manipulates the environment pointed to by environ, and can be used in conjunction with getenv. However, envp, the third argument to main, is not changed [see EXEC(BA_OS)].

A potential error is to call the function putenv with a pointer to an automatic variable as the argument and to then exit the calling function while string is still part of the environment.

SEE ALSO

EXEC(BA_OS), MALLOC(BA_OS), GETENV(BA_LIB).

NAME

　　`putmsg` — send a STREAMS I/O message

SYNOPSIS

```
#include <stropts.h>

int putmsg (fd, ctlptr, dataptr, flags)
int fd;
struct strbuf *ctlptr;
struct strbuf *dataptr;
int flags;
```

DESCRIPTION

The function `putmsg` creates a message from user-specified buffer(s) and sends the message to a STREAMS-device. The message may contain either a data part, a control part or both. The data and control parts to be sent are placed in separate buffers, as described below. The semantics of each part is defined by the STREAMS-module that receives the message.

The argument `fd` is a file-descriptor that denotes an open stream.

The arguments `ctlptr` and `dataptr` each point to a `strbuf` structure which contains the following members:

```
int  maxlen; /* not used */
int  len;    /* length of data */
char *buf;   /* ptr to buffer */
```

The argument `ctlptr` points to the structure describing the control part, if any, to be included in the message. The `buf` field in the `strbuf` structure points to the buffer where the control information resides, and the `len` field indicates the number of bytes to be sent. The `maxlen` field is not used in `putmsg` [see GETMSG(NS_OS)]. In a similar manner, `dataptr` specifies the data, if any, to be included in the message.

To send the data part of a message, `dataptr` must be non-NULL and the `len` field of `dataptr` must have a value of 0 or greater.

To send the control part of a message, the corresponding values must be set for `ctlptr`.

The function `putmsg` sends no data (control) part if either `dataptr` (`ctlptr`) is NULL or the `len` field of `dataptr` (`ctlptr`) equals – 1.

The argument `flags` can equal 0 or `RS_HIPRI` and is used as described below:

　　If a control part is specified and `flags` equals `RS_HIPRI`, `putmsg` sends a priority message.

　　If `flags` equals 0, `putmsg` sends a non-priority message.

　　If no control part is specified and `flags` equals `RS_HIPRI`, `putmsg` fails and `errno` equals `EINVAL`.

　　If no control part and no data part are specified and `flags` equals 0, `putmsg` sends no message and returns 0.

For non-priority messages, `putmsg` blocks if the stream write-queue is full due to internal flow-control conditions. For priority messages, `putmsg` does not block on this condition. For non-priority messages, `putmsg` does not block when the write-queue is full and `O_NDELAY` is set. Instead, it fails and `errno` equals `EAGAIN`.

Unless prevented by lack of internal resources, `putmsg` also blocks waiting for the availability of message blocks in the stream, regardless of priority or whether `O_NDELAY` has been specified. The function `putmsg` sends no partial messages.

RETURN VALUE

On success, `putmsg` returns 0; on failure, it returns -1 and `errno` indicates the error.

ERRORS

The function `putmsg` fails and `errno` equals:

EAGAIN	if a non-priority message is specified, O_NDELAY is set and the stream write-queue is full due to internal flow-control conditions.
EAGAIN	if buffers could not be allocated for the message to be created.
EBADF	if fd is not a valid file-descriptor open for writing.
EFAULT	if ctlptr or dataptr points outside the allocated address space.
EINTR	if a signal is caught during the putmsg operation.
EINVAL	if an undefined value is specified in flags, or flags equals RS_HIPRI and no control part is supplied.
EINVAL	if the stream referenced by fd is linked below a multiplexer.
ENOSTR	if a stream is not associated with fd.
ENXIO	if a hangup occurs downstream for the specified stream.
ERANGE	if the size of the data part of the message falls outside the range specified by the maximum and minimum packet sizes of the topmost stream module.
ERANGE	if the control part of the message is larger than the maximum configured size of the control part of a message.
ERANGE	if the data part of a message is larger than the maximum configured size of the data part of a message.

The function `putmsg` also fails if a STREAMS error message is processed by the stream-head before the call to `putmsg`. The error returned is the value contained in the STREAMS error message.

SEE ALSO

READ(BA_OS), GETMSG(NS_OS), POLL(NS_OS), STREAMIO(NS_ENV), WRITE(BA_OS).

NAME

putpwent — write password file entry

SYNOPSIS

```
#include <pwd.h>

int putpwent(p, f)
struct passwd *p;
FILE *f;
```

DESCRIPTION

The routine putpwent is the inverse of getpwent. Given a pointer to a password structure created by getpwent (or getpwuid or getpwnam), putpwent writes a line on the file f, which must have the format of /etc/passwd.

RETURN VALUE

Returns a non-zero value if an error was detected during its operation, otherwise returns 0.

SEE ALSO

GETPWENT(SD_LIB).

NAME
puts, fputs — put a string onto *stdio*

SYNOPSIS
```
#include <stdio.h>

int puts(s)
char *s;

int fputs(s, stream)
char *s;
FILE *stream;
```

DESCRIPTION
The function puts writes the null-terminated string pointed to by s and followed by a new-line character, onto the standard output stream, stdout.

The function fputs writes the null-terminated string pointed to by s onto the named output stream, stream.

Neither function writes the terminating null-character.

RETURN VALUE
On success, both puts and fputs return the number of characters written; on failure, both return EOF. This occurs if they try to write on a file that is not open for writing.

USAGE
The function puts appends a new-line character while fputs does not.

SEE ALSO
FERROR(BA_OS), FOPEN(BA_OS), FREAD(BA_OS), PRINTF(BA_LIB), PUTC(BA_LIB).

NAME

    `qsort` — quicker sort

SYNOPSIS

    ```
void qsort(base, nel, width, compar)
char *base;
unsigned nel, width;
int (*compar)();
```

DESCRIPTION

    The function `qsort` is a general-sorting algorithm that sorts a table of data in place.

    The argument `base` points to the element at the base of the table.

    The argument `nel` is the number of elements in the table.

    The argument `width` is the size of an element in bytes.

    The argument `compar` is the name of the user-supplied comparison function, which is called with two arguments that point to the elements being compared. The comparison function must return an integer less than, equal to or greater than zero, according as the first argument is to be considered is less than, equal to or greater than the second.

USAGE

    The pointer to the base the table should be of type pointer-to-element, and cast to type pointer-to-character.

    The comparison function need not compare every byte, so arbitrary data may be contained in the elements in addition to the values being compared.

    The relative order in the output of two items which compare as equal is unpredictable.

SEE ALSO

    BSEARCH(BA_LIB), LSEARCH(BA_LIB), STRING(BA_LIB).

NAME

rand, srand — simple random-number generator

SYNOPSIS

```
int rand( )

void srand(seed)
unsigned int seed;
```

DESCRIPTION

The function rand uses a multiplicative congruential random-number generator with period 2^{32} that returns successive pseudo-random numbers in the range from 0 to 32767.

The function srand uses the argument seed as a seed for a new sequence of pseudo-random numbers to be returned by subsequent calls to rand. If srand is then called with the same seed value, the sequence of pseudo-random numbers will be repeated. If rand is called before any calls to srand have been made, the same sequence will be generated as when srand is first called with a seed value of 1.

USAGE

The DRAND48(BA_LIB) routine provides a much more elaborate random-number generator.

The following functions define the semantics of rand and srand.

```
static unsigned long int next = 1;
int rand( )
{
    next = next * 1103515245 + 12345;
    return ((unsigned int)(next/65536) % 32768);
}
void srand(seed)
unsigned int seed;
{
    next = seed;
}
```

Specifying the semantics makes it possible to reproduce the behavior of programs that use pseudo-random sequences. This facilitates the testing of portable programs in different implementations.

SEE ALSO

DRAND48(BA_LIB).

NAME

read — read from file

SYNOPSIS

```
int read(fildes, buf, nbyte)
int fildes;
char *buf;
unsigned nbyte;
```

DESCRIPTION

The function `read` attempts to read `nbyte` bytes from the file denoted by the open file-descriptor `fildes` into the buffer pointed to by `buf`.

On devices capable of seeking, `read` starts at a position in the file given by the file-pointer associated with `fildes`. Upon return from `read`, the file-pointer is incremented by the number of bytes actually read.

Devices incapable of seeking, such as terminals, always read from the current position. The value of a file-pointer associated with such a file is undefined.

If successful, `read` returns the number of bytes read and stored in the buffer; this number may be less than `nbyte` if the file is associated with a communication-line [see IOCTL(BA_OS) and TERMIO(BA_ENV)], or if the number of bytes left in the file is less than `nbyte` bytes, or if the file is a pipe or a special file. When end-of-file is reached, `read` returns 0.

When attempting to read from an ordinary-file with enforced record-locking enabled [see CHMOD(BA_OS)], and all or part of the file to be read has a write-lock owned by another process (i.e., a blocking write-lock):

If `O_NDELAY` is clear, `read` sleeps until all blocking write-locks are removed, or `read` is terminated by a signal.

If `O_NDELAY` is set, `read` returns −1 and `errno` equals **EAGAIN**.

When attempting to read from an empty pipe (or FIFO) that is no longer open for writing, `read` returns 0 indicating end-of-file; otherwise:

If `O_NDELAY` is clear, `read` blocks until data are written to the pipe or the pipe is no longer open for writing.

If `O_NDELAY` is set, `read` returns 0.

When attempting to read a file associated with a character-special file that has no data currently available:

If `O_NDELAY` is clear, `read` blocks until data are available.

If `O_NDELAY` is set, `read` returns 0.

The function `read` reads data previously written to a file. If any portion of an ordinary-file prior to the end-of-file was not written, `read` returns bytes of value 0. For example, the LSEEK(BA_OS) routine allows the file-pointer to be set beyond the end of existing data in the file. If data are later written at this point, subsequent reads in the gap between the previous end of data and newly written data will return bytes of value 0 until data are written into the gap.

RETURN VALUE

On success, `read` returns the number of bytes actually read; on failure, it returns – 1 and `errno` indicates the error.

ERRORS

The function `read` fails and `errno` equals:

EBADF   if `fildes` is not a valid file-descriptor open for reading.

EINTR   if a signal is caught during the `read` operation.

EIO   if a physical I/O error occurs.

ENXIO   if the device associated with the file-descriptor is a block-special or character-special file and the file-pointer is out of range.

EAGAIN   if enforced record-locking is enabled, `O_NDELAY` is set, and there is a write-lock owned by another process.

ENOLCK   if {LOCK_MAX} regions are already locked system-wide.

EDEADLK   if `O_NDELAY` is clear and a deadlock condition is detected.

USAGE

Normally, programs should use the *stdio* routines to open, close, read and write files. Thus, programs that use the FOPEN(BA_OS) *stdio* routine to open a file should use the FREAD(BA_OS) *stdio* routine instead of `read` to read it.

When `O_NDELAY` is set, portable programs should test for two conditions to determine that no data are currently available, for example:

```
fildes = open(path, O_RDONLY ¦ O_NDELAY);
ret = read(fildes, buf, nbyte);
if (ret == 0 ¦¦ (ret == -1 && errno == EAGAIN)) {
        .
        .   /* Data not available now. */
        .
}
```

SEE ALSO

CREAT(BA_OS), DUP(BA_OS), FCNTL(BA_OS), IOCTL(BA_OS), OPEN(BA_OS), PIPE(BA_OS).

NAME

compile, step, advance — regular-expression compile and match
routines

SYNOPSIS

```
#define INIT declarations
#define GETC() getc code
#define PEEKC() peekc code
#define UNGETC() ungetc code
#define RETURN(ptr) return code
#define ERROR(val) error code

#include <regexp.h>

char *compile(instring, expbuf, endbuf, eof)
char *instring, *expbuf, *endbuf;
int eof;

int step(string, expbuf)
char *string, *endbuf;

advance(string, expbuf)
char *string, *expbuf;

extern char *loc1, *loc2, *locs;
```

DESCRIPTION

The function compile takes a regular-expression as input and produces a
compiled-expression that step or advance can use.

The functions step and advance do pattern-matching given a character-
string and a compiled-expression as input.

These functions are general-purpose regular-expression matching routines to
be used in programs that perform regular-expression matching. These
functions are defined by the <regexp.h> header file.

A regular-expression, *re*, specifies a set of character-strings. A member of this
set of strings is said to be *matched* by the *re*. Some characters have special
meaning when used in an *re*; other characters stand for themselves.

Characters that have special meaning except when they appear within square
brackets, [ ], or are preceded by \ are: ., *, [, \. Other special characters,
such as $ have special meaning in more restricted contexts. The special
meaning of the \ operator can be escaped *only* by preceding it with another \
(e.g., \\). The character ^ at the beginning of an expression permits a
successful match only immediately after a new-line, and the character $ at the
end of an expression requires a trailing new-line. Two characters have special
meaning only when used within square brackets. The character – denotes a
range, [c-c], unless it is just after the opening bracket or before the closing
bracket, [-c] or [c-] in which case it has no special meaning. When used
within brackets, the character ^ means *complement of* if it immediately
follows the open bracket, [^c], elsewhere between brackets, [c^], it stands
for the ordinary character ^.

The regular-expressions that `regexp` uses are constructed as follows:

Expression	Meaning
c	any character *c* except special characters.
c	any character *c* except characters in the range 1–9 (i.e., digits).
^	the beginning of the line being compared.
$	the end of the line being compared.
.	any character in the input.
[*s*]	any character in the scanset *s*, where *s* is a set of characters and/or a range of characters (e.g., [*c*–*c*]).
[^*s*]	any character not in the scanset *s*, where *s* is defined as above.
r *	zero or more successive occurrences of regular-expression *r*. The longest match is chosen.
rx	the occurrence of regular-expression *r* followed by the occurrence of regular-expression *x*. (Concatenation)
r\\{ *m* , *n* \\}	any number of *m* through *n* successive occurrences of regular-expression *r*. The regular-expression *r*\\{ *m* \\} matches exactly *m* occurrences; *r*\\{ *m* , \\} matches at least *m* occurrences.
\\(*r* \\)	the regular-expression *r*. When *n* (where *n* is a number greater than zero) appears in a constructed regular-expression, it stands for regular-expression *x* where *x* is the *n*[th] regular-expression enclosed in \\(and \\) strings that appeared earlier in the constructed regular-expression. For example, \\(*r* \\) *x* \\(*y* \\) *z* \\2 is the concatenation of regular-expressions *rxyzy*.

Programs must declare the following five macros before the #include <regexp.h> statement. The function compile uses the macros GETC, PEEKC and UNGETC to operate on the regular-expression given as input.

GETC ( )	returns the next character in the regular-expression. Successive calls to GETC ( ) return successive characters of the regular-expression.
PEEKC ( )	returns the next character in the regular-expression. Successive calls to PEEKC ( ) return the same character, which also is the next character GETC ( ) returns.
UNGETC ( )	causes the next call to GETC ( ) and PEEKC ( ) to return the argument c. No more than one character of pushback is ever needed and this character is guaranteed to be the last character GETC ( ) reads. The value of the macro UNGETC (c) is always ignored.

C Language Interfaces   165

RETURN(ptr)   is used on normal exit from compile. The argument ptr points to the character after the last character of the compiled-expression. This is useful to programs managing memory allocation.

ERROR(val)   is the abnormal return from compile. The argument val is an error number [see ERRORS below for meanings]. This call should never return.

Each program that includes the <regexp.h> header file must have a #define of INIT for dependent declarations and initializations. Most often INIT sets a register variable to point to the start of the regular-expression so that the definitions of GETC(), PEEKC() and UNGETC() can use this register variable. Otherwise, INIT could declare external variables used by GETC(), PEEKC() and UNGETC() [see EXAMPLES].

The syntax of a call to compile is as follows:

```
compile(instring, expbuf, endbuf, eof)
```

The first parameter instring is never used explicitly by compile, but is useful for programs pass different pointers to input characters. It is sometimes used in the INIT declaration [see below]. Programs which call functions to input characters or have characters in an external array can pass down a value of ((char*)0) for this parameter.

The next parameter expbuf is a character pointer. It points to the place where the compiled-expression will be placed.

The parameter endbuf is one more than the highest address where the compiled-expression may be placed. If the compiled-expression cannot fit in (endbuf-expbuf) bytes, a call to ERROR(50) is made.

The parameter eof is the character which marks the end of the regular-expression. For example, *re/*.

The first parameter to step points to a string of characters to be checked for a match. This string should be null-terminated.

The second parameter, expbuf, is the compiled-expression produced by calling compile.

The function step returns non-zero if some sub-string of string matches the regular-expression in expbuf and zero if there is no match. If there is a match, two external character pointers are set as a side effect to the call to step. The variable loc1 points to the first character that matched the regular-expression; the variable loc2 points to the character after the last character that matches the regular-expression. Thus if the regular-expression matches the entire input string, loc1 points to the first character of string and loc2 points to the null at the end of string.

The function advance returns non-zero if the initial substring of string matches the regular-expression in expbuf. If there is a match, an external character pointer, loc2, is set as a side-effect. The variable loc2 points to the next character in string after the last character that matched.

When `advance` gets a * or \{ \} sequence in the regular-expression, it moves its pointer to the string to be matched as far as possible and recursively calls itself trying to match the rest of the string to the rest of the regular-expression. As long as there is no match, `advance` backs up along the string until it finds a match or reaches the point in the string that initially matched the * or \{ \}. It is sometimes desirable to stop this backing-up before reaching the inital point in the string. If the external character pointer `locs` equals the point in the string at sometime during the backing-up, `advance` stops the backing-up and returns zero.

The external variables `circf`, `sed` and `nbra` are reserved.

RETURN VALUE

On success, `compile` uses the macro RETURN; on failure, it uses the macro ERROR [see above]. Both `step` and `advance` return non-zero if there is a match and zero if not.

ERRORS

11	range endpoint too large.
16	bad number.
25	*digit* out of range.
36	illegal or missing delimiter.
41	no remembered search string.
42	\ (\ ) imbalance.
43	too many \ (.
44	more than 2 numbers given in \{ \}.
45	} expected after \.
46	first number exceeds second in \{ \}.
49	[ ] imbalance.
50	regular-expression overflow.

EXAMPLES

A program might use `regexp` macros and calls as follows:

```
#define INIT        register char *sp = instring;
#define GETC()      (*sp++)
#define PEEKC()     (*sp)
#define UNGETC(c)   (--sp)
#define RETURN(c)   return;
#define ERROR(c)    regerr()
#include <regexp.h>
...
(void) compile(*argv, expbuf, &expbuf[ESIZE],'\0');
...
if (step(linebuf, expbuf))
    succeed();
```

NAME

`rmdir` — remove a directory

SYNOPSIS

```
int rmdir(path)
char *path;
```

DESCRIPTION

The function `rmdir` removes a directory.

The argument `path` specifies the path-name of the directory to be removed.

The directory must be empty, that is, not have any directory entries other than, possibly, . (the directory itself) and . . (the parent-directory) [see directory in VOCAB(BA_DEF)].

RETURN VALUE

On success, `rmdir` returns 0; on failure, it returns −1 and `errno` indicates the error.

ERRORS

The function `rmdir` fails and `errno` equals:

`EEXIST`	if the directory to be removed contains directory entries other than . and . . .
`ENOTDIR`	if a component of the path-prefix is not a directory.
`ENOENT`	if the named directory does not exist.
`ENOENT`	if the path-name is longer than {PATH_MAX} characters.
`EACCES`	if a component of the path-prefix denies *search* permission, or if the parent directory of the directory to be removed denies *write* permission
`EBUSY`	if the directory to be removed is currently in use by the system.
`EROFS`	if the directory to be removed resides on a read-only file-system.
`EIO`	if a physical I/O error occurs.

USAGE

The function `rmdir` was added in UNIX System V Release 3.0.

SEE ALSO

MKDIR(BA_OS).

NAME

scanf, fscanf, sscanf — convert formatted input

SYNOPSIS

```
#include <stdio.h>

int scanf(format [ , pointer ...] )
char *format;

int fscanf(stream, format [ , pointer ...] ))
FILE *stream;
char *format;

int sscanf(s, format [ , pointer ...] )
char *s, *format;
```

DESCRIPTION

The function scanf reads from the standard input stream stdin.

The function fscanf reads from the named input stream stream.

The function sscanf reads from the character-string s.

Each function reads characters, interprets them according to a control-string, format described below, and stores the converted input where a set of pointer arguments indicates.

The control-string usually contains conversion-specifications, which direct interpretation of input sequences. The control-string may contain:

1. White-space characters (blanks, tabs, new-lines or form-feeds) which, except in two cases described below, cause input to be read up to the next non-white-space character.

2. Ordinary character (not %), which must match the next character of the input stream.

3. Conversion-specifications, composed of the character %, an optional assignment suppressing the character *, a decimal digit-string specifying an optional numerical maximum field-width, an optional letter l (ell) or h indicating the size of the receiving variable, and a conversion-code.

A conversion-specification directs the conversion of the next input field; the result is stored in the variable pointed to by the corresponding argument unless * appears, thereby suppressing the assignment. Suppressing assignment provides a way of describing an input field to be skipped. An input field is defined as a string of non-space characters; it extends to the next inappropriate character or until the maximum field-width, if one is specified, is exhausted. For all descriptors except the character [and the character c, white space leading an input field is ignored.

The conversion-code indicates the interpretation of the input field; the corresponding pointer argument usually must be of a restricted type. For a suppressed field, no pointer argument is given.

If an invalid conversion-character follows the %, the results of the operation are unpredictable. The following conversion-codes are legal:

%   a single % is expected; no assignment is done.

d   a decimal integer is expected; the corresponding argument must point to an integer.

u   an unsigned decimal integer is expected; the corresponding argument must point to an unsigned integer.

o   an octal integer is expected; the corresponding argument must point to an integer.

x   a hexadecimal integer is expected; the corresponding argument must point to an integer.

i   an integer is expected; the corresponding argument must point to an integer. Store the value of the next input item, interpreted according to C conventions; a leading 0 implies octal, a leading 0x implies hexadecimal; otherwise, decimal is assumed.

n   Store the total number of characters (including white space) scanned so far since the function call; the corresponding argument must point to an integer. No input is consumed.

e,f,g   a floating-point number is expected; the next field is converted accordingly and stored through the corresponding argument, which must point to a **float**. The input format for floating-point numbers is an optionally signed string of digits, possibly containing a decimal-point; followed by an optional exponent field made up of an E or an e, followed by an optionally signed integer.

s   a character-string is expected; the corresponding argument must point to an array of characters large enough to accept the string and a terminating \0, which scanf adds automatically. The input field is terminated by a white-space character.

c   a character is expected; the corresponding argument must point to a character, and the normal skip over white space is suppressed. Use %1s to read the next non-space character. If a field-width is given, the indicated number of characters is read; the corresponding argument must point to a character array.

[indicates string data and the normal skip over leading white space is suppressed. A left bracket is followed by a set of characters called a *scanset* and a right bracket; the input field is the maximal sequence of input characters made up only of characters in the scanset.

There are some conventions for constructing the scanset. The circumflex (^), when it is the first character in the scanset, serves as a complement operator defining the scanset as the set of all characters *not* contained in the rest of the scanset string. The construct *first – last* represents a range of characters; thus, 0123456789 may be expressed 0-9. For this convention, *first* must be lexically less than or equal to *last*, or else the dash stands for itself. The character – also stands for itself whenever it is the first or the last character in the scanset. To include the right square bracket as an element of the scanset, it must appear as the first character (possibly preceded by a circumflex) of the scanset and in this case it is not syntactically interpreted as the closing bracket. The corresponding argument must point to a character array large enough to hold the data field and the terminating \0, which scanf adds automatically. At least one character must match for this conversion to be considered successful.

The conversion-characters d, u, o, x and i may be preceded by l or h to indicate that a pointer to long or to short rather than to int is in the argument list. Similarly, the conversion-characters e, f and g may be preceded by l to indicate that a pointer to double rather than to float is in the argument list. Other conversion-characters ignore the l or h modifier.

The scanf conversion stops at end of file, at the end of the control-string or when an input character conflicts with the control-string. In the latter case, the offending character is left unread in the input stream.

RETURN VALUE

These functions return the number of successfully matched and assigned input items; this number can be zero in the event of an early conflict between an input character and the control-string. If the input ends before the first conflict or conversion, EOF is returned.

USAGE

Trailing white space (including a new-line) is left unread unless matched in the control-string.

The success of literal matches and suppressed assignments is not directly determinable.

EXAMPLES

The call to the function scanf:

```
int i, n; float x; char name[50];
n = scanf("%d%f%s", &i, &x, name);
```

with the input line:

```
25 54.32E-1 thompson
```

assigns to n the value 3, to i the value 25, to x the value 5.432, and name contains thompson\0.

The call to the function scanf:

```
int i; float x; char name[50];
(void) scanf("%2d%f%*d %[0-9]", &i, &x, name);
```

with the input line:

```
56789 0123 56a72
```

assigns 56 to i, 789.0 to x, skips 0123, and stores the string 56\0 in name. The next call to getchar [see GETC(BA_LIB)] returns a.

SEE ALSO

GETC(BA_LIB), PRINTF(BA_LIB), STRTOD(BA_LIB), STRTOL(BA_LIB).

CAVEATS

The function `scanf` will make available character-string representations for ∞ and "Not a Number" (NaN: a symbolic entity encoded in floating-point format) to support the **IEEE 754** standard.

NAME

semctl — semaphore-control-operations

SYNOPSIS

```
#include <sys/types.h>
#include <sys/ipc.h>
#include <sys/sem.h>

int semctl(semid, semnum, cmd, arg)
int semid, cmd;
int semnum;
union semun {
     int val;
     struct semid_ds *buf;
     ushort *array;
} arg;
```

DESCRIPTION

The function semctl provides a variety of semaphore-control-operations, as specified by cmd, that are executed with respect to the semaphore specified by semid and semnum.

The <sys/sem.h> header file defines the symbolic names for values of cmd. The level of permission required for each operation is shown with each command below:

GETVAL   Return the value of semval (needs *read* permission).

SETVAL   Set semval to arg.val (needs *alter* permission). Successfully executing this cmd clears the semadj value corresponding to the specified semaphore in all processes.

GETPID   Return the value of sempid (needs *read* permission).

GETNCNT   Return the value of semncnt (needs *read* permission).

GETZCNT   Return the value of semzcnt (needs *read* permission).

The following cmds operate on each semval in the set of semaphores.

GETALL   Return semvals in the array pointed to by arg.array (needs *read* permission).

SETALL   Set semval values according to the array pointed to by arg.array (needs *alter* permission). Successfully executing this cmd clears the semadj values corresponding to each specified semaphore in all processes.

The following cmds are also available:

IPC_STAT   Put the current value of each member of the semid_ds structure in the structure pointed to by arg.buf (needs *read* permission).

IPC_SET   Set the following members of the `semid_ds` structure to the corresponding value found in the structure pointed to by `arg.buf`:

```
sem_perm.uid
sem_perm.gid
sem_perm.mode /* only low 9-bits */
```

Only a process with an effective-user-ID equal to super-user or either `sem_perm.cuid` or `sem_perm.uid` in the `semid_ds` structure can execute this `cmd`.

IPC_RMID   Remove the semaphore-identifier specified by `semid` from the system and destroy the set of semaphores and the `semid_ds` structure. Only a process with an effective-user-ID equal to super-user or either `sem_perm.cuid` or `sem_perm.uid` in the `semid_ds` structure can execute this `cmd`.

RETURN VALUE

On success, the value `semctl` returns depends on `cmd` as follows:

GETVAL   the value of `semval`.
GETPID   the value of `sempid`.
GETNCNT   the value of `semncnt`.
GETZCNT   the value of `semzcnt`.
All others   a value of `0`.

On failure, `shmctl` returns `-1` and `errno` indicates the error.

ERRORS

The function `semctl` fails and `errno` equals:

EINVAL   if `semid` is not a valid semaphore-identifier; or `semnum` is less than 0 or greater than `sem_nsems`; or `cmd` is not a valid command.

EACCES   if the calling-process is denied operation-permission.

EPERM   if `cmd` is `IPC_RMID` or `IPC_SET` and the effective-user-ID of the calling-process does not equal super-user or either `sem_perm.cuid` or `sem_perm.uid` in the `semid_ds` structure.

ERANGE   if `cmd` is `SETVAL` or `SETALL` and `semval` would exceed the system imposed maximum.

SEE ALSO

SEMGET(KE_OS), SEMOP(KE_OS).

NAME

semget — get set of semaphores

SYNOPSIS

```
#include <sys/types.h>
#include <sys/ipc.h>
#include <sys/sem.h>
int semget(key, nsems, semflg)
key_t key;
int nsems, semflg;
```

DESCRIPTION

The function semget returns the semaphore-identifier associated with the argument key.

A semaphore-identifier with its associated semid_ds structure and its set of nsems semaphores are created for key if one of the following are true:

if key equals IPC_PRIVATE.

if key does not already have a semaphore-identifier associated with it, and (semflg & IPC_CREAT) is "true".

Upon creation, the semid_ds structure is initialized as follows:

In the operation-permissions structure, set sem_perm.cuid and sem_perm.uid to the effective-user-ID of the calling-process; while setting sem_perm.cgid and sem_perm.gid to the effective-group-ID of the calling-process.

Set the low-order 9-bits of sem_perm.mode to the low-order 9-bits of semflg.

Set sem_nsems is set to the value of nsems.

Set sem_otime to 0, and set sem_ctime to the current time.

RETURN VALUE

On success, semget returns a semaphore-identifier (a non-negative integer); on failure, it returns −1 and errno indicates the error.

ERRORS

The function semget fails and errno equals:

EACCES	if a semaphore-identifier exists for key, but operation-permission set by the low-order 9-bits of semflg is denied.
EEXIST	if a semaphore-identifier exists for the argument key but ((semflg & IPC_CREAT) && (semflg & IPC_EXCL)) is "true".
ENOENT	if a semaphore-identifier does not exist for the argument key and (semflg & IPC_CREAT) is "false".
ENOSPC	if a semaphore-identifier is to be created but the system-imposed limit on the maximum number of allowed semaphores system-wide would be exceeded.

EINVAL   if nsems is either less than or equal to 0 or greater than the
          system-imposed limit, or a semaphore-identifier exists for key,
          but the number of semaphores in the set associated with it is less
          than nsems and nsems is not equal to 0.

SEE ALSO

SEMCTL(KE_OS), SEMOP(KE_OS).

NAME

semop — semaphore operations

SYNOPSIS

```
#include <sys/types.h>
#include <sys/ipc.h>
#include <sys/sem.h>

int semop(semid, sops, nsops)
int semid;
struct sembuf *sops;
unsigned nsops;
```

DESCRIPTION

The function semop automatically performs an user-defined array of semaphore-operations on the set of semaphores associated with the semaphore-identifier specified by the argument semid.

The argument sops points to a user-defined array of semaphore-operation structures.

The argument nsops is the number of such structures in the array.

Each structure, sembuf, includes the following members:

```
short sem_num;   /* semaphore number */
short sem_op;    /* semaphore operation */
short sem_flg;   /* operation flags */
```

Each semaphore operation specified by sem_op is performed on the corresponding semaphore specified by semid and sem_num.

The variable sem_op specifies one of three semaphore operations:

1. If sem_op is a negative integer and the calling-process has alter permission, one of the following occurs:

   - If semval is greater than or equal to the absolute value of sem_op, the absolute value of sem_op is subtracted from semval. Also, if (sem_flg & SEM_UNDO) is "true", the absolute value of sem_op is added to the calling-process's semadj value for the specified semaphore [see EXIT(BA_OS) in EFFECTS(KE_ENV)]. The <sys/sem.h> header file defines the symbolic name SEM_UNDO.

   - If semval is less than the absolute value of sem_op and (sem_flg & IPC_NOWAIT) is "true", semop returns immediately.

   - If semval is less than the absolute value of sem_op and (sem_flg & IPC_NOWAIT) is "false", semop increments the semncnt associated with the specified semaphore and suspends execution of the calling-process until one of the following occurs:

C Language Interfaces   177

— The value of semval becomes greater than or equal to the absolute value of sem_op. When this occurs, the value of semncnt associated with the specified semaphore is decremented, the absolute value of sem_op is subtracted from semval and, if (sem_flg & SEM_UNDO) is "true", the absolute value of sem_op is added to the calling-process's semadj value for the specified semaphore.

— The semid for which the calling-process is awaiting action is removed from the system [see SEMCTL(KE_OS)]. When this occurs, errno is set equal to EIDRM, and a value of −1 is returned.

— The calling-process receives a signal that is to be caught. When this occurs, the value of semncnt associated with the specified semaphore is decremented, and the calling-process resumes execution in the manner prescribed in the routines defined in SIGNAL(BA_OS).

2. If sem_op is a positive integer and the calling-process has alter permission, the value of sem_op is added to semval and, if (sem_flg & SEM_UNDO) is "true", the value of sem_op is subtracted from the calling-process's semadj value for the specified semaphore.

3. If sem_op is 0 and the calling-process has read permission, one of the following occurs:

- If semval is 0, semop returns immediately.

- If semval is not equal to 0 and (sem_flg & IPC_NOWAIT) is "true", semop returns immediately.

- If semval is not equal to 0 and (sem_flg & IPC_NOWAIT) is "false", semop increments the semzcnt associated with the specified semaphore and suspends execution of the calling-process until one of the following occurs:

— The value of semval becomes 0, at which time the value of semzcnt associated with the specified semaphore is decremented.

— The semid for which the calling-process is awaiting action is removed from the system. When this occurs, errno is set equal to EIDRM, and a value of −1 is returned.

— The calling-process receives a signal that is to be caught. When this occurs, the value of semzcnt associated with the specified semaphore is decremented, and the calling-process resumes execution in the manner prescribed in the routines defined in SIGNAL(BA_OS).

RETURN VALUE

On success, semop returns 0; on failure, it returns − 1 and errno indicates the error.

ERRORS

The function semop fails and errno equals:

EINVAL   if semid is not a valid semaphore-identifier; or the number of individual semaphores for which the calling-process requests a SEM_UNDO would exceed the limit.

EACCES   if the calling-process is denied operation-permission.

EAGAIN   if the operation would result in suspension of the calling-process but (sem_flg & IPC_NOWAIT) is "true".

EFBIG   if sem_num is less than 0 or greater than or equal to the number of semaphores in the set associated with semid.

E2BIG   if nsops is greater than the system-imposed maximum.

ENOSPC   if the limit on the number of individual processes requesting a SEM_UNDO would be exceeded.

ERANGE   if an operation would cause a semval to overflow the system-imposed limit, or an operation would cause a semadj value to overflow the system-imposed limit.

EINTR   if semop is interrupted by a signal.

EIDRM   if semaphore-identifier semid is removed from the system.

Upon successful completion, the value of sempid for each semaphore specified in the array pointed to by sops is set to the process-ID of the calling-process.

SEE ALSO

EXEC(BA_OS), EXIT(BA_OS), FORK(BA_OS), SEMCTL(KE_OS), SEMGET(KE_OS).

NAME

setbuf, setvbuf — assign buffering for a *stdio*-stream

SYNOPSIS

```
#include <stdio.h>

void setbuf(stream, buf)
FILE *stream;
char *buf;

int setvbuf(stream, buf, type, size)
FILE *stream;
char *buf;
int type, size;
```

DESCRIPTION

The function setbuf may be used after a stream is opened but before it is read or written. If buf is the NULL pointer, input/output is completely unbuffered; otherwise setbuf causes the array pointed to by buf to be used instead of an automatically allocated buffer. A constant BUFSIZ, defined by the <stdio.h> header file, tells how big an array is needed:

```
char buf[BUFSIZ];
```

The function setvbuf may be used after stream is opened but before it is read or written. The value of type determines how stream is buffered. Legal values for type, defined by the <stdio.h> header file, are:

_IOFBF   causes input/output to be fully buffered.

_IOLBF   causes output to be line-buffered; the buffer is flushed when a new-line is written or the buffer is full or input is requested.

_IONBF   causes input/output to be completely unbuffered.

If buf is not the NULL pointer, the array it points to will be used for buffering instead of an automatically allocated buffer. The argument size specifies the size of the buffer to be used. The constant BUFSIZ in the <stdio.h> header file is suggested as a good buffer size. If input/output is unbuffered, buf and size are ignored.

By default, terminal-output is line-buffered and all other input/output is fully buffered, except standard error, stderr, which is normally unbuffered.

RETURN VALUE

If the value for type or size is illegal, setvbuf returns a non-zero value; otherwise, it returns zero.

USAGE

The function setvbuf was added in UNIX System V Release 2.0.

A common source of error is allocating buffer space as an *automatic* variable in a code block, and then failing to close the stream in the same block.

SEE ALSO

FOPEN(BA_OS), MALLOC(BA_OS), GETC(BA_LIB), PUTC(BA_LIB).

NAME
setgid — set group-ID

SYNOPSIS
```
int setgid(gid)
int gid;
```

DESCRIPTION
The function `setgid` sets the real-group-ID and effective-group-ID of the calling-process.

If the effective-user-ID of the calling-process is super-user, `setgid` sets the real-group-ID and effective-group-ID to `gid`.

If the effective-user-ID of the calling-process is not super-user, but its real-group-ID equals `gid`, `setgid` sets the effective-group-ID to `gid`.

If the effective-user-ID of the calling-process is not super-user, but the saved set-group-ID from an EXEC(BA_OS) routine equals `gid`, `setgid` sets the effective-group-ID to `gid`.

RETURN VALUE
On success, `setgid` returns `0`; on failure, it returns `−1` and `errno` indicates the error.

ERRORS
The function `setgid` fails and `errno` equals:

EPERM   if the real-group-ID of the calling-process is not equal to `gid` and its effective-user-ID is not super-user.

EINVAL   if `gid` is out of range.

SEE ALSO
EXEC(BA_OS), GETGID(BA_OS), GETUID(BA_OS), SETUID(BA_OS).

NAME

setjmp, longjmp — non-local goto

SYNOPSIS

```
#include <setjmp.h>

int setjmp(env)
jmp_buf env;

void longjmp(env, val)
jmp_buf env;
int val;
```

DESCRIPTION

These functions are useful for dealing with errors and interrupts encountered in a low-level subroutine of a program.

The function setjmp saves its stack environment in env (whose type, jmp_buf, is defined by the <setjmp.h> header file) for later use by longjmp. The function setjmp returns the value 0.

The function longjmp restores the environment saved by the last call to setjmp with the corresponding env.

After longjmp is completed, program execution continues as if the corresponding call to setjmp (the caller of which must not itself have returned in the interim) had just returned val. All accessible data have values as of the time longjmp was called.

RETURN VALUE

When called by the calling-process, setjmp returns 0.

The function longjmp does not return from where it was called, but rather, program execution continues as if the previous call to setjmp returned val. That is, when setjmp *returns* as a result of calling longjmp, setjmp returns val. However, longjmp cannot cause setjmp to return 0. If longjmp is called with a val of 0, setjmp returns 1.

USAGE

The behavior is undefined when longjmp is called without env having been primed by calling setjmp, or when the last such call was in a function which has since returned.

Register variables may have unpredictable values when the call to longjmp is in a different function from the corresponding call to setjmp.

SEE ALSO

SIGNAL(BA_OS).

NAME

setpgrp — set process-group-ID

SYNOPSIS

int setpgrp()

DESCRIPTION

The function setpgrp sets the process-group-ID of the calling-process to the process-ID of the calling-process and returns the new process-group-ID.

RETURN VALUE

On success, setpgrp returns the new process-group-ID.

SEE ALSO

EXEC(BA_OS), FORK(BA_OS), GETPID(BA_OS), KILL(BA_OS), SIGNAL(BA_OS).

NAME

`setuid` — set user-ID

SYNOPSIS

```
int setuid(uid)
int uid;
```

DESCRIPTION

The function `setuid` sets the real-user-ID and effective-user-ID of the calling-process.

If the effective-user-ID of the calling-process is super-user, `setuid` sets the real-user-ID, effective-user-ID and the saved set-user-ID to `uid`.

If the effective-user-ID of the calling-process is not super-user, but its real-user-ID equals `uid`, `setuid` sets the effective-user-ID to `uid`.

If the effective-user-ID of the calling-process is not super-user, but the saved set-user-ID from an EXEC(BA_OS) routine equals `uid`, `setuid` sets the effective-user-ID to `uid`.

RETURN VALUE

On success, `setuid` returns 0; on failure, it returns −1 and `errno` indicates the error.

ERRORS

The function `setuid` fails and `errno` equals:

EPERM   if the real-user-ID of the calling-process is not equal to `uid` and its effective-user-ID is not super-user.

EINVAL   if `uid` is out of range.

SEE ALSO

EXEC(BA_OS), GETGID(BA_OS), GETUID(BA_OS), SETGID(BA_OS).

NAME

shmctl — shared-memory-control-operations

SYNOPSIS

```
#include <sys/types.h>
#include <sys/ipc.h>
#include <sys/shm.h>

int shmctl(shmid, cmd, buf)
int shmid, cmd;
struct shmid_ds *buf;
```

DESCRIPTION

The function shmctl provides a variety of shared-memory-control-operations as specified by cmd. The following values for cmd are available:

IPC_STAT   Put the current value of each member of the shmid_ds structure in the structure pointed to by buf.

IPC_SET   Set the following members of the shmid_ds structure to the corresponding value found in the structure pointed to by buf:

```
shm_perm.uid
shm_perm.gid
shm_perm.mode /* only low 9-bits */
```

Only a process whose effective-user-ID equals either super-user or either shm_perm.cuid or shm_perm.uid in the shmid_ds structure can execute this cmd.

IPC_RMID   Remove the shared-memory-identifier specified by shmid from the system and destroy the shared-memory-segment and shmid_ds structure associated with it. Only a process whose effective-user-ID equals either super-user or either shm_perm.cuid or shm_perm.uid in the shmid_ds structure can execute this cmd.

RETURN VALUE

On success, shmctl returns 0; on failure, it returns – 1 and errno indicates the error.

ERRORS

The function shmctl fails and errno equals:

EINVAL   if shmid is not a valid shared-memory-identifier; or cmd is not a valid command.

EACCES   if cmd is IPC_STAT and the calling-process does not have read permission.

EPERM   if cmd is IPC_RMID or IPC_SET and the effective-user-ID of the calling-process does not equal either super-user or either shm_perm.cuid or shm_perm.uid in the shmid_ds structure.

USAGE

The functions `shmctl`, `shmget`, and `shmat` and `shmdt` are hardware-dependent and may not be present on all systems. The shared-memory-routines should not be used by programs except when extreme performance considerations demand them.

SEE ALSO

SHMGET(KE_OS), SHMOP(KE_OS).

NAME

    shmget — get shared-memory-segment

SYNOPSIS

    #include <sys/types.h>
    #include <sys/ipc.h>
    #include <sys/shm.h>

    int shmget(key, size, shmflg)
    key_t key;
    int size, shmflg;

DESCRIPTION

The function shmget returns the shared-memory-identifier associated with the argument key.

A shared-memory-identifier with its associated shmid_ds structure and shared-memory-segment of at least size bytes are created for key if one of the following are true:

> if key equals IPC_PRIVATE.

> if key does not already have a shared-memory-identifier associated with it and (shmflg & IPC_CREAT) is "true".

Upon creation, the data structure associated with the new shared-memory-identifier is initialized as follows:

> Set shm_perm.cuid and shm_perm.uid to the effective-user-ID of the calling-process.

> Set shm_perm.cgid and shm_perm.gid to the effective-group-ID of the calling-process.

> Set the low-order 9-bits of shm_perm.mode to the low-order 9-bits of shmflg.

> Set shm_segsz to the value of size.

> Set shm_lpid to 0.

> Set shm_nattch to 0.

> Set shm_atime and shm_dtime to 0.

> Set shm_ctime to the current time.

RETURN VALUE

On success, shmget returns a shared-memory-identifier (a non-negative integer); on failure, it returns – 1 and errno indicates the error.

ERRORS

The function shmget fails and errno equals:

> EACCES   if a shared-memory-identifier exists for the argument key but operation-permission set by the low-order 9-bits of shmflg is denied.

EEXIST   if a shared-memory-identifier exists for the argument `key` but ((`shmflg & IPC_CREAT`) `&&` (`shmflg & IPC_EXCL`)) is "true".

ENOENT   if a shared-memory-identifier does not exist for the argument `key` and (`shmflg & IPC_CREAT`) is "false".

ENOSPC   if a shared-memory-identifier is to be created but the system-imposed limit on the maximum number of allowed shared-memory-identifiers system-wide would be exceeded.

ENOMEM   if a shared-memory-identifier and associated shared-memory-segment are to be created but the amount of available physical memory is not sufficient to fill the request.

EINVAL   if `size` is less than the system-imposed minimum or greater than the system-imposed maximum, or a shared-memory-identifier exists for `key` but the size of the segment associated with it is less than `size` and `size` is not zero.

USAGE

The functions `shmctl`, `shmget` and `shmat` and `shmdt` are hardware-dependent and may not be present on all systems. The shared-memory-routines should not be used by programs except when extreme performance considerations require them.

SEE ALSO

SHMCTL(KE_OS), SHMOP(KE_OS).

NAME

shmat, shmdt — shared-memory-operations

SYNOPSIS

```
#include <sys/types.h>
#include <sys/ipc.h>
#include <sys/shm.h>

char *shmat(shmid, shmaddr, shmflg)
int shmid;
char *shmaddr
int shmflg;

int shmdt(shmaddr)
char *shmaddr
```

DESCRIPTION

The function shmat attaches the shared-memory-segment associated with the shared-memory-identifier specified by shmid to the data segment of the calling-process at the address specified by one of the following criteria:

If shmaddr is zero, attach the shared-memory-segment at the first available address the system selects.

If shmaddr is not zero and (shmflg & SHM_RND) is "false", attach the shared-memory-segment at the address specified by shmaddr.

If shmaddr is not zero and (shmflg & SHM_RND) is "true", attach the shared-memory-segment at the address specified by:

(shmaddr - (shmaddr % SHMLBA))

where % is the C language modulos operator.

The segment is attached for reading if (shmflg & SHM_RDONLY) is "true" and the calling-process has read permission; otherwise, if it is not true and the calling-process has read and write permission, the segment is attached for reading and writing.

The function shmdt detaches the shared-memory-segment located at the address specified by shmaddr from the data segment of the calling-process.

The < sys / shm . h > header file defines the following symbolic names:

Name	Description
SHMLBA	segment low boundary address multiple
SHM_RDONLY	attach read-only (else read-write)
SHM_RND	round attach address to SHMLBA

RETURN VALUE

On success, shmat returns the data segment start address of the attached shared-memory-segment; on failure, it returns – 1 and errno indicates the error.

On success, shmdt returns 0; on failure, it returns – 1 and errno indicates the error.

ERRORS

The function `shmat` fails, it does *not* attach the shared-memory-segment, and `errno` equals:

EACCES　　　if the calling-process is denied operation-permission.

ENOMEM　　　if the available data space is not large enough to accommodate the shared-memory-segment.

EINVAL　　　if `shmid` is not a valid shared-memory-identifier; or if `shmaddr` is non-zero and the address specified by (`shmaddr` - (`shmaddr` % `SHMLBA`)) is illegal; or if `shmaddr` is non-zero and (`shmflg` & `SHM_RND`) is "false" and `shmaddr` is an illegal-address.

EMFILE　　　if the number of shared-memory-segments attached to the calling-process would exceed the system-imposed limit.

The function `shmdt` fails, it does *not* detach the shared-memory-segment, and `errno` equals:

EINVAL　　　if `shmaddr` is not the data-segment-start-address of a shared-memory-segment.

USAGE

The functions `shmctl`, `shmget`, `shmat`, and `shmdt` are hardware dependent and may not be present on all systems. The shared-memory-routines should not be used by programs except when extreme performance considerations require them.

SEE ALSO

EXEC(BA_OS), EXIT(BA_OS), FORK(BA_OS), SHMCTL(KE_OS), SHMGET(KE_OS).

NAME

signal — specify what to do upon receipt of a signal

SYNOPSIS

```
#include <signal.h>

void (*signal(sig, func))()
int sig;
void (*func)();
```

DESCRIPTION

The function signal allows the calling-process to choose one of three ways in which it is possible to handle the receipt of a specific signal.

The argument sig specifies the signal, and the argument func specifies the choice. The argument sig can be assigned any one of the following signals except SIGKILL:

SIGABRT	abort*
SIGALRM	alarm clock
SIGFPE	floating point exception*
SIGHUP	hangup
SIGILL	illegal instruction (not reset when caught)*
SIGINT	interrupt
SIGKILL	kill (cannot be caught or ignored)
SIGPIPE	write on a pipe with no one to read it
SIGQUIT	quit*
SIGSYS	bad argument to routine*
SIGTERM	software termination signal
SIGTRAP	trace trap (not reset when caught)*
SIGUSR1	user-defined signal 1
SIGUSR2	user-defined signal 2

For portability, programs should use or catch *only* the signals listed above; other signals are hardware- and implementation-dependent and may have very different meanings or results across systems. (For example, the UNIX System V signals SIGEMT, SIGBUS, SIGSEGV and SIGIOT are implementation-dependent and are not listed above.) Specific implementations may have other implementation-dependent signals.

The argument func is assigned one of three values:

1. SIG_DFL,

2. SIG_IGN or

3. an *address* of a signal-catching function.

The argument func is declared as a pointer to a function returning void.

---

* The default action for these signals is an abnormal process termination. See SIG_DFL.

The following actions are prescribed by these values:

SIG_DFL   Terminate process upon receipt of a signal.

> Upon receipt of the signal sig, the receiving process is to be terminated with all of the consequences outlined in EXIT(BA_OS). In addition, if sig is one of the signals marked with an asterisk above, implementation-dependent abnormal process termination routines, such as a core dump, may be invoked.

SIG_IGN   Ignore signal.

> The signal sig is to be ignored.

> NOTE: The signal SIGKILL cannot be ignored.

address   Catch signal.

> Upon receipt of the signal sig, the receiving process executes the signal-catching function pointed to by func. The signal number sig is the only argument passed to the signal-catching function. Additional arguments may be passed to the signal-catching function for hardware-generated signals. Before entering the signal-catching function, the value of func for the caught signal is set to SIG_DFL unless the signal is SIGILL or SIGTRAP.

> The function signal will not catch an invalid function argument, func, and results are undefined when an attempt is made to execute the function at the bad address.

> Upon return from the signal-catching function, the receiving process resumes execution at the point at which it was interrupted, except for implementation defined signals where this may not be true.

> NOTE: The signal SIGKILL cannot be caught.

When a signal to be caught occurs during a non-atomic operation such as a call to a READ(BA_OS), WRITE(BA_OS), OPEN(BA_OS) or IOCTL(BA_OS) routine on a slow device (such as a terminal); or occurs during a PAUSE(BA_OS) routine; or occurs during a WAIT(BA_OS) routine that does not return immediately, the signal-catching function is executed and then the interrupted routine may return a − 1 to the calling-process with errno set to EINTR.

A call to signal cancels a pending signal sig except for a pending SIGKILL signal.

RETURN VALUE

On success, signal returns the previous value of func for the specified signal sig; on failure, it returns SIG_ERR and errno indicates the error.

ERRORS

The function `signal` fails and `errno` equals:

`EINVAL`   if `sig` is an illegal signal number or `SIGKILL`.

USAGE

Signals may be sent by the system to a user-level process or signals may be sent by one user-level process to another using the KILL(BA_OS) routine. A program can catch signals and specify the action to be taken using `signal`. The signals that a portable program may *send* are:

`SIGKILL, SIGTERM, SIGUSR1, SIGUSR2`.

For portability, programs should use only the symbolic names of signals rather than their values and use only the set of signals defined here. Specific implementations may have additional signals.

SEE ALSO

KILL(BA_OS), PAUSE(BA_OS), WAIT(BA_OS), SETJMP(BA_LIB).

CAVEATS

The end-user level utility KILL(BU_CMD) will be changed to use symbolic signal names rather than numbers.

NAME
sigset, sighold, sigrelse, sigignore — signal management

SYNOPSIS
```
#include <signal.h>

void (*sigset(sig, func))()
int sig;
void (*func)();

int sighold(sig)
int sig;

int sigrelse(sig)
int sig;

int sigignore(sig)
int sig;
```

DESCRIPTION
The functions sigset, sighold, sigrelse and sigignore enhance
the signal facility and provide signal management for user-processes.

The argument sig specifies the signal and the argument func specifies the
choice. The argument sig can be assigned any one of the following signals
except SIGKILL:

SIGHUP	hangup
SIGINT	interrupt
SIGQUIT	quit*
SIGILL	illegal instruction (not reset when caught)*
SIGTRAP	trace trap (not reset when caught)*
SIGABRT	abort*
SIGFPE	floating point exception*
SIGKILL	kill (cannot be caught or ignored)
SIGSYS	bad argument to routine*
SIGPIPE	write on a pipe with no one to read it
SIGALRM	alarm clock
SIGTERM	software termination signal
SIGUSR1	user-defined signal 1
SIGUSR2	user-defined signal 2

For portability, programs should use or catch *only* the signals listed above;
other signals are hardware- and implementation-dependent and may have very
different meanings or results across systems. (For example, the UNIX System V
signals SIGEMT, SIGBUS, SIGSEGV and SIGIOT are implementation-
dependent and are not listed above.) Specific implementations may have other
implementation-dependent signals.

---

* The default action for these signals is an abnormal process termination. See SIG_DFL.

The argument func is assigned one of four values:

1. SIG_DFL,

2. SIG_IGN,

3. SIG_HOLD or

4. an *address* of a signal-catching function.

The argument func is declared as a pointer to a function returning void. The following actions are prescribed by these values:

SIG_DFL   Terminate process upon receipt of a signal.

Upon receipt of the signal sig, the receiving process is to be terminated with all of the consequences outlined in EXIT(BA_OS). In addition, if sig is one of the signals marked with an asterisk above, implementation-dependent abnormal process termination routines, such as a core dump, may be invoked.

SIG_IGN   Ignore signal.

Any pending signal sig is discarded. A pending signal is a signal that has occurred but for which no action has been taken. The system signal action is set to ignore future occurrences of this signal type.

SIG_HOLD   Hold signal.

The signal sig is to be held. Any pending signal of this type remains held. Only one signal of each type is held.

address   Catch signal.

Upon receipt of the signal sig, the receiving process is to execute the signal-catching function pointed to by func. Any pending signal of this type is released. This address is retained across calls to the other signal management functions, sighold and sigrelse. The signal number sig is passed as the only argument to the signal-catching function. Before entering the signal-catching function, the value of func for the caught signal is set to SIG_HOLD. During normal return from the signal-catching handler, the system signal action is restored to func and any held signal of this type is released. If a non-local goto [see SETJMP(BA_LIB)] is taken, sigrelse must be invoked to restore the system signal action and to release any held signal of this type.

Upon return from the signal-catching function, the receiving process resumes execution at the point at which it was interrupted, except for implementation defined signals where this may not be true.

When a signal to be caught occurs during a non-atomic operation such as a call to the READ(BA_OS), WRITE(BA_OS), OPEN(BA_OS) or IOCTL(BA_OS) routine on a slow device (such as a terminal); or occurs during a PAUSE(BA_OS) routine; or occurs during a WAIT(BA_OS) routine that does not return immediately, the signal-catching function is executed and then the interrupted routine may return a – 1 to the calling-process and `errno` equals `EINTR`.

The function `sigset` specifies the system signal action to be taken upon receipt of `sig`.

The functions `sighold` and `sigrelse` establish critical regions of code. A call to `sighold` is analogous to raising the priority level and deferring or holding a signal until the priority is lowered by `sigrelse`. The function `sigrelse` restores the system signal action to the action previously specified by `sigset`.

The function `sigignore` sets the action for `sig` to `SIG_IGN`.

RETURN VALUE

On success, `sigset` returns the previous value of the system signal action for the specified signal `sig`; on failure, it returns `SIG_ERR` and `errno` indicates the error.

On success, `sighold`, `sigrelse` and `sigignore` return 0; on failure, they return – 1 and `errno` indicates the error.

ERRORS

The functions `sigset`, `sighold`, `sigrelse` and `sigignore` fail and `errno` equals:

`EINVAL`   if `sig` is an illegal signal number or `SIGKILL` or if the default handling of `sig` cannot be changed.

USAGE

The functions `sigset`, `sighold`, `sigrelse` and `sigignore` were added in UNIX System V Release 3.0.

For portability, programs should use only the symbolic names of signals rather than their values and use only the set of signals defined here. Specific implementations may have additional signals.

The other signal management routine, SIGNAL(BA_OS), should not be used in conjunction with these routines for a particular signal type.

SEE ALSO

KILL(BA_OS), PAUSE(BA_OS), SETJMP(BA_LIB), SIGNAL(BA_OS), WAIT(BA_OS).

NAME

sinh, cosh, tanh — hyperbolic functions

SYNOPSIS

```
#include <math.h>

double sinh(x)
double x;

double cosh(x)
double x;

double tanh(x)
double x;
```

DESCRIPTION

The functions sinh, cosh, and tanh return, respectively, the hyperbolic sine, cosine and tangent of their argument.

RETURN VALUE

The functions sinh and cosh return HUGE, and sinh may return −HUGE for negative x, when the correct value would overflow and set errno to ERANGE.

USAGE

The MATHERR(BA_LIB) routine can change these error-handling procedures.

SEE ALSO

MATHERR(BA_LIB).

CAVEATS

A macro HUGE_VAL will be defined by the <math.h> header file. This macro will call a function which returns either +∞ on a system supporting the **IEEE 754** standard or +{MAXDOUBLE} on a system that does not support the **IEEE 754** standard.

The functions sinh and cosh will return HUGE_VAL (sinh will return −HUGE_VAL for negative n) when the correct value overflows.

NAME

`sleep` — suspend execution for interval

SYNOPSIS

```
unsigned sleep(seconds)
unsigned seconds;
```

DESCRIPTION

The function `sleep` suspends the current-process from execution for the number of seconds specified by the argument `seconds`. The actual suspension-time may be less than that requested for two reasons:

1. because scheduled wakeups occur at fixed 1-second intervals (on the second, according to an internal clock) and

2. because any signal caught will terminate `sleep` following execution of the signal-catching routine.

Also, the suspension-time may be longer than requested by an arbitrary amount due to the scheduling of other activity in the system.

The function `sleep` sets an alarm signal and pauses until it (or some other signal) occurs. The previous state of the alarm signal is saved and restored. The calling-process may have set up an alarm signal before calling `sleep`. If the argument `seconds` exceeds the time until such an alarm signal would occur, the process sleeps only until the alarm signal would have occurred. The alarm signal-catching routine of the calling-process is executed just before `sleep` returns. But if the suspension-time is less than the time till such alarm, the prior alarm time remains unchanged.

RETURN VALUE

On success, `sleep` returns the *unslept* amount (the requested time minus the time actually slept) in case the caller had an alarm set to go off earlier than the end of the requested suspension-time or premature arousal due to another caught signal; on failure, `sleep` returns `0`.

SEE ALSO

ALARM(BA_OS), PAUSE(BA_OS), SIGNAL(BA_OS).

NAME

    `sputl, sgetl` — access long integer data in a machine-independent fashion.

SYNOPSIS

```
void sputl(value, buffer)
long value;
char *buffer;

long sgetl(buffer)
char *buffer;
```

DESCRIPTION

    The routine `sputl` takes the four bytes of the long integer `value` and places them in memory starting at the address pointed to by `buffer`. The ordering of the bytes is the same across all machines.

    The routine `sgetl` retrieves the four bytes in memory starting at the address pointed to by `buffer` and returns the long integer value in the byte ordering of the host machine.

    The combination of `sputl` and `sgetl` provides a machine-independent way of storing long numeric data in a file in binary form without conversion to characters.

    A program which uses these functions must be compiled with the object file library, by using the `-lld` option of `cc`.

NAME
ssignal, gsignal — software signals

SYNOPSIS
```
#include <signal.h>

int (*ssignal(sig, action))()
int sig,(*action)();

int gsignal(sig)
int sig;
```

DESCRIPTION
The functions `ssignal` and `gsignal` implement a software facility similar to the SIGNAL(BA_OS) routine.

Software signals available to programs are described in SIGNAL(BA_OS).

A call to `ssignal` associates a procedure, `action`, with the software signal `sig`; a call to `gsignal` raises the software signal, `sig`. Raising a software signal causes the action established for that signal to be taken.

The first argument, `sig`, to the function `ssignal`, is a signal number in the range 1-15 for which an action is to be established. The second argument, `action`, defines the action; it is either the name of a (user-defined) function `action` or one of the manifest constants `SIG_DFL` (default) or `SIG_IGN` (ignore). The function `ssignal` returns the action previously established for that signal type; if no action has been established or the signal is illegal, `ssignal` returns `SIG_DFL`.

The function `gsignal` raises the signal identified by its argument, `sig`:

If an action has been established for `sig`, then `action` is reset to `SIG_DFL` and `action` is entered with `sig`. The function `gsignal` returns the value `action` returns.

If the action for `sig` is `SIG_IGN`, `gsignal` returns 1 and takes no other action.

If the action for `sig` is `SIG_DFL`, `gsignal` returns 0 and takes no other action.

If `sig` has an illegal value or no action was ever specified for `sig`, `gsignal` returns 0 and takes no other action.

SEE ALSO
SIGNAL(BA_OS).

NAME

stat, fstat — get file-status information

SYNOPSIS

```
#include <sys/types.h>
#include <sys/stat.h>

int stat(path, buf)
char *path;
struct stat *buf;

int fstat(fildes, buf)
int fildes;
struct stat *buf;
```

DESCRIPTION

The function stat gets information about the status of the file named by the path-name pointed to by path. Neither read, write, nor execute permission of the named file is required, but all directories listed in the path-name leading to the file must be searchable.

The function fstat gets the status information about an open file associated with the file-descriptor fildes [see file-descriptor in VOCAB(BA_DEF)].

The argument buf points to a structure stat which contains file-status information and includes the following members:

```
ushort st_mode;  /* file-mode */
ino_t  st_ino;   /* i-node number */
dev_t  st_dev;   /* file-system-identifier */
dev_t  st_rdev;  /* device-identifier, only */
                 /* for character-special */
                 /* or block-special files */
short  st_nlink; /* number of links */
ushort st_uid;   /* file-owner user-ID */
ushort st_gid;   /* file-group user-ID */
off_t  st_size;  /* file-size in bytes */
time_t st_atime; /* time data last accessed */
time_t st_mtime; /* time data last modified */
time_t st_ctime; /* time file-status last */
                 /* changed, in seconds since */
                 /* 00:00:00 GMT 1 Jan 70 */
```

st_mode   This field is the file-mode [see MKNOD(BA_OS)].

st_ino   This field uniquely identifies the file in a given file-system.

st_dev   This field uniquely identifies the file-system holding the file. The field has no more significance, but the USTAT(BA_OS) routine uses it to get more information about the file-system. Together, st_ino and st_dev uniquely identify ordinary-files.

st_rdev   This field should not be used by programs. The field is valid for block-special or character-special files and has significance only on the system where the file was configured.

st_nlink This field should not be used by programs.

st_size   For ordinary-files, this field is the address of the end of the file; for pipes or FIFOs, it is the count of the data currently in the file; for block-special or character-special files, it is undefined.

st_atime This field is the time when file-data was last accessed. The following routines change this field:

> CREAT(BA_OS), LOCKF(BA_OS), MKNOD(BA_OS), PIPE(BA_OS), UTIME(BA_OS), READ(BA_OS).

st_mtime This field is the time when file-data was last modified. The following routines change this field:

> CREAT(BA_OS), MKNOD(BA_OS), PIPE(BA_OS), UTIME(BA_OS), WRITE(BA_OS).

st_ctime This field is the time when file-status was last changed. The following routines change this field:

> CHMOD(BA_OS), CHOWN(BA_OS), CREAT(BA_OS), LINK(BA_OS), MKNOD(BA_OS), PIPE(BA_OS), UNLINK(BA_OS), UTIME(BA_OS), WRITE(BA_OS).

The <sys/types.h> header file defines the types ushort, ino_t, dev_t, off_t and time_t.

RETURN VALUE

On success, both stat and fstat return 0; on failure, they return −1 and errno indicates the error.

ERRORS

The function stat fails and errno equals:

ENOTDIR   if a component of the path-prefix is not a directory.

ENOENT   if the named file does not exist.

EACCES   if a component of the path-prefix denies search permission.

The function fstat fails and errno equals:

EBADF   if fildes is not a valid open file-descriptor.

SEE ALSO

CHMOD(BA_OS), CHOWN(BA_OS), CREAT(BA_OS), LINK(BA_OS), MKNOD(BA_OS), PIPE(BA_OS), READ(BA_OS), TIME(BA_OS), UNLINK(BA_OS), UTIME(BA_OS), WRITE(BA_OS).

NAME

stime — set time

SYNOPSIS

```
int stime(tp)
long *tp;
```

DESCRIPTION

The function stime sets the system time and date. The argument tp points to the value of time in seconds since 00:00:00 GMT 1 Jan. 1970.

RETURN VALUE

On success, stime returns 0; on failure, it returns – 1 and errno indicates the error.

ERRORS

The function stime fails and errno equals:

EPERM   if the effective-user-ID of the calling-process is not super-user.

SEE ALSO

TIME(BA_OS).

NAME

strcat, strncat, strcmp, strncmp, strcpy, strncpy,
strdup, strlen, strchr, strrchr, strpbrk, strspn,
strcspn, strtok — string operations

SYNOPSIS

```
#include <string.h>
#include <sys/types.h>

char *strcat(s1, s2)
char *s1, *s2;

char *strncat(s1, s2, n)
char *s1, *s2;
size_t n;

int strcmp(s1, s2)
char *s1, *s2;

int strncmp(s1, s2, n)
char *s1, *s2;
size_t n;

char *strcpy(s1, s2)
char *s1, *s2;

char *strncpy(s1, s2, n)
char *s1, *s2;
size_t n;

char *strdup(s1)
char *s1;

int strlen(s)
char *s;

char *strchr(s, c)
char *s;
int c;

char *strrchr(s, c)
char *s;
int c;

char *strpbrk(s1, s2)
char *s1, *s2;

int strspn(s1, s2)
char *s1, *s2;

int strcspn(s1, s2)
char *s1, *s2;

char *strtok(s1, s2)
char *s1, *s2;
```

DESCRIPTION

The <sys/types.h> header file defines the type size_t.

The arguments s1, s2 and s point to strings, and each string is an array of characters terminated by a null-character.

The functions `strcat`, `strncat`, `strcpy`, `strncpy` and `strtok` all alter s1 without checking for overflow of the array pointed to by s1.

The function `strcat` appends a copy of s2 to the end of s1.

The function `strncat` appends at most n characters. Each returns a pointer to the null-terminated result.

The function `strcmp` compares its arguments and returns an integer less than, equal to or greater than 0, according as s1 is lexicographically less than, equal to or greater than s2.

The function `strncmp` compares at most n characters of its arguments.

The function `strcpy` copies s2 to s1, stopping after the null-character is copied, and returns s1.

The function `strncpy` copies exactly n characters, truncating s2 or adding null-characters to s1 if necessary, and returns s1. The result is not null-terminated if the length of s2 is n or more.

The function `strdup` returns a pointer to a new string, which is a duplicate of the string pointed to by s1, or it returns a NULL pointer if the new string cannot be created. Space for the new string is obtained using MALLOC(BA_OS).

The function `strlen` returns the number of characters in s, not including the terminating null-character.

The function `strchr` (or `strrchr`) returns a pointer to the first (or last) occurrence of character c in s, or it returns a NULL pointer if c does not occur in s. The null-character terminating a string forms part of the string.

The function `strpbrk` returns a pointer to the first occurrence in s1 of any character from s2, or it returns a NULL pointer if no character from s2 occurs in s1.

The function `strspn` (or `strcspn`) returns the size of the initial span of s1 which consists entirely of characters from (or not from) s2.

The function `strtok` considers s1 to consist of a sequence of zero or more text tokens separated by spans of one or more characters from the separator-string s2. The first call (with pointer s1 specified) returns a pointer to the first character of the first token, and writes a null-character into s1 immediately following the returned token. The function `strtok` keeps track of its position in s1 between separate calls, so that subsequent calls (which must be made with the first argument a NULL pointer) work through s1 immediately following that token, returning a pointer to the first character of each subsequent token. Because `strtok` writes a null-character into s1 immediately following the token, the separator-string s2 may differ from call to call. When no token remains in s1, `strtok` returns a NULL pointer.

USAGE

The <string.h> header file declares all these functions.

Both strcmp and strncmp use native character comparison. The sign of the value returned when one of the characters has its high-order bit set is implementation-dependent.

Character movement is performed differently in different implementations. Thus overlapping moves may yield surprises.

SEE ALSO

MEMORY(BA_LIB).

CAVEATS

The type of value returned by strlen will be declared as size_t.

NAME

`strtod, atof` — convert string to double-precision number

SYNOPSIS

```
double strtod( str, ptr )
char *str, **ptr;

double atof( str )
char *str;
```

DESCRIPTION

The function `strtod` returns as a double-precision floating-point number the value represented by the character string pointed to by `str`. The string is scanned up to the first unrecognized character.

The function `strtod` recognizes an optional string of *white-space* characters [as defined by `isspace` in CTYPE(BA_LIB)], then an optional sign, then a string of digits optionally containing a decimal-point, then an optional e or E followed by an optional sign, followed by an integer.

If the value of `ptr` is not `( ( char ** ) 0 )`, the location pointed to by `ptr` contains a pointer to the character terminating the scan. If no number can be formed, `*ptr` is set to `str`, and 0 is returned.

The function call `atof( str )` is equivalent to:

```
strtod( str, ( char ** )0 )
```

RETURN VALUE

If the correct value would cause overflow, ±HUGE is returned (according to the sign of the value) and `errno` is set to ERANGE.

If the correct value would cause underflow, zero is returned and `errno` is set to ERANGE.

USAGE

The function `strtod` was added in UNIX System V Release 2.0.

SEE ALSO

CTYPE(BA_LIB), SCANF(BA_LIB), STRTOL(BA_LIB).

CAVEATS

A macro `HUGE_VAL` will be defined by the `<math.h>` header file. This macro will call a function which returns either $+\infty$ on a system that supports the **IEEE 754** standard or +{MAXDOUBLE} on a system that does not support the **IEEE 754** standard.

If the correct value overflows, ±`HUGE_VAL` will be returned (according to the sign of the value).

NAME

strtol, atol, atoi — convert string to integer

SYNOPSIS

```
long strtol(str, ptr, base)
char *str, **ptr;
int base;

long atol(str)
char *str;

int atoi(str)
char *str;
```

DESCRIPTION

The function strtol returns as a long integer the value represented by the character string pointed to by str. The string is scanned up to the first character inconsistent with the base. Leading *white-space* characters [as defined by isspace in CTYPE(BA_LIB)] are ignored.

If the value of ptr is not ((char **)0), the location pointed to by ptr contains a pointer to the character terminating the scan. If no integer can be formed, that location is set to str and zero is returned.

If base is positive, but not greater than 36, it is used as the base for conversion. After an optional leading sign, leading zeros are ignored and 0x or 0X is ignored if base is 16. If base is zero, the string itself determines the base in the following way: After an optional leading sign, a leading zero causes octal-conversion and a leading 0x or 0X causes hexadecimal-conversion; otherwise, decimal-conversion is used.

Truncation from long to int can, of course, take place upon assignment or by an explicit cast.

The function call atol(str) is equivalent to:

```
strtol(str, (char **)0, 10)
```

The function call atoi(str) is equivalent to:

```
(int)strtol(str, (char **)0, 10)
```

RETURN VALUE

If ptr is a null-pointer, strtol returns the value of the string str as a long integer. If ptr is not NULL, strtol returns the value of the string str as a long integer, and the location pointed to by ptr contains a pointer to the character terminating the scan. If no integer can be formed, that location is set to str and strtol returns 0.

USAGE

Overflow conditions are ignored.

SEE ALSO

CTYPE(BA_LIB), SCANF(BA_LIB), STRTOD(BA_LIB).

CAVEATS

Error handling will be added to strtol.

NAME

swab — swap bytes

SYNOPSIS

```
void swab(from, to, nbytes)
char *from, *to;
int nbytes;
```

DESCRIPTION

The function `swab` copies `nbytes` bytes pointed to by `from` to the array pointed to by `to`, exchanging adjacent even and odd bytes. It is useful for carrying binary data between machines with different low-order/high-order byte arrangements.

The argument `nbytes` should be even and non-negative. If the argument `nbytes` is odd and positive, the function `swab` uses `nbytes-1` instead. If the argument `nbytes` is negative, the function `swab` does nothing.

NAME

    `sync` — update super-block

SYNOPSIS

    `void sync( )`

DESCRIPTION

    The function `sync` causes all information in transient memory that updates a file-system to be written out to the file-system. This includes modified super-blocks, modified i-nodes, and delayed block I/O.

    The function `sync` should be used by programs which examine a file-system.

    The writing, although scheduled, is not necessarily complete upon return from the function `sync`.

USAGE

    The function `sync` is not recommended for use by programs.

NAME

system — issue a command

SYNOPSIS

```
#include <stdio.h>

int system(string)
char *string;
```

DESCRIPTION

The function system causes the argument string to be given as input to a command interpreter and execution process. That is, the argument string is interpreted as a command, and then the command is executed.

Commands

A *blank* is a tab or a space, a *word* is a sequence of characters excluding blanks, and a *simple-command* is a sequence of words separated by blanks. The first word specifies the path-name or file-name of the command to be executed. Except as specified below, the remaining words are passed as arguments to the invoked command. The command-name is passed as argument 0 [see EXEC(BA_OS)]. The *value* of a simple-command is its exit *status* if it terminates normally, or (octal) 200+*status* if it terminates abnormally [see WAIT(BA_OS)].

A *pipeline* is a sequence of two or more simple-commands separated by the character ¦. The standard output of each simple-command (except the last simple-command in the sequence) is connected by a *pipe* [see PIPE(BA_OS)] to the standard input of the next simple-command. Each simple-command is run as a separate process; the command execution process waits for the last simple-command to terminate. The exit status of a pipeline is the exit status of the last command.

A *command* is either a simple-command or a *list* enclosed in parentheses: (*list*). Unless otherwise stated, the value returned by a command is that of the last simple-command executed in the command. A *list* is a command or a pipeline or a sequence of commands and pipelines separated by the characters ; or & or the character-pairs && or ¦ ¦. Of these, the characters ; and &, which have equal precedence, have a precedence lower than that of the character-pairs && and ¦ ¦, which have equal precedence. A *list* may optionally be terminated by the characters ; or &. An arbitrarily long sequence of newlines may appear in a *list*, instead of the character ;, to delimit commands.

A series of commands and/or pipelines separated by the character ; are executed sequentially, while commands and pipelines terminated by the character & are executed asynchronously. The character-pair && or ¦ ¦ causes the command or pipeline following it to be executed only if the preceding pipeline returns a zero (non-zero) exit status.

Comments

A word beginning with the character # causes that word and all the following characters up to a new-line to be ignored.

Command Substitution

The standard output from a command bracketed by grave-accents (the character `) may be used as part or all of a word; trailing new-lines are removed.

Parameter Substitution

A *parameter-name* is a sequence of letters, digits or underscores beginning with a letter or underscore. A *parameter* is a parameter-name, a digit or any of the characters ?, $ or !.

The character $ is used to introduce substitutable keyword-parameters.

${ *parameter* }   The value, if any, of the *parameter* is substituted. The braces are required only when *parameter* is followed by a letter, digit or underscore that is not to be interpreted as part of its name.

Keyword-parameters (also known as variables) may be assigned values by writing:

   parameter-name = *value*

The following parameters are automatically set:

Parameter	Description
?	The decimal value returned by the last synchronously executed command in this call to system.
$	The process-number of this process.
!	The process-number of the last background command invoked in this call to system.

The following parameters are used by the command execution process:

Parameter	Description
HOME	The initial working (home) directory, initially set from the 6th-field in the /etc/passwd file [see PASSWD(BA_ENV)].
PATH	The search path for commands (see Execution below).

Blank Interpretation

After parameter and command substitution, the results of substitution are scanned for internal field separator characters (*space*, *tab* and *new-line*) and split into distinct arguments where such characters are found. Explicit null arguments (" " or ' ') are retained. Implicit null arguments (those resulting from parameters that have no values) are removed.

File Name Generation

Following substitution, each word in the command is scanned for the characters *, ?, and [. If one of these characters appears the word is regarded as a *pattern*. The word is replaced with alphabetically sorted file-names that match the pattern. If no file-name is found that matches the pattern, the word is left unchanged. The character . at the start of a file-name or immediately following the character /, as well as the character / itself, must be matched explicitly.

Parameter	Description
*	Matches any string, including the null-string.
?	Matches any single character.
[...]	Matches any one of the enclosed characters.
	A pair of characters separated by the character – matches any character lexically between the pair, inclusive. If the first character following the opening [is the character ! any character *not* enclosed is matched.

Quoting

The following characters have special meaning and cause termination of a word unless enclosed in quotation marks as explained below:

> ; & ( ) ¦ < > *newline space tab*

A character may be *quoted* (i.e., made to stand for itself) by preceding it with the character \. The character-pair \ *new-line* is ignored. All characters enclosed between a pair of single quote marks (' '), except a single quote, are quoted. Inside double quote marks (" "), parameter and command substitution occurs and the character \ quotes the characters \, *, ", and $.

Input/Output

Before a command is executed, its input and output may be redirected using a special notation. The following may appear anywhere in a simple-command, or may precede or follow a command and are *not* passed on to the invoked command; substitution occurs before *word* or *digit* is used:

Notation	Description
<*word*	Use file *word* as standard input (file-descriptor 0).
>*word*	Use file *word* as standard output (file-descriptor 1). If the file does not exist it is created; otherwise, it is truncated to zero length.
>>*word*	Use file *word* as standard output. If the file exists, output is appended to it (by first seeking to the end-of-file); otherwise, the file is created.
<&*digit*	Use the file associated with file-descriptor *digit* as standard input. Similarly for the standard output using >&*digit*.
<&–	The standard input is closed. Similarly for the standard output using >&–.

If a digit precedes any of the above, the digit specifies the file-descriptor to be associated with the file (instead of the default 0 or 1). For example:

> ... 2>&1

associates file-descriptor 2 with the file associated with file-descriptor 1.

The order in which redirections are specified is significant. Redirections are evaluated left-to-right. For example:

> ... 1>*xxx* 2>&1

first associates file-descriptor 1 with file *xxx*. It associates file-descriptor 2 with the file associated with file-descriptor 1 (i.e., *xxx*). If the order of redirections were reversed, file-descriptor 2 would be associated with the terminal (assuming file-descriptor 1 had been) and file-descriptor 1 would be associated with file *xxx*.

If a command is followed by the character & the default standard input for the command is the empty file `/dev/null`. Otherwise, the environment for the execution of a command contains the file-descriptors of the invoking process as modified by input/output specifications.

Environment

The *environment* [see EXEC(BA_OS)] is a list of parameter-name-value pairs passed to an executed program in the same way as a normal argument list. On invocation, the environment is scanned and a parameter is created for each name found, giving it the corresponding value.

The environment for any simple-command may be augmented by prefixing it with one or more assignments to parameters. For example:

```
TERM=450 cmd;
```

Signals

The `SIGINT` and `SIGQUIT` signals for an invoked command are ignored if the command is followed by the character &; otherwise signals have the values inherited by the command execution process from its parent.

Execution

The above substitutions are carried out each time a command is executed. A new process is created and an attempt is made to execute the command via EXEC(BA_OS).

The parameter `PATH` defines the search path for the directory containing the command. The character : separates path-names. The default path is `:/bin:/usr/bin` (specifying the current directory, `/bin`, and `/usr/bin`, in that order). If the command-name contains the character / the search path is not used. Otherwise, each directory in the path is searched for an executable file.

> NOTE: The current directory is specified by a null path-name, which can appear immediately after the equal sign or between the colon delimiters anywhere else in the path-list.

Conventionally, `system` has been implemented with the Bourne shell [see SH(BU_CMD)].

Commands and Utilities

The current definition of `system` is not intended to preclude that or its implementation by another command-line interpreter that provides the minimum functionality described here. Of course, any implementation may provide a superset of the functionality described.

RETURN VALUE

On success, `system` returns the exit status of the last simple-command executed. Errors, such as syntax errors, cause a non-zero return value and execution of the command is abandoned.

FILES

    /dev/null

USAGE

If possible, programs should use the function `system`, which is easier to use and has more functionality than the FORK(BA_OS) and EXEC(BA_OS) routines.

SEE ALSO

DUP(BA_OS), EXEC(BA_OS), FORK(BA_OS), PIPE(BA_OS), SIGNAL(BA_OS), ULIMIT(BA_OS), UMASK(BA_OS), WAIT(BA_OS).

NAME

    `time` — get time

SYNOPSIS

    `#include <sys/types.h>`

    `time_t time(tloc)`
    `time_t *tloc;`

DESCRIPTION

    The function `time` returns the value of time in seconds since 00:00:00 GMT
    1 Jan. 1970.

    As long as `tloc` is not a null-pointer, the return value is also stored in the
    location to which `tloc` points.

    The actions of `time` are undefined if `tloc` points to an invalid address.

RETURN VALUE

    On success, `time` returns the value of time; on failure, it returns − 1.

SEE ALSO

    STIME(BA_OS).

NAME

times — get process and child-process elapsed times

SYNOPSIS

```
#include <sys/types.h>
#include <sys/times.h>

long times(buffer)
struct tms *buffer;
```

DESCRIPTION

The function times fills the structure pointed to by buffer with time-accounting information. The action of times is undefined if buffer points to an illegal address.

The following are the contents of the structure tms, which is defined by the <sys/times.h> header file to include:

```
time_t   tms_utime;
time_t   tms_stime;
time_t   tms_cutime;
time_t   tms_cstime;
```

This information comes from the calling-process and each of its terminated child-processes for which it has executed a WAIT(BA_OS) routine. All times are defined in units of 1/{CLK_TCK}'s of a second.

The type time_t is defined by the <sys/types.h> header file.

The value of tms_utime is the CPU time used while executing instructions in the user-space of the calling-process.

The value of tms_stime is the CPU time used by the system on behalf of the calling-process.

The value of tms_cutime is the sum of the tms_utime and tms_cutime of the child-processes.

The value of tms_cstime is the sum of the tms_stime and tms_cstime of the child-processes.

RETURN VALUE

On success, times returns the elapsed real time, in units of 1/{CLK_TCK}'s of a second, since an arbitrary point in the past (e.g., system start-up time). This point does not change from one invocation of times to another. When times fails, it returns −1.

SEE ALSO

EXEC(BA_OS), FORK(BA_OS), TIME(BA_OS), WAIT(BA_OS).

NAME

  tmpfile — create a temporary file

SYNOPSIS

  #include <stdio.h>

  FILE *tmpfile()

DESCRIPTION

  The function tmpfile creates a temporary file using a name generated by
  the TMPNAM(BA_LIB) library routine, and returns a corresponding pointer to the
  FILE structure associated with the stream [see stdio-stream in
  VOCAB(BA_DEF)]. The temporary file will automatically be deleted when the
  process that opened it terminates or the temporary file is closed. The
  temporary file is opened for update (w+) [see FOPEN(BA_OS)].

RETURN VALUE

  If the temporary file cannot be opened, an error message is written and a
  NULL pointer is returned.

SEE ALSO

  CREAT(BA_OS), UNLINK(BA_OS), FOPEN(BA_OS), MKTEMP(BA_LIB),
  TMPNAM(BA_LIB).

NAME

tmpnam, tempnam — create a name for a temporary file

SYNOPSIS

```
#include <stdio.h>

char *tmpnam(s)
char *s;

char *tempnam(dir, pfx)
char *dir, *pfx;
```

DESCRIPTION

These functions create file-names that can safely be used for a temporary file.

The function tmpnam always generates a file-name using the path-prefix defined as P_tmpdir by the <stdio.h> header file. If s is NULL, tmpnam stores its result in an internal static area and returns a pointer to that area. The next call to tmpnam destroys the contents of the area. The function tmpnam stores its result in an array of at least L_tmpnam bytes, where L_tmpnam is a constant defined by the <stdio.h> header file. If s is not NULL, tmpnam stores its result in the array pointed to by s and returns s.

The function tempnam allows the user to control the choice of a directory. If defined in the user's environment, the value of the environmental variable TMPDIR is used as the name of the desired temporary file directory. The argument dir points to the name of the directory in which the file is to be created. If dir is NULL or points to a string that is not a name for an appropriate directory, tempnam uses the path-prefix defined as P_tmpdir by the <stdio.h> header file. If that directory is not accessible, the directory /tmp is used as a last resort.

The function tempnam uses the MALLOC(BA_OS) routine to get space for the constructed file-name, and returns a pointer to this area. Thus, any pointer value tempnam returns may serve as an argument to the function free defined in MALLOC(BA_OS). If tempnam cannot return the expected result for any reason, for example, the MALLOC(BA_OS routine failed or none of the above-mentioned attempts to find an appropriate directory succeeded, tempnam returns a NULL pointer.

USAGE

Many programs prefer their temporary-files to have certain favorite initial letter sequences in their names. Use the argument pfx for this. This argument may be NULL or point to a string of up to five characters to be used as the first few characters of the temporary-file name.

The functions tmpnam and tempnam create a different file-name each time they are called. If called more than {TMP_MAX} times in a single process, these functions start recycling previously used names.

Files created using these functions and either the FOPEN(BA_OS) routine or the CREAT(BA_OS) routine are temporary only in the sense that they reside in a directory intended for temporary use, and their names are unique. The user is responsible for using the UNLINK(BA_OS) routine to remove the file when done.

Between the time a file-name is created and the file is opened, some other process can create a file with the same name. This can never happen if that other process uses these functions or `mktemp`, and the file-names are chosen so as to render duplication by other means unlikely.

SEE ALSO

CREAT(BA_OS), UNLINK(BA_OS), FOPEN(BA_OS), MALLOC(BA_OS), MKTEMP(BA_LIB), TMPFILE(BA_LIB).

NAME

sin, cos, tan, asin, acos, atan, atan2 — trigonometric functions

SYNOPSIS

```
#include <math.h>

double sin(x)
double x;

double cos(x)
double x;

double tan(x)
double x;

double asin(x)
double x;

double acos(x)
double x;

double atan(x)
double x;

double atan2(y, x)
double y, x;
```

DESCRIPTION

The functions sin, cos and tan return respectively the sine, cosine and tangent of their argument, x, measured in radians.

The function asin returns the arc-sine of x in the range $-\pi/2$ to $\pi/2$.

The function acos returns the arc-cosine of x in the range 0 to π.

The function atan returns the arc-tangent of x in the range $-\pi/2$ to $\pi/2$.

The function atan2 returns the arc-tangent of y / x in the range $-\pi$ to π, using the signs of both y and x to get the quadrant of the return value.

RETURN VALUE

Both sin and cos lose accuracy when their argument is far from zero. For arguments sufficiently large, these functions return zero when there would otherwise be a complete loss of significance, and a TLOSS error message is printed on the standard error output [see MATHERR(BA_LIB)]. For arguments causing only partial loss of significance, a PLOSS error occurs but no message is printed. In both cases, errno equals ERANGE.

If the magnitude of the argument to asin or acos is greater than one, they return 0, print a DOMAIN error message on the standard error output, and errno equals EDOM.

If both arguments to atan2 are zero, it returns 0, prints a DOMAIN error message on the standard error output, and errno equals EDOM.

USAGE

The MATHERR(BA_LIB) routine can change these error-handling procedures.

SEE ALSO

MATHERR(BA_LIB).

NAME

tsearch, tfind, tdelete, twalk — manage binary search trees

SYNOPSIS

```
#include <search.h>

char *tsearch(key, rootp, compar)
char *key;
char **rootp;
int (*compar)();

char *tfind(key, rootp, compar)
char *key;
char **rootp;
int (*compar)();

char *tdelete(key, rootp, compar)
char *key;
char **rootp;
int (*compar)();

void twalk(root, action)
char *root;
void(*action)();
```

DESCRIPTION

The functions tsearch, tfind, tdelete, and twalk manipulate binary search trees. All comparisons are done with a user-supplied function, compar. The comparison function is called with two arguments, the pointers to the elements being compared. It returns an integer less than, equal to or greater than 0, according to whether the first argument is to be considered less than, equal to or greater than the second argument. The comparison function need not compare every byte, the elements may contain arbitrary data in addition to the values being compared.

The function tsearch can build and access the tree. The argument key points to a datum to be accessed or stored. If a datum in the tree equals *key (the value pointed to by key), tsearch returns a pointer to this found datum. Otherwise, tsearch inserts *key, and returns a pointer to it. Only pointers are copied, so the calling routine must store the data. The argument rootp points to a variable that points to the root of the tree. A NULL value for the variable pointed to by rootp denotes an empty tree; in this case, the variable is set to point to the datum which will be at the root of the new tree.

Like tsearch, tfind searchs for a datum in the tree, and returns a pointer to it if found. However, if it is not found, tfind returns a NULL pointer. The arguments for tfind are the same as for tsearch.

The function tdelete deletes a node from a binary search tree. The arguments are the same as for tsearch. The variable pointed to by rootp is changed if the deleted node was the root of the tree.

The function `twalk` traverses a binary search tree. The argument `root` is the root of the tree to be traversed. (Any node in a tree may be used as the root for a walk below that node.) The argument `action` names a user-defined routine to be called at each node. This routine is, in turn, called with three arguments.

The first argument is the address of the node being visited.

The second argument is a value from an enumeration data type, `VISIT` defined by the `<search.h>` header file. The values `preorder`, `postorder`, `endorder`, indicate whether this is the first, second or third time that the node has been visited (during a depth-first, left-to-right traversal of the tree), or the value `leaf` indicates that the node is a leaf.

The third argument is an integer that identifies the level of the node in the tree, with the root being level zero.

RETURN VALUE

If enough space is not available to create a new node, `tsearch` returns a `NULL` pointer.

If `rootp` is `NULL` on entry, `tsearch`, `tfind` and `tdelete` return a `NULL` pointer.

If the datum is found, both `tsearch` and `tfind` return a pointer to it. If not, `tfind` returns `NULL`, and `tsearch` returns a pointer to the inserted item. If the node is not found, `tdelete` returns a pointer to the parent of the deleted node, or a `NULL` pointer.

USAGE

The function `tfind` was added in UNIX System V Release 2.0.

The pointers to the key and the root of the tree must be of type pointer-to-element, and cast to type pointer-to-character. Similarly, although declared as type pointer-to-character, the value returned must be cast to type pointer-to-element.

The argument `root` to `twalk` is one level of indirection less than the argument `rootp` to `tsearch` and `tdelete`.

There are two nomenclatures used to refer to the order in which tree nodes are visited. The function `tsearch` uses preorder, postorder and endorder to respectively refer to visiting a node before any of its children, after its left child and before its right, and after both its children. The alternate nomenclature uses preorder, inorder and postorder to refer to the same visits, which could result in some confusion over the meaning of postorder.

If the calling function alters the pointer to the root, results are unpredictable.

EXAMPLES

The following code reads in strings and stores structures containing a pointer to each string and a count of its length. It then walks the tree, printing out the stored strings and their lengths in alphabetical order.

```c
#include <search.h>
#include <stdio.h>
/*
 * The tree stores pointers to the following structure:
 */
struct node {
   char *string;
   int length;
};
char string_space[10000]; /* space to store strings */
struct node nodes[500];   /* nodes to store */
struct node *root = NULL; /* this points to the root */
main()
{
    char *strptr = string_space;
    struct node *nodeptr = nodes;
    void print_node(), twalk();
    int i = 0, node_compare();

    while (gets(strptr) != NULL && i++ < sizeof(nodes[0]) {
        /* set node */
        nodeptr->string = strptr;
        nodeptr->length = strlen(strptr);
        /* put node into the tree */
        (void) tsearch((char *)nodeptr, &root, node_compare);
        /* adjust pointers, to not overwrite tree */
        strptr += nodeptr->length + 1;
        nodeptr++;
    }
    twalk(root, print_node);
}
/* This routine compares two nodes, based on an */
/* alphabetical ordering of the string field. */
int node_compare(node1, node2)
struct node *node1, *node2;
{
    return strcmp(node1->string, node2->string);
}
/* This routine prints out a node, the */
/* first time twalk encounters it. */
void print_node(node, order, level)
struct node **node;
VISIT order;
int level;
{
    if (order == preorder || order == leaf) {
        (void) printf("string = %20s,  length = %d\n",
            (*node)->string, (*node)->length);
    }
}
```

SEE ALSO

BSEARCH(BA_LIB), HSEARCH(BA_LIB), LSEARCH(BA_LIB).

NAME

ttyname, isatty — find name of a terminal

SYNOPSIS

```
char *ttyname(fildes)
int fildes;

int isatty(fildes)
int fildes;
```

DESCRIPTION

The function ttyname returns a pointer to a string containing the null-terminated path-name of the terminal-device associated with file-descriptor, fildes.

The function isatty returns 1 if fildes is associated with a terminal-device, 0 otherwise.

RETURN VALUE

The function ttyname returns a null-pointer if fildes does not describe a terminal device.

USAGE

The return value points to static data that is overwritten by each call.

NAME

    `t_accept` — accept a connect-request

SYNOPSIS

    `#include <tiuser.h>`

    `int t_accept(fd, resfd, call)`
    `int fd;`
    `int resfd;`
    `struct t_call *call;`

DESCRIPTION

The function `t_accept` is called by a transport-user to accept a connect-request. The argument `fd` identifies the local transport-endpoint where the connect-indication arrived, `resfd` specifies the local transport-endpoint where the connection is to be established, and `call` contains information required by the transport-provider to complete the connection. The argument `call` points to a `t_call` structure which contains the following members:

```
struct netbuf addr;
struct netbuf opt;
struct netbuf udata;
int sequence;
```

In `call`, `addr` is the address of the caller, `opt` indicates any protocol-specific parameters associated with the connection, `udata` points to any user-data to be returned to the caller, and `sequence` is the value returned by T_LISTEN(NS_LIB) that uniquely associates the response with a previously received connect-indication.

A transport-user may accept a connection on either the same, or on a different, local transport-endpoint than the one on which the connect-indication arrived. If the same endpoint is specified (i.e., `resfd=fd`), the connection can be accepted unless the following condition is true: The user has received other indications on that endpoint but has not responded to them (with `t_accept` or T_SNDDIS(NS_LIB)). In this case, `t_accept` fails and `t_errno` equals TBADF.

If a different transport-endpoint is specified (`resfd!=fd`), the endpoint must be bound to a protocol address and must be in the `T_IDLE` state [see T_GETSTATE(NS_LIB)] before `t_accept` is called.

For both types of endpoints, `t_accept` fails and `t_errno` equals TLOOK if there are indications (e.g., a connect or disconnect) waiting to be received on that endpoint.

The values of parameters specified by `opt` and the syntax of those values are protocol specific. The `udata` argument enables the called transport-user to send user-data to the caller and the amount of user-data must not exceed the limits supported by the transport-provider as returned in the `connect` field of the `info` argument of T_OPEN(NS_LIB) or T_GETINFO(NS_LIB). If the `len` field of `udata` is zero, no data is sent to the caller.

RETURN VALUE

On success, `t_accept` returns `0`; on failure, it returns `-1`, and `t_errno` indicates the error.

ERRORS

On failure, `t_errno` equals:

`TBADF`	if `fd` or `resfd` fails to refer to a transport-endpoint, or the user is illegally accepting a connection on the same transport-endpoint on which the connect-indication arrived.
`TOUTSTATE`	if `t_accept` is called in the wrong sequence on the transport-endpoint referenced by `fd`, or the transport-endpoint referred to by `resfd` is in the wrong state.
`TACCES`	if the user lacks permission to accept a connection on the responding transport-endpoint or to use the specified options.
`TBADOPT`	if the specified options are in the wrong format or contain illegal information.
`TBADDATA`	if the amount of user-data specified falls outside the bounds allowed by the transport-provider.
`TBADSEQ`	if an invalid sequence number is specified.
`TLOOK`	if an asynchronous event occurs on the transport-endpoint referenced by `fd` and requires immediate attention.
`TNOTSUPPORT`	if the transport-provider fails to support `t_accept`.
`TSYSERR`	if a system error occurs during `t_accept`.

SEE ALSO

T_CONNECT(NS_LIB), T_GETSTATE(NS_LIB), T_LISTEN(NS_LIB), T_OPEN(NS_LIB), T_RCVCON(NS_LIB).

NAME

   t_alloc — allocate a library structure

SYNOPSIS

```
#include <tiuser.h>

char *t_alloc(fd, struct_type, fields)
int fd;
int struct_type;
int fields;
```

DESCRIPTION

   The function t_alloc dynamically allocates memory for various transport
   function argument structures (specified below), and also allocates memory for
   buffers referenced by the structure. The structure to allocate is specified by
   struct_type, and must be one of the following:

T_BIND	struct t_bind
T_CALL	struct t_call
T_OPTMGMT	struct t_optmgmt
T_DIS	struct t_discon
T_UNITDATA	struct t_unitdata
T_UDERROR	struct t_uderr
T_INFO	struct t_info

   where each of these structures may subsequently be used as an argument to
   one or more transport functions.

   Each of the above structures, except T_INFO, contains at least one field of
   type struct netbuf. For each field of this type, the user may specify
   that the buffer for that field should be allocated as well. The length of the
   buffer allocated is based on the size information returned in the info
   argument of **T_OPEN(NS_LIB)** or **T_GETINFO(NS_LIB)**. The relevant fields of
   the info argument are described in the following list. The fields
   argument specifies which buffers to allocate, where the argument is the
   bitwise-OR of any of the following:

   T_ADDR   The addr field of the t_bind, t_call, t_uderr or
                   t_unitdata structures (size obtained from
                   info_addr).

   T_OPT   The opt field of the t_optmgmt, t_call, t_uderr or
                   t_unitdata structures (size obtained from
                   info_options).

   T_UDATA   The udata field of the t_call, t_discon or
                   t_unitdata structures (for T_CALL, size is the
                   maximum value of info_connect and info_discon;
                   for T_DIS, size is the value of info_discon; for
                   T_UNITDATA, size is the value of info_tsdu).

   T_ALL   All relevant fields of the given structure.

For each field specified in fields, t_alloc allocates memory for the buffer associated with the field, and initializes the len field to zero and the buf pointer and maxlen field accordingly. Because the length of the buffer allocated is based on the same size information returned to the user by T_OPEN(NS_LIB) and T_GETINFO(NS_LIB), fd must refer to the transport-endpoint on which the newly allocated structure is passed. In this way the appropriate size information can be accessed. If the size value associated with any specified field is -1 or -2 [see T_OPEN(NS_LIB) or T_GETINFO(NS_LIB)], t_alloc can not determine the size of the buffer to allocate and fails with t_errno set to TSYSERR and errno set to EINVAL. For any field not specified in fields, buf is set to NULL and maxlen is set to zero.

Use of t_alloc to allocate structures helps ensure the compatibility of user programs with future releases of the transport-interface functions.

RETURN VALUE

On success, t_alloc returns a pointer to the newly allocated structure; on failure, it returns NULL, and t_errno indicates the error.

ERRORS

On failure, t_errno equals:

TBADF   if fd fails to refer to a transport-endpoint.

TSYSERR   if a system error occurs during t_alloc.

SEE ALSO

T_FREE(NS_LIB), T_GETINFO(NS_LIB), T_OPEN(NS_LIB).

NAME

t_bind — bind an address to a transport-endpoint

SYNOPSIS

```
#include <tiuser.h>

int t_bind(fd, req, ret)
int fd;
struct t_bind *req;
struct t_bind *ret;
```

DESCRIPTION

The function t_bind associates a protocol address with the transport-endpoint specified by fd and activates that transport-endpoint. In connection-mode, the transport-provider may begin accepting or requesting connections on the transport-endpoint. In connectionless-mode, the transport-user may send or receive data-units through the transport-endpoint.

The req and ret arguments point to a t_bind structure containing the following members:

```
struct netbuf addr;
unsigned qlen;
```

The addr field of the t_bind structure specifies a protocol address and the qlen field indicates the maximum number of outstanding connect-indications.

The argument req requests that an address, represented by the netbuf structure, be bound to the given transport-endpoint.

The argument len specifies the number of bytes in the address and buf points to the address buffer.

The argument maxlen is meaningless for the req argument.

On return, ret contains the address that the transport-provider actually bound to the transport-endpoint; this may be different from the address specified by the user in req. In ret, the user specifies maxlen which is the maximum size of the address buffer and buf which points to the buffer where the address is to be placed.

On return, len specifies the number of bytes in the bound address and buf points to the bound address. If maxlen is not large enough to hold the returned address, an error results.

If the requested address is not available or if no address is specified in req (the len field of addr in req is zero), the transport-provider assigns an appropriate address to be bound and returns that address in the addr field of ret. The user can compare the addresses in req and ret to determine whether the transport-provider bound the transport-endpoint to a different address than that requested.

The argument `req` may be NULL if the user does not wish to specify an address to be bound. Here, the value of `qlen` is assumed to be zero, and the transport-provider must assign an address to the transport-endpoint. Similarly, `ret` may be NULL if the user does not care what address the provider bound and is not interested in the value of `qlen` negotiated. It is valid to set `req` and `ret` to NULL for the same call, in which case the provider chooses the address to bind to the transport-endpoint and does not return that information to the user.

The `qlen` field is only meaningful when initializing a connection-mode service. It specifies the number of outstanding connect-indications the transport-provider should support for the given transport-endpoint. An outstanding connect-indication is one passed to the transport-user by the transport-provider. A value of `qlen` greater than zero is only meaningful when issued by a passive transport-user that expects other users to call it. The value of `qlen` is negotiated by the transport-provider and may be changed if the transport-provider cannot support the specified number of outstanding connect-indications. On return, the `qlen` field in `ret` contains the negotiated value.

The function `t_unbind` allows more than one transport-endpoint to be bound to the same protocol address (however, the transport-provider must support this capability also), but it is not allowable to bind more than one protocol address to the same transport-endpoint. If a user binds more than one transport-endpoint to the same protocol address, only one endpoint can be used to listen for connect-indications associated with that protocol address. In other words, only one `t_bind` for a given protocol address may specify a value of `qlen` greater than zero. In this way, the transport-provider can identify which transport-endpoint should be notified of an incoming connect-indication. If a user attempts to bind a protocol address to a second transport-endpoint with a value of `qlen` greater than zero, the transport-provider assigns another address to be bound to that endpoint. If a user accepts a connection on the transport-endpoint being used as the listening endpoint, the bound protocol address will be found to be busy for the duration of that connection. No other transport-endpoints may be bound for listening while that initial listening endpoint is in the data-transfer phase. This prevents more than one transport-endpoint bound to the same protocol address from accepting connect-indications.

RETURN VALUE

On success, `t_bind` returns 0; on failure, it returns −1, and `t_errno` indicates the error.

ERRORS

On failure, `t_errno` equals:

TBADF	if `fd` fails to refer to a transport-endpoint.
TOUTSTATE	if `t_bind` is called in the wrong sequence.

TBADADDR	if the specified protocol address is in the wrong format or contained illegal information.
TNOADDR	if the transport-provider could not allocate an address.
TACCES	if the user lacks permission to use the specified address.
TBUFOVFLW	if the number of bytes allowed for an incoming argument are too few to store the value of that argument. The provider's state changes to T_IDLE and the information to be returned in ret is discarded.
TSYSERR	if a system error occurs during t_bind.

SEE ALSO

T_ALLOC(NS_LIB), T_OPEN(NS_LIB), T_OPTMGMT(NS_LIB), T_UNBIND(NS_LIB).

NAME

   t_close — close a transport-endpoint

SYNOPSIS

```
#include <tiuser.h>

int t_close(fd)
int fd;
```

DESCRIPTION

The function t_close informs the transport-provider that the user is
finished with the transport-endpoint specified by fd, and frees any local
library resources associated with the endpoint. In addition, t_close closes
the file associated with the transport-endpoint.

The function t_close should be called from the T_UNBND state [see
T_GETSTATE(NS_LIB)]. However, t_close does not check state information,
so it may be called from any state to close a transport-endpoint. If this
occurs, the local library resources associated with the endpoint are freed
automatically. In addition, CLOSE(BA_OS) is issued for that file-descriptor; the
close fails if no other process has that file open, and breaks any transport-
connection that may be associated with that endpoint.

RETURN VALUE

On success, t_close returns 0; on failure, it returns − 1, and t_errno
indicates the error.

ERRORS

On failure, t_errno equals:

TBADF   if fd fails to refer to a transport-endpoint.

SEE ALSO

T_GETSTATE(NS_LIB), T_OPEN(NS_LIB), T_UNBIND(NS_LIB).

NAME

`t_connect` — establish a connection with another transport-user

SYNOPSIS

```
#include <tiuser.h>

int t_connect(fd, sndcall, rcvcall)
int fd;
struct t_call *sndcall;
struct t_call *rcvcall;
```

DESCRIPTION

The function `t_connect` requests a connection to the specified destination transport-user.

The argument `fd` identifies the local transport-endpoint where communication is to be established, while `sndcall` and `rcvcall` point to a `t_call` structure which contains the following members:

```
struct netbuf addr;
struct netbuf opt;
struct netbuf udata;
int sequence;
```

The argument `sndcall` specifies information needed by the transport-provider to establish a connection and `rcvcall` specifies information that is associated with the newly established connection.

In `sndcall`, `addr` specifies the protocol address of the destination transport-user, `opt` presents any protocol-specific information that might be needed by the transport-provider, `udata` points to optional user-data that may be passed to the destination transport-user during connection-establishment, and `sequence` is meaningless for this function.

On return in `rcvcall`, `addr` returns the protocol address associated with the responding transport-endpoint, `opt` presents any protocol-specific information associated with the connection, `udata` points to optional user-data that may be returned by the destination transport-user during connection-establishment, and `sequence` is meaningless for this function.

The argument `opt` implies no structure on the options that may be passed to the transport-provider. The transport-provider is free to specify the structure of any options passed to it. These options are specific to the underlying protocol of the transport-provider. The user may choose not to negotiate protocol options by setting the `len` field of `opt` to zero. In this case, the provider may use default options.

The argument `udata` enables the caller to pass user-data to the destination transport-user and receive user-data from the destination user during connection-establishment. However, the amount of user-data must not exceed the limits supported by the transport-provider as returned in the `connect` field of the `info` argument of T_OPEN(NS_LIB) or T_GETINFO(NS_LIB). If the `len` of `udata` is zero in `sndcall`, no data is sent to the destination transport-user.

On return, the `addr`, `opt`, and `udata` fields of `rcvcall` are updated to reflect values associated with the connection. Thus, the `maxlen` field of each argument must be set before calling `t_connect`, to indicate the maximum size of the buffer for each. However, `rcvcall` may be NULL, in which case no information is given to the user on return from `t_connect`.

By default, `t_connect` executes in synchronous mode, and waits for the destination user's response before returning control to the local-user. A successful return (i.e., return value of zero) indicates that the requested connection has been established. However, if O_NDELAY is set [via T_OPEN(NS_LIB) or FCNTL(BA_OS)], `t_connect` executes in asynchronous mode. In this case, the call does not wait for the remote-user's response, but returns control immediately to the local-user and returns – 1 with `t_errno` set to TNODATA to indicate that the connection has not yet been established. In this way, `t_connect` simply initiates the connection-establishment procedure by sending a connect-request to the destination transport-user. The T_RCVCON(NS_LIB) component is used in conjunction with `t_connect` to determine the status of the requested connection.

RETURN VALUE

On success, `t_connect` returns 0; on failure, it returns – 1, and `t_errno` indicates the error.

ERRORS

On failure, `t_errno` equals:

TBADF	if `fd` fails to refer to a transport-endpoint.
TOUTSTATE	if `t_connect` is called in the wrong sequence.
TNODATA	if O_NDELAY is set, so `t_connect` successfully initiated the connection-establishment procedure, but did not wait for a response from the remote-user.
TBADADDR	if the specified protocol address is in the wrong format or contains illegal information.
TBADOPT	if the specified protocol options are in the wrong format or contain illegal information.
TBADDATA	if the amount of user-data specified falls outside the bounds allowed by the transport-provider.
TACCES	if the user lacks permission to use the specified address or options.
TBUFOVFLW	if the number of bytes allocated for an incoming argument are too few to store the value of that argument. When executed in synchronous mode, the provider's state, as seen by the user, changes to T_DATAXFER, and the connect-indication information to be returned in `rcvcall` is discarded.

`TLOOK`	if an asynchronous event occurs on this transport-endpoint and requires immediate attention.
`TNOTSUPPORT`	if the transport-provider fails to support `t_connect`.
`TSYSERR`	if a system error occurs during `t_connect`.

SEE ALSO

T_ACCEPT(NS_LIB), T_ALLOC(NS_LIB), T_GETINFO(NS_LIB), T_LISTEN(NS_LIB), T_OPEN(NS_LIB), T_OPTMGMT(NS_LIB), T_RCVCON(NS_LIB).

NAME
t_error − produce error message

SYNOPSIS
```
#include <tiuser.h>

void t_error(errmsg)
char *errmsg;
extern int t_errno;
extern char *t_errlist[];
extern int t_nerr;
```

DESCRIPTION
The function t_error produces a message on the standard error output
which describes the last error encountered during a call to a transport
function. The argument string errmsg is a user-supplied error message that
gives context to the error.

The function t_error prints the user-supplied error message followed by a
colon and a standard error message for the current error defined in
t_errno. If t_errno equals TSYSERR, t_error also prints a
standard error message for the current value contained in errno [see
ERRNO(BA_ENV)].

To simplify variant formatting of messages, the array of message strings,
t_errlist, is provided; t_errno can be used as an index in this table to
get the message string without the newline.

The value of t_nerr is the largest message number provided for in the
t_errlist table.

The value of t_errno is set only when an error occurs and is not cleared on
successful calls.

EXAMPLES
If T_CONNECT(NS_LIB) fails on transport-endpoint fd2 because a bad address
was given, the following call might follow the failure:

```
t_error("t_connect failed on fd2");
```

The diagnostic message to be printed would look like:

```
t_connect failed on fd2:   Incorrect transport
                           address format
```

where "Incorrect transport-address format" identifies the
specific error that occurred, and "t_connect failed on fd2" tells
the user which function failed on which transport-endpoint.

SEE ALSO
T_LOOK(NS_LIB).

NAME

t_free — free a library structure

SYNOPSIS

```
#include <tiuser.h>

int t_free(ptr, struct_type)
char *ptr;
int struct_type;
```

DESCRIPTION

The function t_free frees memory previously allocated by T_ALLOC(NS_LIB). The function t_free frees memory for the specified structure, and also frees memory for buffers referenced by the structure.

The argument ptr points to one of the seven structure types described for T_ALLOC(NS_LIB), and struct_type identifies the type of that structure which must be one of the following:

T_BIND	struct t_bind
T_CALL	struct t_call
T_OPTMGMT	struct t_optmgmt
T_DIS	struct t_discon
T_UNITDATA	struct t_unitdata
T_UDERROR	struct t_uderr
T_INFO	struct t_info

where each of these structures is used as an argument to one or more transport functions.

The function t_free checks the addr, opt and udata fields of the given structure (as appropriate) and frees the buffers pointed to by the buf field of the netbuf structure. If buf is NULL, t_free does not attempt to free memory. After all buffers are freed, t_free frees the memory associated with the structure pointed to by ptr.

Undefined results occur if ptr or any of the buf pointers points to a block of memory not previously allocated by T_ALLOC(NS_LIB).

RETURN VALUE

On success, t_free returns 0; on failure, it returns −1, and t_errno indicates the error.

ERRORS

On failure, t_errno equals:

TSYSERR   if a system error occurs during t_free.

SEE ALSO

T_ALLOC(NS_LIB).

NAME

t_getinfo — get protocol-specific service information

SYNOPSIS

```
#include <tiuser.h>

int t_getinfo(fd, info)
int fd;
struct t_info *info;
```

DESCRIPTION

The function t_getinfo returns the current characteristics of the
underlying transport-protocol associated with file-descriptor fd. The info
structure returns the same information returned by T_OPEN(NS_LIB). The
function t_getinfo enables a transport-user to access this information
during any phase of communication.

The argument info points to a t_info structure which contains the
following members:

```
long addr;      /* max size of the transport-protocol */
                /* address */
long options;   /* max number of bytes of */
                /* protocol-specific options */
long tsdu;      /* max size of a transport-service data */
                /* unit (TSDU) */
long etsdu;     /* max size of an expedited transport */
                /* service data-unit (ETSDU) */
long connect;   /* max amount of data allowed on */
                /* connection-establishment functions */
long discon;    /* max amount of data allowed on */
                /* t_snddis and t_rcvdis functions */
long servtype;  /* service type supported by the */
                /* transport-provider */
```

The value of each field may change as a result of option negotiation, and
t_getinfo enables a user to retrieve the current characteristics of the
underlying transport-protocol.

The values of the fields have the following meanings:

addr   A value greater than or equal to zero indicates the maximum
         size of a transport-protocol address; a value of − 1 specifies that
         there is no limit on the address size; and a value of − 2 specifies
         that the transport-provider does not provide user access to
         transport-protocol addresses.

options A value greater than or equal to zero indicates the maximum
         number of bytes of protocol-specific options supported by the
         provider; a value of − 1 specifies that there is no limit on the
         option size; and a value of − 2 specifies that the transport-
         provider does not support user-settable options.

tsdu   A value greater than zero specifies the maximum size of a
         transport-service data-unit (TSDU); a value of zero specifies that
         the transport-provider does not support the concept of TSDU,

although it does support the sending of a data stream with no
logical boundaries preserved across a connection; a value of – 1
specifies that there is no limit on the size of a TSDU; and a value
of – 2 specifies that the transfer of normal data is not supported
by the transport-provider.

etsdu   A value greater than zero specifies the maximum size of an
expedited transport-service data-unit (ETSDU); a value of zero
specifies that the transport-provider does not support the concept
of ETSDU, although it does support the sending of an expedited
data stream with no logical boundaries preserved across a
connection; a value of – 1 specifies that there is no limit on the
size of an ETSDU; and a value of – 2 specifies that the transfer of
expedited data is not supported by the transport-provider.

connect   A value greater than or equal to zero specifies the maximum
amount of data that may be associated with connection-
establishment functions; a value of – 1 specifies that there is no
limit on the amount of data sent during connection-
establishment; and a value of – 2 specifies that the transport-
provider does not allow data to be sent with connection-
establishment functions.

discon   A value greater than or equal to zero specifies the maximum
amount of data that may be associated with the
T_SNDDIS(NS_LIB) and T_RCVDIS(NS_LIB) components; a value of
– 1 specifies that there is no limit on the amount of data sent
with these abortive-release functions; and a value of – 2 specifies
that the transport-provider does not allow data to be sent with
the abortive-release functions.

servtype   This field specifies the service type supported by the transport-
provider, as described below.

If a transport-user is concerned with protocol independence, the above sizes
may be accessed to determine how large the buffers must be to hold each
piece of information. Alternatively, the T_ALLOC(NS_LIB) component may be
used to allocate these buffers. An error results if a transport-user exceeds the
allowed data size on any function.

The servtype field of info specifies one of the following values on return:

T_COTS   connection-mode service without optional orderly-release.
T_COTS_ORD   connection-mode service with optional orderly-release.
T_CLTS   connectionless-mode service.

A single transport-endpoint offers only one of the above services at one time.
For connectionless-mode service, T_OPEN(NS_LIB) returns – 2 for etsdu,
connect and discon.

RETURN VALUE

On success, t_getinfo returns 0; on failure, it returns – 1 and t_errno
indicates the error.

ERRORS

On failure, `t_errno` equals:

TBADF	if `fd` fails to refer to a transport-endpoint.
TSYSERR	if a system error occurs during `t_getinfo`.

SEE ALSO

T_OPEN(NS_LIB).

NAME

t_getstate — get the current state

SYNOPSIS

```
#include <tiuser.h>

int t_getstate(fd)
int fd;
```

DESCRIPTION

The function t_getstate returns the current state of the provider associated with the transport-endpoint specified by fd.

RETURN VALUE

On success, t_getstate returns the current state; on failure, it returns − 1 and t_errno indicates the error.

The current state is one of the following:

T_UNBND	unbound
T_IDLE	idle
T_OUTCON	outgoing connection pending
T_INCON	incoming connection pending
T_DATAXFER	data-transfer
T_OUTREL	outgoing orderly-release (awaiting orderly-release indication)
T_INREL	incoming orderly-release (waiting to request orderly-release)

The function t_getstate fails if the provider is undergoing a state transition when t_getstate is called.

ERRORS

On failure, t_errno equals:

TBADF	if fd fails to refer to a transport-endpoint.
TSTATECHNG	if the transport-provider is undergoing a state change or t_getstate is called after an exec, t_sync sequence.
TSYSERR	if a system error occurs during t_getstate.

SEE ALSO

T_OPEN(NS_LIB).

NAME

    t_listen — listen for a connect-request

SYNOPSIS

    `#include <tiuser.h>`

    `int t_listen(fd, call)`
    `int fd;`
    `struct t_call *call;`

DESCRIPTION

The function t_listen listens for a connect-request from a calling transport-user.

The argument fd identifies the local transport-endpoint on which connect-indications arrive.

On return, call specifies information describing the connect-indication by pointing to a t_call structure which contains the following members:

    `struct netbuf addr;`
    `struct netbuf opt;`
    `struct netbuf udata;`
    `int sequence;`

In call, addr returns the protocol address of the calling transport-user, opt returns protocol-specific parameters associated with the connect-request, udata returns any user-data sent by the caller on the connect-request, and sequence is a number that uniquely identifies the returned connect-indication. The value of sequence enables the user to listen for multiple connect-indications before responding to any of them.

Since t_listen returns values for the addr, opt and udata fields of call, the maxlen field of each must be set before issuing the t_listen to indicate the maximum size of the buffer for each.

By default, t_listen executes in synchronous mode and waits for a connect-indication to arrive before returning to the user. However, if O_NDELAY is set [via T_OPEN(NS_LIB) or FCNTL(BA_OS)], t_listen executes asynchronously, reducing to a poll for existing connect-indications. If none are available, it returns – 1 and sets t_errno to TNODATA.

RETURN VALUE

On success, t_listen returns 0; on failure, it returns – 1 and t_errno indicates the error.

ERRORS

On failure, t_errno equals:

TBADF	if fd fails to refer to a transport-endpoint.
TBUFOVFLW	if the number of bytes allocated for an incoming argument are too few to store the value of that argument. The provider's state, as seen by the user, goes to T_INCON, and the connect-indication in call is discarded.

TLOOK	if an asynchronous event occurs on this transport-endpoint and requires immediate attention.
TNODATA	if O_NDELAY is set, but no connect-indications is queued.
TNOTSUPPORT	if the transport-provider fails to support t_listen.
TSYSERR	if a system error occurs during t_listen.

CAVEATS

If a user calls t_listen in synchronous mode on a transport-endpoint not bound for listening (i.e., qlen is zero on T_BIND(NS_LIB)), the call waits forever because no connect-indications ever arrive on that endpoint.

SEE ALSO

T_ACCEPT(NS_LIB), T_ALLOC(NS_LIB), T_BIND(NS_LIB), T_CONNECT(NS_LIB), T_OPEN(NS_LIB), T_RCVCON(NS_LIB).

NAME
t_look — look at the current event on a transport-endpoint

SYNOPSIS
```
#include <tiuser.h>

int t_look(fd)
int fd;
```

DESCRIPTION
The function t_look returns the current event on the transport-endpoint specified by fd. The function t_look enables a transport-provider to notify a transport-user of an asynchronous event when the user is issuing functions in synchronous mode. Certain events require immediate notification of the user and are indicated by a specific error, TLOOK, on the current or next function to be executed.

The function t_look also enables a transport-user to poll a transport-endpoint periodically for asynchronous events.

RETURN VALUE
On success, t_look returns a value that indicates which of the allowable events occurred, or returns zero if no event exists. One of the following events is returned:

T_LISTEN	connection indication received
T_CONNECT	connect-confirmation received
T_DATA	normal data received
T_EXDATA	expedited data received
T_DISCONNECT	disconnect received
T_ERROR	fatal error indication
T_UDERR	datagram error indication
T_ORDREL	orderly-release indication

On failure, t_look returns −1 and t_errno indicates the error.

ERRORS
On failure, t_errno equals:

TBADF   if fd fails to refer to a transport-endpoint.

TSYSERR   if a system error occurs during t_look.

SEE ALSO
T_OPEN(NS_LIB).

NAME

t_open — establish a transport-endpoint

SYNOPSIS

```
#include <tiuser.h>
#include <fcntl.h>
int t_open(path, oflag, info)
char *path;
int oflag;
struct t_info *info;
```

DESCRIPTION

The function t_open must be called as the first step in the initialization of a transport-endpoint. The function t_open establishes a transport-endpoint by opening a UNIX System V file that identifies a particular transport-provider (i.e., transport-protocol) and returning a file-descriptor that identifies that endpoint. For example, opening the file /dev/iso_cots identifies an OSI connection-oriented transport layer protocol as the transport-provider.

The argument path points to the path name of the file to open, and oflag identifies any open flags [as in OPEN(BA_OS)].

The argument oflag may be constructed from O_NDELAY OR-ed with either O_RDONLY, O_WRONLY or O_RDWR. The header file <fcntl.h> defines these flags.

The function t_open returns a file-descriptor that will be used by all subsequent functions to identify the particular local transport-endpoint.

The function t_open also returns various default characteristics of the underlying transport-protocol by setting fields in the t_info structure.

The argument info points to a t_info structure [see T_GETINFO(NS_LIB)]. If the transport-user sets info to NULL, t_open returns no protocol information.

RETURN VALUE

On success, t_open returns a valid file-descriptor; on failure, it returns − 1 and t_errno indicates the error.

ERRORS

On failure, t_errno equals:

TSYSERR   if a system error occurs during t_open.

SEE ALSO

OPEN(BA_OS).

NAME

`t_optmgmt` — manage options for a transport-endpoint

SYNOPSIS

```
#include <tiuser.h>

int t_optmgmt(fd, req, ret)
int fd;
struct t_optmgmt *req;
struct t_optmgmt *ret;
```

DESCRIPTION

The function `t_optmgmt` enables a transport-user to retrieve, verify or negotiate protocol options with the transport-provider.

The argument `fd` identifies a bound transport-endpoint.

The arguments `req` and `ret` point to a `t_optmgmt` structure containing the following members:

```
struct netbuf opt;
long          flags;
```

The `opt` field identifies protocol options and the `flags` field specifies the action to take with those options.

The options are represented by a `netbuf` structure in a manner similar to the address in T_BIND(NS_LIB). The argument `req` requests a specific action of and sends options to the transport-provider. For `req`, `len` specifies the number of bytes in the options, `buf` points to the options buffer, but `maxlen` is meaningless. The transport-provider may return options and flag values to the user through `ret`. For `ret`, `maxlen` specifies the maximum size of the options buffer and `buf` points to the buffer where the options are to be placed. On return, `len` specifies the number of bytes of options returned. Although `maxlen` lacks a meaning in `req`, it must be set in `ret` to specify the maximum number of bytes the options buffer can hold. The actual structure and content of the options is imposed by the transport-provider.

The `flags` field of `req` must specify one of the following actions:

`T_NEGOTIATE`	Negotiate the values of the options specified in `req` with the transport-provider. The transport-provider evaluates the requested options and negotiates the values, returning the negotiated values through `ret`.
`T_CHECK`	Verify whether the options specified in `req` are supported by the transport-provider. On return, the `flags` field of `ret` has either `T_SUCCESS` or `T_FAILURE` set to indicate whether the options are supported. These flags are only meaningful for the `T_CHECK` request.
`T_DEFAULT`	Retrieve the default options supported by the transport-provider and return them in the `opt` field of `ret`. In `req`, the `len` field of `opt` must be zero and the `buf` field may be NULL.

If called as part of the connectionless-mode service, `t_optmgmt` may block due to flow-control constraints. The function `t_optmgmt` does *not* complete until the transport-provider processes all previously sent data-units.

RETURN VALUE

On success, `t_optmgmt` returns 0; on failure, it returns − 1 and `t_errno` indicates the error.

ERRORS

On failure, `t_errno` equals:

TBADF	if `fd` fails to refer to a transport-endpoint.
TOUTSTATE	if `t_optmgmt` is called in the wrong sequence.
TACCES	if the user lacks permission to negotiate the specified options.
TBADOPT	if the specified protocol options are in the wrong format or contain illegal information.
TBADFLAG	if an invalid flag is specified.
TBUFOVFLW	if the number of bytes allowed for an incoming argument are too few to store the value of that argument. The information to be returned in `ret` is discarded.
TSYSERR	if a system error occurs during `t_optmgmt`.

SEE ALSO

T_ALLOC(NS_LIB), T_GETINFO(NS_LIB), T_OPEN(NS_LIB).

NAME

t_rcv — receive data or expedited data sent over a connection

SYNOPSIS

```
int t_rcv(fd, buf, nbytes, flags)
int fd;
char *buf;
unsigned nbytes;
int *flags;
```

DESCRIPTION

The function t_rcv receives either normal or expedited data.

The argument fd identifies the local transport-endpoint on which data arrives.

The argument buf points to a receive buffer where user-data are placed.

The argument nbytes specifies the size of the receive buffer.

On return, t_rcv may set flags which specifies optional flags as described below.

By default, t_rcv operates in synchronous mode and waits for data to arrive if no data are now available. However, if O_NDELAY is set (via T_OPEN(NS_LIB) or FCNTL(BA_OS)), t_rcv executes in asynchronous mode and fails if no data are now available [see TNODATA below].

On return from the call, T_MORE set in flags means there is more data and the current transport-service data-unit (TSDU) or expedited transport-service data-unit (ETSDU) must be received in multiple t_rcv calls. Each t_rcv with T_MORE set means that another t_rcv must follow immediately to get more data for the current TSDU. The end of the TSDU is identified by the return of a t_rcv call with T_MORE clear. If the transport-provider fails to support the concept of a TSDU as indicated in info on return from T_OPEN(NS_LIB) or T_GETINFO(NS_LIB), T_MORE is meaningless and should be ignored.

On return, the data returned is expedited data if T_EXPEDITED is set in flags. If the number of bytes of expedited data exceeds nbytes, t_rcv sets both T_EXPEDITED and T_MORE on return from the initial call. Subsequent calls to retrieve the remaining ETSDU set T_EXPEDITED on return. The end of the ETSDU is identified by the return of a t_rcv call with T_MORE clear.

If expedited data arrives after part of a TSDU is retrieved, receipt of the remainder of the TSDU is suspended until the ETSDU is processed. Only after the full ETSDU is retrieved (T_MORE clear) will the remainder of the TSDU be available to the user.

RETURN VALUE

On success, t_rcv returns the number of bytes received; on failure, it returns -1 and t_errno indicates the error.

ERRORS

On failure, t_errno equals:

TBADF   if fd fails to refer to a transport-endpoint.

TNODATA   if O_NDELAY is set, but no data are now available from
                      the transport-provider.

TLOOK   if an asynchronous event occurs on this transport-endpoint
                      and requires immediate attention.

TNOTSUPPORT   if the transport-provider fails to support t_rcv.

TSYSERR   if a system error occurs during t_rcv.

SEE ALSO

T_OPEN(NS_LIB), T_SND(NS_LIB).

NAME

t_rcvconnect — receive the confirmation from a connect-request

SYNOPSIS

```
#include <tiuser.h>

int t_rcvconnect(fd, call)
int fd;
struct t_call *call;
```

DESCRIPTION

The function t_rcvconnect enables a calling transport-user to determine the status of a previously sent connect-request and is used in conjunction with T_CONNECT(NS_LIB) to establish a connection in asynchronous mode. The connection is established on successful completion of t_rcvconnect.

The argument fd identifies the local transport-endpoint on which to establish communication.

The argument call contains information associated with the newly established connection. The argument call points to a t_call structure which contains the following members:

```
struct netbuf addr;
struct netbuf opt;
struct netbuf udata;
int sequence;
```

In call, addr returns the protocol address associated with the responding transport-endpoint, opt presents any protocol-specific information associated with the connection, udata points to optional user-data that may be returned by the destination transport-user during connection-establishment, and sequence is meaningless for t_rcvconnect.

Before calling t_rcvconnect, the maxlen field of each argument must equal the maximum size of the buffer for each. However, if call is NULL, no information is given to the user on return from t_rcvconnect. By default, t_rcvconnect executes in synchronous mode and waits for the connection to be established before returning. On return, the addr, opt, and udata fields reflect values associated with the connection.

If O_NDELAY is set (via T_OPEN(NS_LIB) or FCNTL(BA_OS)), t_rcvconnect executes in asynchronous mode, and reduces to a poll for existing connect-confirmations. If none are available, t_rcvconnect fails and returns immediately without waiting for the connection to be established [see TNODATA below]. The function t_rcvconnect must be called again at a later time to complete the connection-establishment phase and retrieve the information returned in call.

RETURN VALUE

On success, t_rcvconnect returns 0; on failure, it returns −1 and t_errno indicates the error.

ERRORS

On failure, `t_errno` equals:

TBADF	if `fd` fails to refer to a transport-endpoint.
TBUFOVFLW	if the number of bytes allocated for an incoming argument are too few to store the value of that argument and the connect information to be returned in `call` is discarded. The provider's state, as seen by the user, is changed to DATAXFER.
TNODATA	if O_NDELAY is set, but a connect-confirmation has not yet arrived.
TLOOK	if an asynchronous event occurs on this transport-connection and requires immediate attention.
TNOTSUPPORT	if the transport-provider fails to support `t_rcvconnect`.
TSYSERR	if a system error occurs during `t_rcvconnect`.

SEE ALSO

T_ACCEPT(NS_LIB), T_ALLOC(NS_LIB), T_BIND(NS_LIB), T_CONNECT(NS_LIB), T_LISTEN(NS_LIB), T_OPEN(NS_LIB).

NAME
`t_rcvdis` — retrieve information from disconnect

SYNOPSIS
```
#include <tiuser.h>

t_rcvdis(fd, discon)
int fd;
struct t_discon *discon;
```

DESCRIPTION
The function `t_rcvdis` identifies the cause of a disconnect, and retrieves any user-data sent with the disconnect.

The argument `fd` identifies the local transport-endpoint on which the connection existed.

The argument `discon` points to a `t_discon` structure containing the following members:
```
struct netbuf udata;
int reason;
int sequence;
```

In `t_discon`, `reason` specifies the reason for the disconnect through a protocol-dependent reason code, `udata` identifies any user-data sent with the disconnect, and `sequence` may identify an outstanding connect-indication associated with the disconnect.

The `sequence` field is only meaningful when `t_rcvdis` is called by a passive transport-user who has executed one or more T_LISTEN(NS_LIB) functions and is processing the resulting connect-indications. If a disconnect-indication occurs, `sequence` identifies which of the outstanding connect-indications is associated with the disconnect.

If a user does not care if there are incoming data and does not need to know the value of `reason` or `sequence`, by setting `discon` equal to NULL any user-data associated with the disconnect are discarded. However, if a user retrieved more than one outstanding connect-indication (via T_LISTEN(NS_LIB)) and `discon` is NULL, the user can not identify with which connect-indication the disconnect is associated.

RETURN VALUE
On success, `t_rcvdis` returns 0; on failure, it returns − 1 and `t_errno` indicates the error.

ERRORS
On failure, `t_errno` equals:

TBADF	if `fd` fails to refer to a transport-endpoint.
TBUFOVFLW	if the number of bytes allocated for incoming data are too few to store the data. The provider's state, as seen by the user, goes to `T_IDLE`, and the disconnect-indication information to be returned in `discon` is discarded.

TNODIS   if no disconnect-indication already exists on the specified transport-endpoint.

TNOTSUPPORT   if the transport-provider fails to support `t_rcvdis`.

TSYSERR   if a system error occurs during `t_rcvdis`.

SEE ALSO

T_ALLOC(NS_LIB), T_CONNECT(NS_LIB), T_LISTEN(NS_LIB), T_OPEN(NS_LIB), T_SNDDIS(NS_LIB).

NAME

t_rcvrel — acknowledge receipt of an orderly-release indication

SYNOPSIS

```
#include <tiuser.h>

t_rcvrel(fd)
int fd;
```

DESCRIPTION

The function t_rcvrel acknowledges receipt of an orderly-release indication.

The argument fd identifies the local transport-endpoint where the connection exists.

After receipt of this indication, the user may not attempt to receive more data because such an attempt will block forever. However, the user may continue to send data over the connection if T_SNDREL(NS_LIB) is not issued by the user.

The function t_rcvrel is an optional service of the transport-provider supported if and only if the transport-provider returned service type T_COTS_ORD on T_OPEN(NS_LIB) or T_GETINFO(NS_LIB).

RETURN VALUE

On success, t_rcvrel returns 0; on failure, it returns −1 and t_errno indicates the error.

ERRORS

On failure, t_errno equals:

TBADF	if fd fails to refer to a transport-endpoint.
TNOREL	if no orderly-release indication already exists on the specified transport-endpoint.
TLOOK	if an asynchronous event occurs on this transport-endpoint and requires immediate attention.
TNOTSUPPORT	if the transport-provider fails to support t_rcvrel.
TSYSERR	if a system error occurs during t_rcvrel.

SEE ALSO

T_OPEN(NS_LIB), T_SNDREL(NS_LIB).

NAME

t_rcvudata — receive a data-unit

SYNOPSIS

```
#include <tiuser.h>

int t_rcvudata(fd, unitdata, flags)
int fd;
struct t_unitdata *unitdata;
int *flags;
```

DESCRIPTION

The function t_rcvudata receives a data-unit in connectionless-mode from another transport-user.

The argument fd identifies the local transport-endpoint on which data are received.

The argument unitdata holds information associated with the received data-unit.

On return, flags indicates if the complete data-unit was received.

The argument unitdata points to a t_unitdata structure containing the following members:

```
struct netbuf addr;
struct netbuf opt;
struct netbuf udata;
```

Before calling t_rcvudata, the maxlen field of addr, opt and udata must equal the maximum size of the buffer for each.

On return from this call, addr specifies the protocol address of the sending user, opt identifies protocol-specific options associated with this data-unit, and udata specifies the user-data received.

By default, t_rcvudata operates in synchronous mode and waits for a data-unit to arrive if no data are now available. However, if O_NDELAY is set (via T_OPEN(NS_LIB) or FCNTL(BA_OS)), t_rcvudata executes in asynchronous mode and fails if no data-units are available.

If the buffer defined in the udata field of unitdata is too small to hold the current data-unit, the buffer is filled and T_MORE is set in flags on return to indicate that another call to t_rcvudata should be made to retrieve the rest of the data-unit. Subsequent t_rcvudata calls return zero for the length of the address and options until the full data-unit is received.

RETURN VALUE

On success, t_rcvudata returns 0; on failure, it returns − 1 and t_errno indicates the error.

ERRORS

On failure, t_errno equals:

TBADF   if fd fails to refer to a transport-endpoint.

TNODATA	if O_NDELAY is set, but no data-units are now available from the transport-provider.
TBUFOVFLW	if the number of bytes allocated for the incoming protocol address or options are too few to store the information. The unit data information to be returned in `unitdata` is discarded.
TLOOK	if an asynchronous event occurs on this transport-endpoint and requires immediate attention.
TNOTSUPPORT	if the transport-provider fails to support `t_rcvudata`.
TSYSERR	if a system error occurs during `t_rcvudata`.

SEE ALSO

T_ALLOC(NS_LIB), T_RCVUDERR(NS_LIB), T_SNDUDATA(NS_LIB).

NAME

t_rcvuderr — receive a unit-data error-indication

SYNOPSIS

```
#include <tiuser.h>

int t_rcvuderr(fd, uderr)
int fd;
struct t_uderr *uderr;
```

DESCRIPTION

The function t_rcvuderr receives information concerning an error on a data-unit previously sent in connectionless-mode, and should be called only after a unit-data error-indication. It informs the transport-user that a data-unit with a specific destination address and protocol options produced an error.

The argument fd identifies the local transport-endpoint on which to receive the error report.

The argument uderr points to a t_uderr structure containing the following members:

```
struct netbuf addr;
struct netbuf opt;
long error;
```

Before calling t_rcvuderr, the maxlen field of addr and opt must equal the maximum size of the buffer for each. On return from this call, the addr structure contains the destination protocol address of the erroneous data-unit, the opt structure contains protocol-specific options associated with the data-unit, and error contains a protocol-specific error code.

If uderr equals NULL, t_rcvuderr simply clears the error-indication without reporting any information to the user.

RETURN VALUE

On success, t_rcvuderr returns 0; on failure, it returns −1 and t_errno indicates the error.

ERRORS

On failure, t_errno equals:

TBADF	if fd fails to refer to a transport-endpoint.
TNOUDERR	if no unit-data error-indication already exists on the specified transport-endpoint.
TBUFOVFLW	if the number of bytes allocated for the incoming protocol address or options are too few to store the information. The unit-data error-indication in uderr is discarded.
TNOTSUPPORT	if the transport-provider fails to support t_rcvuderr.
TSYSERR	if a system error occurs during t_rcvuderr.

SEE ALSO

T_RCVUDATA(NS_LIB), T_SNDUDATA(NS_LIB).

NAME

t_snd — send data or expedited data over a connection

SYNOPSIS

```
#include <tiuser.h>

int t_snd(fd, buf, nbytes, flags)
int fd;
char *buf;
unsigned nbytes;
int flags;
```

DESCRIPTION

The function t_snd sends either normal or expedited data.

The argument fd identifies the local transport-endpoint on which to send data.

The argument buf points to the user-data, nbytes specifies the number of bytes of user-data to send, and flags specifies any optional flags described below.

By default, t_snd operates in synchronous mode and may wait if flow-control restrictions prevent the data from being accepted by the local transport-provider at the time the call is made. However, if O_NDELAY is set (via T_OPEN(NS_LIB) or FCNTL(BA_OS)), t_snd executes in asynchronous mode and fails immediately if there are flow-control restrictions.

On success, t_snd returns the number of bytes accepted by the transport-provider. Normally this equals the number of bytes specified in nbytes. However, if O_NDELAY is set, the transport-provider may accept only part of the data. When this occurs, t_snd returns some value less than the value of nbytes and sets T_MORE for the data sent [see below]

If nbytes is zero, no data is passed to the provider, and t_snd returns zero.

If T_EXPEDITED is set in flags, the data is sent as expedited data and is subject to the interpretations of the transport-provider.

If T_MORE is set in flags, or as described above, this indicates to the transport-provider that the transport-service data-unit (TSDU) or expedited transport-service data-unit (ETSDU) is being sent through multiple t_snd calls. Each t_snd with T_MORE set indicates that another t_snd follows with more data for the current TSDU. The end of the TSDU (or ETSDU) is identified by a t_snd call with T_MORE clear. Use of T_MORE enables a user to break up large logical data-units without losing the boundaries of those units at the other end of the connection. The flag implies nothing about how the data is packaged for transfer below the transport-interface. If the transport-provider does not support the concept of a TSDU as indicated in the info argument on return from T_OPEN(NS_LIB) or T_GETINFO(NS_LIB), T_MORE is meaningless and should be ignored.

The size of each TSDU or ETSDU must not exceed the limits of the transport-provider as returned in the TSDU or ETSDU fields of the `info` argument of T_OPEN(NS_LIB) or T_GETINFO(NS_LIB). Failure to comply results in protocol error EPROTO [see TSYSERR below].

If `t_snd` is called from the `T_IDLE` state, the provider may silently discard the data.

If `t_snd` is called from any state other than `T_DATAXFER`, `T_INREL` or `T_IDLE`, the transport-provider generates an EPROTO error.

RETURN VALUE

On success, `t_snd` returns the number of bytes accepted by the transport-provider; on failure, it returns −1 and `t_errno` indicates the error.

ERRORS

On failure, `t_errno` equals:

TBADF	if `fd` fails to refer to a transport-endpoint.
TFLOW	if `O_NDELAY` is set, but the flow-control mechanism prevents the transport-provider from accepting data at this time.
TNOTSUPPORT	if the transport-provider fails to support `t_snd`.
TSYSERR	if a system error occurs during `t_snd`. An EPROTO error may not cause `t_snd` to fail until a subsequent access of the transport-endpoint.

SEE ALSO

T_OPEN(NS_LIB), T_RCV(NS_LIB).

NAME

   t_snddis — send user-initiated disconnect-request

SYNOPSIS

```
#include <tiuser.h>

int t_snddis(fd, call)
int fd;
struct t_call *call;
```

DESCRIPTION

   The function t_snddis initiates an abortive-release on an already
   established connection or rejects a connect-request.

   The argument fd identifies the local transport-endpoint of the connection.

   The argument call specifies information associated with the abortive-release
   by pointing to a t_call structure which contains the following members:

```
struct netbuf addr;
struct netbuf opt;
struct netbuf udata;
int sequence;
```

   The values in call have different semantics, depending on the context of the
   call to t_snddis. When rejecting a connect-request, call must be non-
   NULL and contain a valid value of sequence to uniquely identify the
   rejected connect-indication to the transport-provider. The addr and opt
   fields of call are ignored. In all other cases, call need only be used when
   data is being sent with the disconnect-request. The addr, opt and
   sequence fields of the t_call structure are ignored. If the user does not
   wish to send data to the remote-user, the value of call may be NULL.

   The argument udata specifies the user-data to be sent to the remote-user.
   The amount of user-data must not exceed the limits supported by the
   transport-provider as returned in the discon field of the info argument of
   T_OPEN(NS_LIB) or T_GETINFO(NS_LIB). If the len field of udata is zero, no
   data is sent to the remote-user.

RETURN VALUE

   On success, t_snddis returns 0; on failure, it returns −1 and t_errno
   indicates the error.

ERRORS

   On failure, t_errno equals:

   TBADF   if fd fails to refer to a transport-endpoint.

   TOUTSTATE   if t_snddis is called in the wrong sequence. The
                    transport-provider's outgoing queue is flushed, so data
                    may be lost.

   TBADDATA   if the amount of user-data specified falls outside the
                    bounds set by the transport-provider. The transport-
                    provider's outgoing queue is flushed, so data may be lost.

TBADSEQ	if an invalid sequence number is specified, or a NULL call structure is specified when rejecting a connect-request. The transport-provider's outgoing queue is flushed, so data may be lost.
TLOOK	if an asynchronous event occurs on this transport-endpoint and requires immediate attention.
TNOTSUPPORT	if the transport-provider fails to support t_snddis.
TSYSERR	if a system error occurs during t_snddis.

SEE ALSO

T_CONNECT(NS_LIB), T_GETINFO(NS_LIB), T_LISTEN(NS_LIB), T_OPEN(NS_LIB).

NAME

t_sndrel — initiate an orderly-release

SYNOPSIS

```
#include <tiuser.h>

int t_sndrel(fd)
int fd;
```

DESCRIPTION

The function t_sndrel initiates an orderly-release of a transport-connection and indicates to the transport-provider that the transport-user has no more data to send.

The argument fd identifies the local transport-endpoint where the connection exists.

After calling t_sndrel, the user may not send any more data over the connection; however, a user may continue to receive data if an orderly-release indication is received.

The function t_sndrel is an optional service of the transport-provider supported if and only if the transport-provider returned service type T_COTS_ORD on T_OPEN(NS_LIB) or T_GETINFO(NS_LIB).

RETURN VALUE

On success, t_sndrel returns 0; on failure, it returns – 1 and t_errno indicates the error.

ERRORS

On failure, t_errno equals:

TBADF	if fd fails to refer to a transport-endpoint.
TFLOW	if O_NDELAY is set, but the flow-control mechanism prevents the transport-provider from accepting the function at this time.
TNOTSUPPORT	if the transport-provider fails to support t_sndrel.
TSYSERR	if a system error occurs during t_sndrel.

SEE ALSO

T_OPEN(NS_LIB), T_RCVREL(NS_LIB).

NAME

t_sndudata — send a data-unit

SYNOPSIS

```
#include <tiuser.h>

int t_sndudata(fd, unitdata)
int fd;
struct t_unitdata *unitdata;
```

DESCRIPTION

The function t_sndudata sends a data-unit in connectionless-mode to another transport-user.

The argument fd identifies the local transport-endpoint on which to send data.

The argument unitdata points to a t_unitdata structure containing the following members:

```
struct netbuf addr;
struct netbuf opt;
struct netbuf udata;
```

In unitdata, addr specifies the protocol address of the destination user, opt identifies protocol-specific options the user wants associated with this request, and udata specifies the user-data to be sent.

The user may choose not to specify what protocol options are associated with the transfer by setting the len field of opt to zero. In this case, the provider may use default options. If the len field of udata is zero, no data-unit is passed to the transport-provider; t_sndudata does *not* send zero-length data-units.

By default, t_sndudata operates in synchronous mode and may wait if flow-control restrictions prevent the data from being accepted by the local transport-provider at the time the call is made. However, if O_NDELAY is set (via T_OPEN(NS_LIB) or FCNTL(BA_OS)), t_sndudata executes in asynchronous mode and fails under such conditions.

If t_sndudata is called from an invalid state, or if the amount of data specified in udata exceeds the TSDU size as returned in the tsdu field of the info argument of T_OPEN(NS_LIB) or T_GETINFO(NS_LIB), the provider generates an EPROTO protocol error [see TSYSERR below]. If t_sndudata is called before the destination user has activated its transport-endpoint [see T_BIND(NS_LIB)], the data-unit may be discarded.

RETURN VALUE

On success, t_sndudata returns 0; on failure, it returns −1 and t_errno indicates the error.

ERRORS

On failure, t_errno equals:

TBADF	if fd fails to refer to a transport-endpoint.
TFLOW	if O_NDELAY is set, but the flow-control mechanism prevents the transport-provider from accepting data at this time.
TNOTSUPPORT	if the transport-provider fails to support t_sndudata.
TSYSERR	if a system error occurs during t_sndudata. An EPROTO error may not cause t_sndudata to fail until a subsequent access of the transport-endpoint.

SEE ALSO

T_ALLOC(NS_LIB), T_RCVUDATA(NS_LIB), T_RCVUDERR(NS_LIB).

NAME

  t_sync — synchronize transport library

SYNOPSIS

  #include <tiuser.h>

  int t_sync(fd)
  int fd;

DESCRIPTION

  The function t_sync synchronizes the data structures managed by the
  transport library with information from the underlying transport-provider for
  the transport-endpoint specified by fd. In doing so, it can convert a raw file-
  descriptor (obtained via OPEN(BA_OS), DUP(BA_OS), or as a result of
  FORK(BA_OS) and EXEC(BA_OS)) to an initialized transport-endpoint, assuming
  the file-descriptor refers to a transport-provider. The function t_sync also
  allows two cooperating processes to synchronize their interaction with a
  transport-provider.

  For example, if a process forks a new process and calls an exec, the new
  process must call t_sync to build the private library data structure
  associated with a transport-endpoint and to synchronize the data structure
  with the relevant provider information.

  It is important to remember that the transport-provider treats all users of a
  transport-endpoint as a single user. If multiple processes are using the same
  endpoint, they should coordinate their activities so as not to violate the state of
  the provider. The function t_sync returns the current state of the provider
  to the user, thereby enabling the user to verify the state before taking further
  action. This coordination is only valid among cooperating processes; it is
  possible that a process or an incoming event could change the provider's state
  after t_sync is called.

  If the provider is undergoing a state transition when t_sync is called,
  t_sync fails.

RETURN VALUE

  On success, t_sync returns the state of the transport-provider; on failure, it
  returns -1 and t_errno indicates the error.

  The state returned is one of the following:

T_UNBND	unbound
T_IDLE	idle
T_OUTCON	outgoing connection pending
T_INCON	incoming connection pending
T_DATAXFER	data-transfer
T_OUTREL	outgoing orderly-release (awaiting orderly-release indication)
T_INREL	incoming orderly-release (awaiting orderly-release request)

ERRORS

On failure, `t_errno` equals:

TBADF	if `fd` fails to refer to a transport-endpoint.
TSTATECHNG	if the transport-provider is undergoing a state change.
TSYSERR	if a system error occurs during `t_sync`.

SEE ALSO

DUP(BA_OS), EXEC(BA_OS), FORK(BA_OS), OPEN(BA_OS).

NAME

t_unbind — disable a transport-endpoint

SYNOPSIS

```
#include <tiuser.h>

int t_unbind(fd)
int fd;
```

DESCRIPTION

The function t_unbind disables the transport-endpoint specified by fd previously bound by T_BIND(NS_LIB). On completion of this call, no further data or events destined for this transport-endpoint will be accepted by the transport-provider.

RETURN VALUE

On success, t_unbind returns 0; on failure, it returns – 1 and t_errno indicates the error.

ERRORS

On failure, t_errno equals:

TBADF	if fd fails to refer to a transport-endpoint.
TOUTSTATE	if t_unbind is called in the wrong sequence.
TLOOK	if an asynchronous event occurs on this transport-endpoint and requires immediate attention.
TSYSERR	if a system error occurs during t_unbind.

SEE ALSO

T_BIND(NS_LIB).

NAME

ulimit — get and set user limits

SYNOPSIS

```
long ulimit( cmd, newlimit )
int cmd;
long newlimit;
```

DESCRIPTION

The function ulimit provides for control over process limits.

Values available for the argument cmd are:

1   Get the file-size limit of the process. The limit is in units of 512-byte blocks and is inherited by child-processes. Files of any size can be read.

2   Set the file-size limit of the process equal to newlimit. Any process may decrease this limit, but only a process with an effective-user-ID of super-user may increase the limit.

RETURN VALUE

On success, ulimit returns a non-negative value; on failure, it returns − 1, it does *not* change the limit, and errno indicates the error.

ERRORS

The function ulimit fails and errno equals:

EPERM   if a process with an effective-user-ID other than super-user attempts to increase its file-size limit.

SEE ALSO

WRITE(BA_OS).

NAME

umask — set and get file-mode-creation-mask

SYNOPSIS

```
int umask(cmask)
int cmask;
```

DESCRIPTION

The function umask sets the process's file-mode-creation-mask [see CREAT(BA_OS)] equal to cmask and returns the previous value of the mask. Only the *owner*, *group*, *other* permission-bits of cmask and the file-mode-creation-mask are used.

RETURN VALUE

On success, umask returns the previous value of the file-mode-creation-mask.

SEE ALSO

CHMOD(BA_OS), CREAT(BA_OS), MKNOD(BA_OS), OPEN(BA_OS).

NAME

umount — unmount a file-system

SYNOPSIS

```
int umount( spec )
char *spec;
```

DESCRIPTION

The function umount requests that a previously mounted file-system contained on the block-special device identified by spec be unmounted.

The argument spec points to a path-name. After unmounting the file-system, the directory upon which the file-system was mounted reverts to its ordinary interpretation.

The function umount may be invoked only by the super-user.

RETURN VALUE

On success, umount returns 0; on failure, it returns − 1 and errno indicates the error.

ERRORS

The function umount fails and errno equals:

EPERM	if the process's effective-user-ID is not super-user.
ENXIO	if the device identified by spec does not exist.
ENOTDIR	if a component of the path-prefix is not a directory.
ENOENT	if the named file does not exist.
ENOTBLK	if the device identified by spec is not block-special.
EINVAL	if the device identified by spec is not mounted.
EBUSY	if a file on the device identified by spec is busy.

USAGE

The function umount is not recommended for use by programs.

SEE ALSO

MOUNT(BA_OS).

NAME

uname — get name of current operating system

SYNOPSIS

```
#include <sys/utsname.h>

int uname(name)
struct utsname *name;
```

DESCRIPTION

The function uname stores information identifying the current operating system in the structure pointed to by name.

The <sys/utsname.h> header file defines the structure that uname uses and that includes the following members:

```
char sysname[{SYS_NMLN}];
char nodename[{SYS_NMLN}];
char release[{SYS_NMLN}];
char version[{SYS_NMLN}];
char machine[{SYS_NMLN}];
```

The function uname returns a null-terminated character string naming the current operating system in the character array sysname.

Similarly, the character array nodename contains the name that the system is known by on a communications network.

The members release and version further identify the operating system.

The member machine contains a standard name that identifies the hardware that the operating system is running on.

RETURN VALUE

On success, uname returns a non-negative value; on failure, it returns − 1 and errno indicates the error.

NAME

ungetc — push character back onto *stdio* input

SYNOPSIS

```
#include <stdio.h>

int ungetc(c, stream)
int c;
FILE *stream;
```

DESCRIPTION

The function ungetc inserts the character c into the buffer associated with an input stream. That character, c, will be returned by the next call to the GETC(BA_LIB) routine on that stream. The function ungetc returns c, and leaves the file corresponding to stream unchanged.

One character of pushback is guaranteed, provided something has already been read from the stream and the stream is actually buffered.

If c equals EOF, ungetc does nothing to the buffer and returns EOF.

The FSEEK(BA_OS) routine erases all memory of inserted characters.

RETURN VALUE

On success, ungetc returns c; ungetc returns EOF if it cannot insert the character.

SEE ALSO

FSEEK(BA_OS), GETC(BA_LIB), SETBUF(BA_LIB).

NAME

unlink — remove directory entry

SYNOPSIS

```
int unlink(path)
char *path;
```

DESCRIPTION

The function unlink removes the directory entry named by the path-name pointed to by the argument path. When all links to a file have been removed and no process has the file open, the space occupied by the file is freed and the file ceases to exist. If one or more processes have the file open when the last link is removed, space occupied by the file is not released until all references to the file have been closed.

RETURN VALUE

On success, unlink returns 0; on failure, it returns − 1 and errno indicates the error.

ERRORS

The function unlink fails and errno equals:

ENOTDIR   if a component of the path prefix is not a directory.

ENOENT   if the named file does not exist.

EACCES   if a component of the path-prefix denies search permission.

EACCES   if the directory containing the link to be removed denies write permission.

EPERM   if the named file is a directory and the effective-user-ID of the process is not super-user.

EBUSY   if the entry to be unlinked is the mount point for a mounted file-system.

ETXTBSY   if the entry to be unlinked is the last link to a pure procedure (shared text) file being executed.

EROFS   if the entry to be unlinked is part of a read-only file-system.

SEE ALSO

CLOSE(BA_OS), LINK(BA_OS), OPEN(BA_OS).

NAME

ustat — get file-system statistics

SYNOPSIS

```
#include <sys/types.h>
#include <ustat.h>

int ustat(dev, buf)
dev_t dev;
struct ustat *buf;
```

DESCRIPTION

The function ustat returns information about a mounted file-system.

The argument dev is a device number identifying a device containing a mounted file-system. The value of dev comes from the field st_dev of the structure stat [see STAT(BA_OS)].

The argument buf points to a ustat structure that includes the following elements:

```
daddr_t f_tfree;    /* total free blocks */
ino_t   f_tinode;   /* number of free i-nodes */
char    f_fname[6]; /* file-system name or null */
char    f_fpack[6]; /* file-system pack or null */
```

The last two fields, f_fname and f_fpack may not have significant information on all systems, and, in that case, will contain the null-character.

RETURN VALUE

On success, ustat returns 0; on failure, it returns − 1 and errno indicates the error.

ERRORS

The function ustat fails and errno equals:

EINVAL　　　if dev is not the device number of a device containing a mounted file-system.

SEE ALSO

STAT(BA_OS).

NAME
utime — set file access and modification times

SYNOPSIS
```
#include <sys/types.h>

int utime(path, times)
char *path;
struct utimbuf *times;
```

DESCRIPTION
The function utime sets the access and modification times of the file named by the path-name pointed to by path; hence, utime updates the time of the last file-status change (st_ctime) for that file [see STAT(BA_OS)].

If times is NULL, the access and modification times are set to the current time; a process must be the owner of the file or have write permission to do this. If times is not NULL, it must point to a utimbuf structure (see below) and the access and modification times are set to the values in that structure; only the owner of the file or the super-user may do this.

RETURN VALUE
On success, utime returns 0; on failure, it returns −1 and errno indicates the error.

ERRORS
The function utime fails and errno equals:

ENOENT   if the named file does not exist.

ENOTDIR   if a component of the path-prefix is not a directory.

EACCES   if a component of the path-prefix denies search permission, or if the effective-user-ID is not super-user and not the owner of the file and times is NULL and write access is denied.

EPERM   if the effective-user-ID is not super-user and not the owner of the file and times is not NULL.

EROFS   if the file-system containing the file is mounted read-only.

USAGE
A program must declare the structure utimbuf as follows:
```
struct utimbuf {
        time_t actime;   /* access time */
        time_t modtime;  /* modification time */
};
```

The structure utimbuf gives times in seconds since 00:00:00 GMT 1 Jan. 1970. The <sys/types.h> header file defines the type time_t.

SEE ALSO
STAT(BA_OS).

NAME

vprintf, vfprintf, vsprintf — print formatted output of a varargs argument list

SYNOPSIS

```
#include <stdio.h>
#include <varargs.h>

int vprintf(format, ap)
char *format;
va_list ap;

int vfprintf(stream, format, ap)
FILE *stream;
char *format;
va_list ap;

int vsprintf(s, format, ap)
char *s, *format;
va_list ap;
```

DESCRIPTION

The functions vprintf, vfprintf, and vsprintf are the same as printf, fprintf, and sprintf respectively, except they are called with an argument list ap of type va_list as defined by the <varargs.h> header file.

The <varargs.h> header file defines the type va_list and a set of macros for advancing through a list of arguments whose number and types may vary. The argument ap is used with the <varargs.h> header file macros va_start, va_arg and va_end. The EXAMPLE section below shows their use with vprintf.

The macro va_alist is used as the parameter list in a function definition as in the function called error in the example below.

The macro va_dcl is the declaration for va_alist and should not be followed by a semicolon.

The macro va_start(ap), where ap is of type va_list, must be called before any attempt to traverse and access the list of arguments.

Calls to va_arg(ap, atype) traverse the argument list. Each execution of va_arg expands to an expression with the value of the next argument in the list ap. The argument atype is the type that the returned argument is expected to be.

The macro va_end(ap) must be executed when all desired arguments have been accessed. (The argument list in ap can be traversed again if va_start is called again after va_end).

USAGE

The functions vprintf, vfprintf and vsprintf were added in UNIX System V Release 2.0.

EXAMPLES

The following shows how `vfprintf` can be used to write an error routine.
In it, `va_arg` is executed first to return the function name passed to `error`
and it is called again to retrieve the format passed to `error`. The remaining
`error` arguments, `arg1`, `arg2`, ..., are given to `vfprintf` in `ap`.

```
#include <stdio.h>
#include <varargs.h>
...
/*
 *    error should be called like
 *          error(function_name, format, arg1, arg2...);
 */
void error(va_alist)
   va_dcl
{
   va_list ap;
   char *fmt;

   va_start(ap);
   /* print out name of function causing error */
   (void) fprintf(stderr, "ERR in %s:", va_arg(ap, char *));
   fmt = va_arg(ap, char *);
   /* print out remainder of message */
   (void) vfprintf(stderr, fmt, ap);
   va_end(ap);
   (void) abort();
}
```

SEE ALSO

PRINTF(BA_LIB).

NAME

`wait` — wait for child-process to stop or terminate

SYNOPSIS

```
int wait( stat_loc )
int *stat_loc;

int wait( (int *)0 )
```

DESCRIPTION

The function `wait` suspends the calling-process until one of the immediate children terminates. If a child-process terminates prior to the call to `wait`, return is immediate.

If `stat_loc` (taken as an integer) is non-zero, 16-bits of information called *status* are stored in the low-order 16-bits of the location pointed to by `stat_loc`. The status differentiates between stopped and terminated child-processes and if the child-process terminated, identifies the cause of termination and passes useful information to the parent-process as follows:

If the child-process terminated due to a call to the EXIT(BA_OS) routine, the low-order 8-bits of status will be zero and the next 8-bits will contain the low-order 8-bits of the argument that the child-process passed to the EXIT(BA_OS) routine.

If the child-process terminated due to a signal, the low-order 7-bits (i.e., bits 177) will contain the number of the signal that caused the termination. Also, if abnormal-process-termination routines [see SIGNAL(BA_OS)] successfully completed, the low-order eighth-bit (i.e., bit 200) will be set. The next 8-bits of status will be zero.

If a parent-process terminates without waiting for its child-processes to terminate, a special system-process inherits them [see EXIT(BA_OS)].

The function `wait` fails and its actions are undefined if the argument `stat_loc` points to an illegal address.

RETURN VALUE

If `wait` returns due to the receipt of a signal, it returns – 1 to the calling-process and `errno` to `EINTR`.

If `wait` returns due to a terminated child-process, it returns the process-ID of the child-process to the calling-process; otherwise, it returns immediately with a value of – 1 and `errno` indicates the error.

ERRORS

The function `wait` fails and `errno` equals:

`ECHILD`   if the calling-process has no more unwaited-for child-processes.

SEE ALSO

EXEC(BA_OS), EXIT(BA_OS), FORK(BA_OS), SIGNAL(BA_OS).

NAME

write — write on a file

SYNOPSIS

```
int write(fildes, buf, nbyte)
int fildes;
char *buf;
unsigned nbyte;
```

DESCRIPTION

The function `write` attempts to write `nbyte` bytes from the buffer pointed to by `buf` to the file denoted by the open file-descriptor `fildes`.

On devices capable of seeking, writing proceeds from the position in the file indicated by the file-pointer associated with `fildes`. On return, `write` increments the file-pointer by the number of bytes actually written.

On devices incapable of seeking, such as a terminal, writing always proceeds from the current position. The value of a file-pointer associated with such a device is undefined [see OPEN(BA_OS)].

If `O_APPEND` is set, the file-pointer is set to the end of the file prior to each `write` operation.

In a `write` of {PIPE_BUF} bytes or less to a pipe (or FIFO) with less than `nbytes` bytes of free space available in the pipe, one of the following occurs:

If `O_NDELAY` is clear, the process blocks until at least `nbytes` of space becomes available in the pipe, at which point `write` proceeds; or

If `O_NDELAY` is set, the process does *not* block and `write` returns 0.

A `write` of more than {PIPE_BUF} bytes to a pipe (or FIFO) behaves differently. In a `write` of more than {PIPE_BUF} bytes to a pipe (or FIFO), one of the following occurs:

If `O_NDELAY` is clear, the process blocks if the pipe is full and:

As space becomes available in the pipe, the data from the `write` are written piecemeal, in multiple smaller amounts until the `write` is fulfilled. Thus, data from a `write` of more than {PIPE_BUF} bytes may be interleaved on arbitrary byte boundaries with data written by other processes.

If `O_NDELAY` is set, the process does *not* block and:

If the pipe is full, `write` returns 0.

If the pipe is *not* full, as much data as currently fits in the pipe are written and `write` returns the number of bytes written. In this case, only part of the data are written, but what data are written are *not* interleaved with data from other processes.

In contrast to a `write` of more than {PIPE_BUF} bytes, data from a `write` of {PIPE_BUF} bytes or less are *never* interleaved in the pipe with data from other processes.

When attempting to write to an ordinary-file with enforced record-locking enabled [see CHMOD(BA_OS)], and all or part of the file to be written has a read or write lock owned by another process (i.e., a blocking record-lock):

If O_NDELAY is clear, write sleeps until all blocking record-locks are removed, or write is terminated by a signal.

If O_NDELAY is set, write returns − 1 and errno equals EAGAIN.

If a write requests that more bytes be written than there is room for (e.g., beyond the user-process's file-size limit [see ULIMIT(BA_OS)] or the physical end of a medium), only as many bytes as there is room for are written. For example, when there is space for 20 bytes more in a file before reaching a limit, a write of 512-bytes returns 20-bytes. The next write of a non-zero number of bytes returns failure (except as noted for pipes and FIFOs below).

For ordinary-files, if O_SYNC is set, write should not return until both the file-data and file-status are physically updated.

For block-special files, if O_SYNC is set, write should not return until the file-data are physically updated.

The way file-data reaches the physical media depends on the implementation and hardware.

RETURN VALUE

On success, write returns the number of bytes actually written; on failure, it returns − 1, it does *not* change the file-pointer, and errno indicates the error.

ERRORS

The function write fails and errno equals:

EBADF   if fildes is not a valid file-descriptor open for writing.

EPIPE and SIGPIPE signal
     if attempting to write to a pipe not open for reading by any process.

EFBIG   if attempting to write a file that exceeds the process's file-size limit or the system's maximum file-size [see ULIMIT(BA_OS)].

EINTR   if a signal is caught during the write operation.

ENOSPC   if there is no free space remaining on the device holding the file.

EIO   if a physical I/O error occurs.

ENXIO   if the device associated with the file-descriptor is a block-special or character-special file and the file-pointer value is out of range.

EAGAIN   if enforced record-locking is enabled, O_NDELAY is set and there are record-locks on the file.

ENOLCK   if enforced record-locking is enabled and {LOCK_MAX} regions are already locked in the system.

EDEADLK   if enforced record-locking is enabled, O_NDELAY is clear and a deadlock condition is detected.

USAGE

Normally, programs should use the *stdio* routines to open, close, read and write files. Thus, programs that use the FOPEN(BA_OS) *stdio* routine to open a file should use the FWRITE(BA_OS) *stdio* routine instead of `write` to write it.

Because it is not atomic, a `write` of more than {PIPE_BUF} bytes to a pipe (or FIFO) should be used only when two cooperating processes, one reader and one writer, are using a pipe.

When O_NDELAY is set, portable programs should test for two conditions to determine that no data are currently available, for example:

```
fildes = open(path, O_WRONLY | O_NDELAY);
ret = write(fildes, buf, nbyte);
if (ret == 0 || (ret == -1 && errno == EAGAIN)) {
      .
      .   /* Data not available now. */
      .
}
```

A program that requires extra reliability should use O_SYNC, but at some cost in performance.

SEE ALSO

CREAT(BA_OS), DUP(BA_OS), LSEEK(BA_OS), OPEN(BA_OS), PIPE(BA_OS), ULIMIT(BA_OS).

Environment

NAME

intro — introduction to the UNIX System V Environment

DESCRIPTION

(BA_ENV) — Base System Environment

The Base System Environment defines terminolgy, error conditions, environmental variables, directory tree structures, system data files and special device files present in the Base System; these definitions also apply to the Extensions because the Base System is a prerequisite for any Extension.

Table (BA_ENV) lists components of the Base System Environment.

TABLE (BA_ENV) — Base System Environment

bin	FILSYS(BA_ENV)	PATH	ENVVAR(BA_ENV)
console	DEVCON(BA_ENV)	TERM	ENVVAR(BA_ENV)
dev	FILSYS(BA_ENV)	termio	TERMIO(BA_ENV)
errno	ERRNO(BA_ENV)	tmp	FILSYS(BA_ENV)
etc	FILSYS(BA_ENV)	tty	DEVTTY(BA_ENV)
HOME	ENVVAR(BA_ENV)	TZ	ENVVAR(BA_ENV)
null	DEVNUL(BA_ENV)	usr	FILSYS(BA_ENV)
passwd	PASSWD(BA_ENV)		

(KE_ENV) — Kernel Extension Environment

The Kernel Extension Environment defines terms, error conditions and other extensions to the Base System Environment relating to message-queues, semaphores, shared-memory and the inter-process communication mechanisms introduced by the Kernel Extension, including additional behavior of Base System Routines when Kernel Extension Routines are present on a system [see EFFECTS(KE_ENV)].

Table (KE_ENV) lists components of the Kernel Extension Environment.

TABLE (KE_ENV) — Kernel Extension Environment

errno	ERRNO(KE_ENV)	exit	EFFECTS(KE_ENV)
exec	EFFECTS(KE_ENV)	fork	EFFECTS(KE_ENV)

(NS_ENV) — Network Services Environment

The Network Services Environment defines terms, error conditions and other extensions relating to streams, open systems networking, transport layer services and remote file-sharing provided by the Network Services Extension. Network Services Environment includes additional behavior of Base System Routines when the Network Services Extension is present on a system [see EFFECTS(NS_ENV)].

Table (NS_ENV) lists components of the Network Services Environment.

TABLE (NS_ENV) — Network Services Environment

effects	EFFECTS(NS_ENV)	stropts	STREAMIO(NS_ENV)
errno	ERRNO(NS_ENV)		

NAME
`console` — system console interface

SYNOPSIS
`/dev/console`

DESCRIPTION
`/dev/console` is a generic name given to the system console. It is usually linked to a particular machine-dependent special file, and provides a basic I/O interface to the system console through the *termio* interface [see TERMIO(BA_ENV)].

SEE ALSO
TERMIO(BA_ENV).

NAME

null — the null file

SYNOPSIS

/dev/null

DESCRIPTION

Data written on a null special file are discarded.

Read operations from a null special file always return 0 bytes.

Output of a command is written to the special file /dev/null when the command is executed for its side effects and not for its output.

SEE ALSO

FILSYS(BA_ENV).

NAME

`tty` — controlling terminal interface

SYNOPSIS

`/dev/tty`

DESCRIPTION

The file `/dev/tty` is, in each process, a synonym for the control-terminal associated with the process group of that process, if any. It is useful for programs that wish to be sure of writing messages on the terminal no matter how output has been redirected [see SYSTEM(BA_OS)]. It can also be used for programs that demand the name of a file for output when typed output is desired and as an alternative to identifying what terminal is currently in use.

USAGE

Normally, programs should not need to use this file interface. The standard input, standard output and standard error files should be used instead. These files are accessed through the `stdin`, `stdout` and `stderr` *stdio* interfaces [see **stdio-stream** in VOCAB(BA_DEF)].

SEE ALSO

TERMIO(BA_ENV).

NAME

`exec`, `exit`, `fork` — effects of the Kernel Extension

DESCRIPTION

Kernel Extension Routines affect Base System Routines as follows:

EXEC(BA_OS)

The `AFORK` flag in the `ac_flag` field of the accounting-record is turned off and the `ac_comm` field reset by an `exec` routine [see ACCT(KE_OS)].

Any process-lock, data-lock or text-lock is removed and not inherited by the new process [see PLOCK(KE_OS)].

Profiling is disabled for the new process [see PROFIL(KE_OS)].

The shared-memory-segments attached to the calling-process are not attached to the new process [see SHMOP(KE_OS)].

The new process inherits these added attributes from the calling-process:

> nice-value [see NICE(KE_OS)];
> `semadj` values [see SEMOP(KE_OS)];
> trace flag [see request 0 in PTRACE(KE_OS)].

EXIT(BA_OS)

An accounting-record is written on the accounting-file if the system's accounting-routine is enabled [see ACCT(KE_OS)].

Any process-lock, data-lock or text-lock is removed [see PLOCK(KE_OS)].

Each attached shared-memory-segment is detached and the value of `shm_nattch` in the data structure associated with its shared-memory-identifier is decremented by 1.

Each semaphore with a `semadj` value set by the calling-process has that value added to the `semval` for the semaphore [see SEMOP(KE_OS)].

FORK(BA_OS)

The `AFORK` flag is turned on when the function `fork` is executed.

The child-process inherits these added attributes from the parent-process:

> The `ac_comm` contents of the accounting-record [see ACCT(KE_OS)];
> nice-value [see NICE(KE_OS)];
> profiling on/off status [see PROFIL(KE_OS)];
> all attached shared-memory-segments [see SHMOP(KE_OS)].

The child-process differs from the parent-process in these other ways:

> All `semadj` values are cleared [see SEMOP(KE_OS)].
> No process-lock, data-lock or text-lock is inherited [see PLOCK(KE_OS)].

SEE ALSO

ACCT(KE_OS), NICE(KE_OS), PLOCK(KE_OS), PROFIL(KE_OS), PTRACE(KE_OS), SEMOP(KE_OS), SHMOP(KE_OS).

NAME

    `effects` — effects of the Network Services

DESCRIPTION

Effects on the Base System

Components in the Base System may return a new values for `errno` as listed in ERRNO(NS_ENV). A program that checks the value of `errno` must include the header file `<errno.h>`.

Under the Shared Resource Environment, components in the Base System may return a new value for `errno`. In addition, some operating system service routines may return the `errno` value of `EINTR` when accessing a remote resource. The operating system service routines that do not return this value of `errno` except under the Shared Resource Environment are:

access	creat	mknod
chdir	dup	stat
chmod	exec	unlink
chown	fcntl	ustat
close	link	utime

The symbolic names and descriptions of these additional error return conditions are listed in ERRNO(NS_ENV). These errors may be returned by the system functions `open`, `close`, `read`, `write`, `ioctl`, `getmsg`, `putmsg` and `poll` only when accessing STREAMS devices and as described in the component interface definitions for the Newtork Services Extension.

A new signal has been defined by the header file `<signal.h>`. This signal is used to support asynchronous processing of events on STREAMS devices.

The following symbolic name defines the additional signal:

Name	*Description*
`SIGPOLL`	Signals STREAMS events

Effects on the Software Development Extension

In a software development environment, a program *file*.`c` that accesses any function defined in this part of the extension must be compiled in one of the following ways:

    `cc` *file*.`c -lnsl_s`

    `cc` *file*.`c -lnsl`

SEE ALSO

    ERRNO(BA_ENV).

NAME

HOME, PATH, TERM, TZ — environmental variables

DESCRIPTION

When a process begins execution, the EXEC(BA_OS) routines make available an array of strings called the *environment* [see also SYSTEM(BA_OS)]. These strings take the form *variable=value*, for example, PATH=/bin/usr/bin. These environmental variables provide a way to make information about an end-user's environment available to programs. The following environmental variables can be used by programs and are expected to be set in the target run-time environment.

Name	*Description*
HOME	Full path-name of the user's home-directory, the user's initial-working-directory [see PASSWD(BA_ENV)].
PATH	Colon-separated ordered list of path-names that determine the search sequence used in locating files [see SYSTEM(BA_OS)].
TERM	The kind of terminal for which output is prepared. This information is used by programs that may exploit special capabilities of the terminal.
TZ	Time-zone information. TZ must be a three-letter, local time-zone abbreviation, followed by a number (an optional minus sign, for time-zones east of Greenwich, followed by a series of digits) that is the difference in hours between this time-zone and Greenwich Mean Time. This may be followed by an optional three-letter daylight local time-zone. For example, EST5EDT for Eastern Standard, Eastern Daylight Saving Time.

Other variables might be set in a particular environment but are not required to be included in the Base System.

SEE ALSO

EXEC(BA_OS), SYSTEM(BA_OS), FILSYS(BA_ENV).

CAVEATS

The number in TZ will be defined as an optional minus sign followed by two hour digits and two minute digits, hhmm, in order to represent fractional time-zones.

NAME

`errno` — error codes and conditions

SYNOPSIS

```
#include <errno.h>

extern int errno;
```

DESCRIPTION

The numerical value represented by the symbolic name of an error condition is assigned to the external variable `errno` for errors that occur when executing a system service routine or general library routine.

The component interface definitions list possible error conditions for each function and the meaning of the error in that *context*. The order in which possible errors are listed is not significant and does not imply precedence. The value of `errno` should be checked only *after* an error is indicated; that is, when the return value of the component indicates an error, and the component interface definition specifies that `errno` is set. A program that checks the value of `errno` must include the `<errno.h>` header file. The `errno` value 0 is reserved; no error condition will equal zero. Additional error conditions may be defined by Extensions to the Base System or by particular implementations.

The following list describes the *general* meaning of each error:

E2BIG　　　Argument list too long
　　　　　An argument list longer than {ARG_MAX} bytes was presented to
　　　　　a member of the EXEC(BA_OS) family of routines.

EACCES　　Permission denied
　　　　　An attempt was made to access a file in a way forbidden by the
　　　　　protection system.

EAGAIN　　Resource temporarily unavailable, try again later
　　　　　For example, the FORK(BA_OS) routine failed because the
　　　　　system's process table is full.

EBADF　　　Bad file number
　　　　　Either a file-descriptor fails to denote an open file, or an attempt
　　　　　was made to read (respectively, write) a file that is open only for
　　　　　writing (respectively, reading).

EBUSY　　　Device or resource busy
　　　　　An attempt was made to mount a device that was already
　　　　　mounted or an attempt was made to dismount a device on which
　　　　　there is an active file (open file, current directory, mounted-on
　　　　　file, active text segment). It also occurs if an attempt was made
　　　　　to enable accounting when it is already enabled. The device or
　　　　　resource is currently unavailable.

ECHILD　　No child-processes
　　　　　The WAIT(BA_OS) routine was executed by a process that had no
　　　　　existing or unwaited-for child-processes.

EDEADLK　　Deadlock avoided
　　　　　　The request would have caused a deadlock; the situation was
　　　　　　detected and avoided.

EDOM　　　　Math argument
　　　　　　The argument of a function in the math package is out of the
　　　　　　domain of the function.

EEXIST　　File exists
　　　　　　An existing file was specified in an inappropriate context (e.g., a
　　　　　　call to the LINK(BA_OS) routine).

EFAULT　　Bad address
　　　　　　The system encountered a hardware fault in attempting to use
　　　　　　an argument of a routine. For example, errno potentially may
　　　　　　be set to EFAULT any time a routine that takes a pointer
　　　　　　argument is passed an invalid address, if the system can detect
　　　　　　the condition. Because systems differ in their ability to reliably
　　　　　　detect a bad address, on some implementations passing a bad
　　　　　　address to a routine results in undefined behavior.

EFBIG　　　File too large
　　　　　　The size of a file exceeded the maximum file-size, {FCHR_MAX}
　　　　　　[see ULIMIT(BA_OS)].

EINTR　　　Interrupted system service
　　　　　　An asynchronous signal (such as interrupt or quit), which the
　　　　　　user elected to catch, occurred during a system service routine.
　　　　　　If execution is resumed after processing the signal, it will appear
　　　　　　as if the interrupted routine returned this error condition.

EINVAL　　Invalid argument
　　　　　　Some invalid argument (e.g., dismounting a non-mounted device;
　　　　　　specifying an undefined signal in a call to the SIGNAL(BA_OS) or
　　　　　　KILL(BA_OS) routine). Also set by math routines.

EIO　　　　I/O error
　　　　　　Some physical I/O error occurred. This error may, in some
　　　　　　cases, occur on a call following the one to which it actually
　　　　　　applies.

EISDIR　　Is a directory
　　　　　　An attempt was made to write on a directory.

ELIBACC　　Reserved.

ELIBBAD　　Reserved.

ELIBEXEC　Reserved.

ELIBMAX　　Reserved.

ELIBSCN　　Reserved.

EMFILE　　Too many open files in a process
　　　　　　No process may have more than {OPEN_MAX} file-descriptors
　　　　　　open at a time.

EMLINK　　Too many links
　　　　　　An attempt was made to make more than the maximum number
　　　　　　of links, {LINK_MAX}, to a file.

ENFILE　　Too many open files in the system
　　　　　　The system file table is full (i.e., {SYS_OPEN} files are open, and
　　　　　　temporarily no more *opens* can be accepted).

ENODEV　　No such device
　　　　　　An attempt was made to apply an inappropriate operation to a
　　　　　　device (e.g., read a write-only device).

ENOENT　　No such file or directory
　　　　　　A file-name is specified and the file should exist but does not, or
　　　　　　one of the directories in a path-name does not exist, or a path-
　　　　　　name is longer than {PATH_MAX} characters.

ENOEXEC　Exec format error
　　　　　　An attempt was made to execute a file which, although it has
　　　　　　the appropriate permissions, does not start with a valid format.

ENOLCK　　No locks available
　　　　　　There are no more locks available. The system lock table is full.

ENOMEM　　Not enough space
　　　　　　During execution of an EXEC(BA_OS) routine, a program asks for
　　　　　　more space than the system is able to supply. This is not a
　　　　　　temporary condition; the maximum space size is a system
　　　　　　parameter. The error may also occur if the arrangement of text,
　　　　　　data, and stack segments requires too many segmentation
　　　　　　registers, or if there is not enough swap space during execution
　　　　　　of the FORK(BA_OS) routine.

ENOSPC　　No space left on device
　　　　　　While writing an ordinary-file or creating a directory entry,
　　　　　　there is no free space left on the device.

ENOTBLK　Block device required
　　　　　　A non-block file was specified where a block device was required
　　　　　　(e.g., in a call to the MOUNT(BA_OS) routine).

ENOTDIR　Not a directory
　　　　　　A non-directory was specified where a directory is required (e.g.,
　　　　　　in a path-prefix or in a call to the CHDIR(BA_OS) routine).

ENOTTY　　Not a character device
　　　　　　A call was made to the IOCTL(BA_OS) routine specifying a file
　　　　　　that is not a special character device.

ENXIO   No such device or address
             I/O on a special file specifies a subdevice which does not exist, or
             exists beyond the limits of the device. It may also occur when,
             for example, a tape drive is not on-line or no disk pack is loaded
             on a drive.

EPERM   No permission match
             Typically this error indicates an attempt was made to modify a
             file in some way forbidden except to its owner or super-user. It
             is also returned for attempts by ordinary users to do things
             allowed only to the super-user.

EPIPE   Broken pipe
             A write on a pipe for which there is no process to read the data.
             This condition normally generates a signal; the error is returned
             if the signal is ignored.

ERANGE   Result too large
             The value of a function in the math package is not representable
             within machine precision.

EROFS   Read-only file-system
             An attempt was made to modify a file or directory on a device
             mounted read-only.

ESPIPE   Illegal seek
             A call to the LSEEK(BA_OS) routine was issued to a pipe.

ESRCH   No such process
             No process can be found corresponding to that specified by pid
             in the KILL(BA_OS) or PTRACE(KE_OS) routine.

ETXTBSY   Text file busy
             An attempt was made to execute a pure-procedure program that
             is currently open for writing. Also an attempt was made to open
             for writing a pure-procedure program being executed.

EXDEV   Cross-device link
             An attempt was made to link to a file on another device.

USAGE

Because a few routines may not have an error return value, a program may set
errno to zero, call the routine, and then check errno again to see if an
error occurred.

NAME

    `errno` — error codes and conditions

SYNOPSIS

    `#include <errno.h>`

    `extern int errno;`

DESCRIPTION

    In addition to the values defined in the Base System for the external variable `errno` [see ERRNO(BA_ENV)], two additional error conditions are defined in the Kernel Extension:

    `EIDRM`   Identifier removed.
                This error is returned to processes that resume execution because of the removal of an identifier [see MSGCTL(KE_OS), SEMCTL(KE_OS), and SHMCTL(KE_OS)].

    `ENOMSG`   No message of desired type.
                An attempt was made to receive a message of a type that does not exist on the specified message queue.

SEE ALSO

    ERRNO(BA_ENV).

NAME

errno — error codes and conditions

SYNOPSIS

```
#include <errno.h>

extern int errno;
```

DESCRIPTION

In addition to the errno values defined in ERRNO(BA_ENV), the Network Services Extension adds new values to the header file errno.h to define the following symbolic names:

EBADMSG   Trying to read unreadable message

ECOMM   Communications error
occurs on any operating system service routine that references a remote resource (through a file-descriptor or path name), whenever there is a communications error while trying to send the request for that service routine to the server machine.

EMULTIHOP   Multihop not allowed
may occur on any operating system service routine that has a path name as one of its arguments, and indicates that resolution of that path name involves multihop access to a remote resource, when multihop access is not supported by the underlying implementation. Multihop access is implementation-specific, but if it is not supported, the EMULTIHOP error code must be returned on any attempted multihop access.

ENOLINK   The link is severed
occurs on any operating system service routine that references a remote file, when the communications link to the server for that resource is lost; any file-descriptor associated with this remote file should not be used for further I/O.

ENOSR   Out of stream resources

ENOSTR   Device not a stream

EPROTO   Protocol error occurred

EREMOTE   The object is remote
occurs on the MOUNT(BA_OS) operating system service routine when the requested mount point resides on a remote resource.

ETIME   Timer expired

SEE ALSO

ERRNO(BA_ENV), ERRNO(KE_ENV).

NAME

`bin, dev, etc, tmp, usr` — directory tree structure

DESCRIPTION

Directory Tree Structure

Below is a diagram of the minimal directory tree structure expected to be on any UNIX System V operating system.

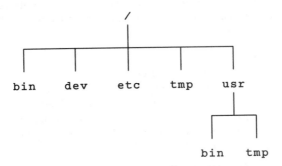

- `/bin`, `/dev`, `/etc`, and `/tmp` are primarily for the use of the system. Most applications should never *create* files in any of these directories, though they may read and execute them. Applications, as well as the system, can use `/usr/bin` and `/usr/tmp`.

- `/bin` holds executable system-commands (utilities), if any.

- `/dev` holds special device files.

- `/etc` holds system-data-files, such as `/etc/passwd`.

- `/tmp` holds temporary files created by utilities in `/bin` and by other system-processes.

- `/usr/bin` holds (user-level) executable application and system commands.

- `/usr/tmp` holds temporary files created by applications and the system.

Some Extensions to the Base System will have additional requirements on the tree structure when the Extension is installed on a system. Directory tree requirements specific to an Extension will be identified when the Extension is defined in detail.

System Data Files

The Base System Definition specifies only these system-resident data files:

```
/etc/passwd
/etc/profile
```

The `/etc/passwd` and `/etc/profile` files are owned by the system and are readable but not writable by ordinary users.

PASSWD(BA_ENV) defines the format and contents of `/etc/passwd`. This is a generally useful file, readable by user-programs, that makes available to applications some basic information about end-users on a system. It has one entry for each user. Minimally, each user's entry contains a string that is the name by which the user is known on the system, a numerical user-ID, and the home-directory or initial-working-directory of the user.

Conventionally, the information in this file is used during the initialization of the environment for a particular user. However, the `/etc/passwd` file is also useful as a standardly formatted database of information about users, which can be used independently of the mechanisms that maintain the data file.

The `/etc/profile` file may contain a string assignment of the **PATH** and **TZ** variables defined in ENVVAR(BA_ENV).

CAVEATS

The following directory structure and guidelines are proposed for applications ("add-ons") that are to be installed on a system:

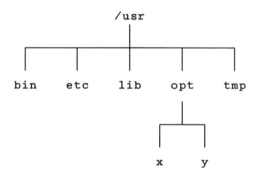

- `/usr/etc` would hold data and log files for commands in `/usr/bin`.

- `/usr/lib` would hold any executable files for commands in `/usr/bin`.

- `/usr/opt` would hold sub-directories for each add-on to hold data files private to the add-on (e.g., add-on **x**)

- `/usr/opt/x` would hold files and/or directories private to add-on **x**, `/usr/opt/y` would hold files and/or directories private to add-on **y**.

NAME

passwd — password file

SYNOPSIS

/etc/passwd

DESCRIPTION

The file /etc/passwd contains the following information for each user:

name
encrypted password (may be empty)
numerical user-ID
numerical group-ID (may be empty)
free field
initial-working-directory
program to use as command interpreter (may be empty)

This ASCII file resides in directory /etc. It has general read permission and can be used, for example, to map *numerical user-ID*s to *name*s.

Each field within each user's entry is separated from the next by a colon. Fields 2, 4, and 7 may be empty. However, if they are not empty, they must be used for their stated purpose. Field 5 is a free field that is implementation-specific. Fields beyond 7 are also free but may be standardized in the future. Each user's entry is separated from the next by a new-line.

The *name* is a character string that identifies a user. Its composition should follow the same rules used for file-names.

By convention, the last element in the path-name of the initial-working-directory is typically *name*.

SEE ALSO

CRYPT(BA_LIB).

NAME

stropts — STREAMS I/O interface

DESCRIPTION

STREAMS I/O provides a uniform mechanism for implementing networking services and other I/O in the kernel, and for directly controlling I/O modules implemented in the kernel.

A stream is a full-duplex connection between a user-process and an open device or pseudo-device. The stream itself exists entirely within the kernel and provides a general character I/O interface for user-processes. It optionally includes one or more intermediate processing modules that are interposed between the user-process end of the stream and the device-driver (or pseudo-device-driver) end of the stream.

STREAMS I/O is based on messages that flow in both directions in a stream. A given module may not understand and process every message in the stream, but every module in the stream handles every message. Each module accepts messages from one of its neighbor modules in the stream, and passes them to the other neighbor. A line discipline module may transform the data. Data flow through the intermediate modules is symmetrical, with all modules handling, and optionally processing, all messages.

STREAMS-modules use many types of messages classified according to queueing priority:

Ordinary-messages are always placed at the tail of a queue behind all other messages already in the queue.

Priority-messages are always placed at the head of a queue before all ordinary-messages but behind any other priority-messages already in the queue.

Priority-messages send control and data information outside the normal flow-control constraints. Other types of messages are used between modules and are not accessible to users.

Accessing STREAMS Devices

A user-process accesses STREAMS I/O using the Base System components open, close, read, write and ioctl described below, as well as the Network Services components putmsg, getmsg and poll. Refer to the component interface definitions OPEN(BA_OS), CLOSE(BA_OS), READ(BA_OS), WRITE(BA_OS) and IOCTL(BA_OS), as well as PUTMSG(NS_OS), GETMSG(NS_OS) and POLL(NS_OS) for general properties and errors.

The interface between the stream and the rest of the operating system is provided by a set of routines at the *stream-head* (upstream) end of the stream. User-process write, putmsg and ioctl calls become messages that are sent down the stream; while, read and getmsg calls accept data from the stream and pass it to a user-process. Data intended for the device at the downstream end of the stream are packaged into messages and sent downstream, while data and signals from the device are composed into messages by the device-driver and sent upstream to the stream-head.

A user may access STREAMS-messages that contain a data part, control part or both. The data part is that information which is sent out over the network and the control information is used by the local STREAMS-modules. Messages containing only a data part are accessible via `putmsg`, `getmsg`, `read` and `write` routines. Messages containing a control part with or without a data part are accessible via calls to the `putmsg` and `getmsg` routines.

When a STREAMS-device is opened, the system creates a stream that contains two modules: the stream-head module and the stream end (driver) module. Other modules are added to the stream using the IOCTL(BA_OS) routine. New modules are "pushed" onto the stream one at a time in Last-In, First-Out (LIFO) style, as if the stream were a push-down stack.

OPEN(NS_OS)

Calls to `open` have the format:

```
int open (path, oflag)
char *path;
int oflag;
```

The function `open` attempts to open a STREAMS-device. When opening a STREAMS-device, `oflag` is constructed from O_NDELAY OR-ed with either O_RDONLY, O_WRONLY or O_RDWR. These values are defined by `<fcntl.h>`, and a program must contain the following line:

```
#include <fcntl.h>
```

Other flag values are not applicable to STREAMS-drivers and have no effect on them. The value of O_NDELAY affects the operation of STREAMS-drivers and certain system calls [see READ(BA_OS), GETMSG(NS_OS), PUTMSG(NS_OS) and WRITE(BA_OS)]. For STREAMS-drivers, the implementation of O_NDELAY is device-specific, and each driver may treat this option differently. Certain flag values can be set following a call to `open` as described in FCNTL(BA_OS).

On success, `open` returns a file-descriptor for the open stream; on failure, it returns − 1 and `errno` equals:

EINTR	if a signal is caught during the `open` operation.
ENXIO	if a module or driver open procedure failed.
ENOSR	if unable to allocate a stream.
EIO	if a hangup or error occurs during the `open` operation.

CLOSE(NS_OS)

Calls to `close` have the format:

```
int close (fd)
int fd;
```

The function `close` is used to close a STREAMS-device. If a STREAMS-device is closed and the calling-process previously registered to receive a SIGPOLL signal [see SIGNAL(BA_OS) and SIGSET(BA_OS)] for events associated with that device, the calling-process is unregistered for events associated with the device.

For STREAMS-devices, the last `close` dismantles the stream denoted by `fd`.

If `O_NDELAY` is clear and no signals are posted for the stream, `close` waits up to 15 seconds (for each module and driver) for any output to drain before dismantling the stream.

If `O_NDELAY` is set or any signals are pending, `close` does not wait for output to drain, and dismantles the stream immediately.

On success, `close` returns 0; on failure, it returns – 1 and `errno` equals:

EBADF   if `fd` is not a valid open file-descriptor.

EINTR   if a signal is caught during the `close` operation.

READ(NS_OS)

Calls to `read` have the format:

```
int read (fd, buf, nbyte)
int fd;
char *buf;
unsigned nbyte;
```

The function `read` attempts to read `nbyte` bytes of data from the stream denoted by `fd` into the buffer pointed to by `buf`. The function `read` can operate in three different modes:

1. "byte-stream" mode,
2. "message-nondiscard" mode and
3. "message-discard" mode.

The default read-mode is byte-stream mode. This can be changed using the `ioctl` command `I_SRDOPT`, and can be tested with the `ioctl` command `I_GRDOPT` [see IOCTL(BA_OS)]. In byte-stream mode, `read` accepts data from the stream until it gets `nbyte` bytes, or until there are no more data available. Byte-stream mode ignores message boundaries.

In message-nondiscard mode, `read` accepts data until it gets `nbyte` bytes, or until it reaches a message boundary. If `read` does not retrieve all the data in a message, the remaining data are replaced on the stream, and can be retrieved by the next `read` (or `getmsg`) call.

In message-discard mode, `read` also accepts data until it gets `nbyte` bytes, or it reaches a message boundary. However, unread data remaining in a message after `read` returns are discarded, and are not available for a subsequent `read` (or `getmsg`) call.

The read-mode setting determines how `read` handles zero-byte messages:

In byte-stream mode, `read` accepts data until it gets `nbyte` bytes, or until there are no more data to read, or until a zero-byte message block is encountered. The function `read` then returns the number of bytes read, and places the zero-byte message back on the stream for the next `read` (or `getmsg`) call to retrieve.

In the two other modes, a zero-byte message returns a value of 0 and the message is removed from the stream.

When a zero-byte message is read as the first message on a stream, `read` returns 0 regardless of the read-mode.

When attempting to read from a stream that has no data currently available:

If `O_NDELAY` is clear, `read` blocks until data becomes available.

If `O_NDELAY` is set, `read` returns – 1 and `errno` equals `EAGAIN`.

With a STREAMS-device, `read` can only process messages with data and without control information. The function `read` fails if a message containing control information is encountered at the stream-head.

On success, `read` returns the number of bytes actually read; on failure, it returns – 1 and `errno` equals:

`EBADF`	if `fd` is not a valid open file-descriptor.
`EFAULT`	if `buf` points outside the allocated space.
`EBADMSG`	if the message waiting to be read is not a data message.
`EAGAIN`	if `O_NDELAY` is set and no message is waiting to be read.
`EINVAL`	if attempting to read from a stream linked to a multiplexer.
`EINTR`	if a signal is caught during the `read` operation.

The function `read` also fails if an error message is received at the stream-head. In this case, `errno` equals the value returned in the error message. If a hangup occurs on the stream being read, `read` continues to operate normally until the stream-head read-queue is empty; thereafter, it returns 0.

WRITE(NS_OS)

Calls to `write` have the format:

```
int write(fd, buf, nbyte)
int fd;
char *buf;
unsigned nbyte;
```

The function `write` attempts to write `nbyte` bytes from the buffer `buf` onto the stream denoted by `fd`.

The values of the minimum and maximum `nbyte` range ("packet size") accepted by the stream determine how `write` operates. These values are contained in the topmost stream module. Unless the user pushes the topmost module, these values cannot be set or tested from user level.

If `nbyte` falls within the packet size range, `nbyte` bytes are written.

If `nbyte` falls outside the range and the minimum packet size value is zero, `write` breaks the buffer into maximum packet size segments prior to sending the data downstream (the last segment may contain less than the maximum packet size).

If `nbyte` falls outside the range and the minimum value is non-zero, `write` fails and `errno` equals `ERANGE`.

Writing a zero-length buffer (nbyte is zero) sends zero bytes with zero returned.

When the stream cannot accept data (e.g., the stream write-queue is full due to internal flow-control conditions):

If O_NDELAY is clear, write blocks until data can be accepted.

If O_NDELAY is set, write returns – 1 and errno equals EAGAIN.

If O_NDELAY is set and part of the buffer is written, write terminates and returns the number of bytes written.

On success, write returns the number of bytes actually written; on failure, it returns – 1 and errno equals:

EBADF   if fd is not a valid open file-descriptor.

EFAULT   if buf points outside the allocated space.

ERANGE   if attempting to write to a stream and nbyte falls outside the specified minimum and maximum write range, and the minimum value is non-zero.

EAGAIN   if attempting to write to a stream that cannot accept data with O_NDELAY set.

EINVAL   if attempting to read from a stream linked to a multiplexer.

EINTR   if a signal is caught during the write operation.

ENXIO   if a hangup occurs on the stream being written to.

The function write also fails if an error message is received at the stream-head. In this case, errno equals the value included in the error message.

IOCTL(NS_OS)

Calls to ioctl have the format:

```
int ioctl(fd, cmd, arg)
int fd;
int cmd;
int arg;
```

The function ioctl is used to control the stream denoted by fd.

The argument fd is an open file-descriptor denoting a stream.

The argument cmd determines the ioctl command to be performed as described below.

The argument arg represents additional information needed by the ioctl command. The type of arg depends upon the ioctl command, but generally is an integer or a pointer to the ioctl command-specific data structure.

The arguments cmd and arg are passed to the stream denoted by fd and are interpreted by the stream-head. Certain combinations of these arguments may be passed to a module or driver in the stream.

To use `ioctl`, a program must contain the following line:

```
#include <stropts.h>
```

Described below are the `ioctl` commands (with their arguments and error values) that apply to all STREAMS-devices:

I_PUSH   Pushes the module whose name is pointed to by `arg` onto the top of the current stream, just below the stream-head; then calls the open procedure of the newly-pushed module.

On failure, `errno` equals:

EINVAL	if the module name is invalid.
EFAULT	if `arg` points outside the allocated space.
ENXIO	if the open procedure of new module failed.
ENXIO	if a hangup occurs on `fd`.

I_POP   Removes the module just below the stream-head of the stream pointed to by `fd`.

The argument `arg` should be 0 for I_POP.

On failure, `errno` equals:

EINVAL	if no module is present in the stream.
ENXIO	if a hangup occurs on `fd`.

I_LOOK   Retrieves the name of the module just below the stream-head of the stream pointed to by `fd`, and places it in a character string pointed to by `arg`.

The buffer pointed to by `arg` should be at least **FMNAMESZ** bytes long where **FMNAMESZ** is defined by `#include <sys/conf.h>`.

On failure, `errno` equals:

EFAULT	if `arg` points outside the allocated space.
EINVAL	if no module is present in the stream.

I_FLUSH   Flushes all input and/or output queues, depending on the value of `arg`. Legal `arg` values are:

FLUSHR	Flush read-queues.
FLUSHW	Flush write-queues.
FLUSHRW	Flush read-queues and write-queues.

On failure, `errno` equals:

EINVAL	if the value of `arg` is invalid.
EAGAIN	if unable to allocate buffers for the flush message.
ENXIO	if a hangup occurs on `fd`.

I_SETSIG   Informs the stream-head that the user wishes the kernel to
             issue the SIGPOLL signal [see SIGNAL(BA_OS) and
             SIGSET(BA_OS)] when a particular event occurs on the stream
             denoted by fd. I_SETSIG supports an asynchronous
             processing capability in STREAMS.

             The value of arg is a bitmask that specifies the events for
             which the user should be signaled. It is the bitwise-OR of
             any combination of the following constants:

             S_INPUT   An ordinary-message arrived on a stream-head
                         read-queue, and no other messages were on
                         that queue before this message arrived. This is
                         set even if the message is of zero length.

             S_HIPRI   A priority-message arrived on a stream-head
                         read-queue. This is set even if the message is
                         zero length.

             S_OUTPUT   The write-queue just below the stream-head is
                         no longer full. This notifies the user that the
                         queue has room for sending (or writing) data
                         downstream.

             S_MSG   A STREAMS signal message that contains the
                         SIGPOLL signal reached the front of the
                         stream-head read-queue.

             A user-process may choose to handle asynchronously only
             priority-messages by setting the arg bitmask to S_HIPRI.

             Processes that wish to receive SIGPOLL signals must
             explicitly register to receive them using I_SETSIG. If
             several processes register to receive this signal for the same
             event on the same stream, each process is signaled when the
             event occurs.

             If arg is zero, the calling-process is unregistered and does
             not receive further SIGPOLL signals.

             On failure, errno equals:

             EINVAL   if the value of arg is invalid or if arg is zero
                         and the process is not registered to receive the
                         SIGPOLL signal.

             EAGAIN   if allocation of a data structure to store the
                         signal request failed.

I_GETSIG   Returns the events for which the calling-process is currently
             registered to receive a SIGPOLL signal.

             The events are returned as a bitmask pointed to by arg,
             where the events are those specified in I_SETSIG above.

On failure, `errno` equals:

EINVAL   if the process is not registered to receive the SIGPOLL signal.

EFAULT   if `arg` points outside the allocated space.

I_FIND   Compares the names of all modules currently present in the stream to the name pointed to by `arg`, and returns 1 if the named module is present in the stream.

I_FIND returns 0 if the named module is not present.

On failure, `errno` equals:

EFAULT   if `arg` points outside the allocated space.

EINVAL   if `arg` does not contain a valid module name.

I_NREAD   Counts the number of data bytes in data blocks in the first message on the stream-head read-queue and places this value in the location pointed to by `arg`.

I_NREAD returns the number of messages on the stream-head read-queue. For example, if I_NREAD returns zero in `arg`, but the return value from `ioctl` is positive, this means a zero-length message is next on the queue.

On failure, `errno` equals:

EFAULT   if `arg` points outside the allocated space.

I_PEEK   Retrieves the information in the first message on the stream-head read-queue without taking the message off the queue.

The argument `arg` points to a `strpeek` structure which contains the following members:

```
struct strbuf ctlbuf;
struct strbuf databuf;
long          flags;
```

where `strbuf` is a structure with the following members:

```
int maxlen;
int len;
char *buf;
```

The `maxlen` field in the `strbuf` structures `ctlbuf` and `databuf` [see GETMSG(NS_OS)] must equal the number of bytes of control information and/or data information, respectively, to retrieve.

If the user sets `flags` to RS_HIPRI, I_PEEK only looks for a priority-message on the stream-head read-queue.

I_PEEK returns 1 if a message is found, and returns 0 if no message is on the stream-head read-queue, or if RS_HIPRI is set in `flags` and no priority-message is on the stream-head read-queue. It does not wait for a message to arrive.

On return, `ctlbuf` specifies information in the control buffer, `databuf` specifies information in the data buffer, and `flags` contains the value 0 or `RS_HIPRI`.

On failure, `errno` equals:

EFAULT if `arg` points, or the buffer area specified in `ctlbuf` or `databuf` is, outside the allocated space.

I_SRDOPT Sets the current read-mode using the value of `arg`. Legal `arg` values are:

RNORM   Byte-stream mode, the default.
RMSGD   Message-discard mode.
RMSGN   Message-nondiscard mode.

Read-modes are described in READ(BA_OS).

On failure, `errno` equals:

EINVAL if `arg` is not one of the above legal values.

I_GRDOPT Returns the current read-mode setting in an `int` pointed to by `arg`.

Read-modes are described in READ(BA_OS).

On failure, `errno` equals:

EFAULT if `arg` points outside the allocated space.

I_FDINSERT Creates a message from user specified buffer(s), adds information about another stream, and sends the message downstream.

The message contains a control part and an optional data part. The data and control parts to be sent are placed in separate buffers, as described below.

The argument `arg` points to a `strfdinsert` structure which contains the following members:

```
struct strbuf ctlbuf;
struct strbuf databuf;
long          flags;
int           fildes;
int           offset;
```

The `len` field in the `strbuf` structure `ctlbuf` must equal the size of a pointer plus the number of bytes in the control part sent with the message [see PUTMSG(NS_OS)].

The `fildes` field is the file-descriptor of the other stream.

The `offset` field, which must be word-aligned, gives the number of bytes beyond the beginning of the control buffer where I_FDINSERT will store a pointer to the `fildes` stream's driver read-queue structure.

The `len` field in the `strbuf` structure `databuf` must equal the number of bytes of data information sent with the message or zero if no data part is sent.

The `flags` field specifies the type of message to be created. An ordinary-message is created if `flags` equals `0`, and a priority-message is created if `flags` equals `RS_HIPRI`.

For ordinary-messages, `I_FDINSERT` blocks if the stream write-queue is full due to internal flow-control conditions; for priority-messages, `I_FDINSERT` does *not* block on this condition.

For ordinary-messages, `I_FDINSERT` does *not* block if `O_NDELAY` is set and the write-queue is full; instead, it fails and `errno` equals `EAGAIN`.

Unless prevented by lack of internal resources, `I_FDINSERT` also blocks awaiting the availability of message-blocks in the stream, regardless of priority or whether `O_NDELAY` is set. `I_FDINSERT` does *not* send partial messages.

On failure, `errno` equals:

`EAGAIN`	if `O_NDELAY` is set, an ordinary-message is specified and the stream write-queue is full due to internal flow-control conditions.
`EAGAIN`	if unable to allocate buffers for the message to be created.
`EFAULT`	if `arg` points, or the buffer area specified in `ctlbuf` or `databuf` is, outside the allocated space.
`EINVAL`	if the `fildes` field in the `strfdinsert` structure is not a valid open stream file-descriptor.
`EINVAL`	if the size of a pointer plus `offset` is greater than the `len` field for the buffer specified through `ctlbuf`.
`EINVAL`	if `offset` does not specify a properly-aligned location in the data buffer.
`EINVAL`	if an undefined value is stored in `flags`.
`ENXIO`	if a hangup occurs on `fd`.
`ERANGE`	if the `len` field for the buffer specified through `databuf` falls outside the range set by the maximum and minimum packet sizes of the topmost stream module.

ERANGE   if the len field for the buffer specified through databuf is larger than the maximum configured size of the data part of a message.

ERANGE   if the len field for the buffer specified through ctlbuf is larger than the maximum configured size of the control part of a message.

I_STR   Constructs a STREAMS-message for an internal ioctl command from the data pointed to by arg, and sends that message downstream.

This mechanism is provided for users to send ioctl commands to downstream modules and drivers. I_STR allows information to be sent with the ioctl command, and returns to the user any information sent upstream by the downstream recipient. I_STR blocks until the system responds with either a positive or negative acknowledgment message, or until the ioctl command "times-out" after some period of time. If the ioctl command times out, it fails and errno equals ETIME.

At most, one I_STR can be active on a stream. Any further I_STR blocks until the active I_STR completes at the stream-head. The default time-out for I_STR is 15 seconds. O_NDELAY has no effect on I_STR [see OPEN(BA_OS)].

To send ioctl commands downstream, arg must point to a strioctl structure which contains the following members:

```
int    ic_cmd;    /* downstream command */
int    ic_timout; /* ACK/NAK time-out */
int    ic_len;    /* length of data arg */
char *ic_dp;      /* ptr to data arg */
```

The ic_cmd field is the internal ioctl command intended for a downstream module or driver.

The ic_timout field is the number of seconds (-1 = infinite, 0 = use default, > 0 = as specified) I_STR waits for an acknowledgment message before timing out.

The ic_len field is the number of bytes in the data argument, and ic_dp is a pointer to the data argument. The ic_len field has two uses: on input, it contains the length of the data argument passed in, and on return from the internal ioctl command, it contains the number of bytes being returned to the user (the buffer pointed to by ic_dp should be large enough to contain the maximum amount of data that any module or the driver in the stream can return).

The stream-head converts the information pointed to by the strioctl structure to a STREAMS-message for the internal ioctl command and sends it downstream.

On failure, errno equals:

EAGAIN   if unable to allocate buffers for the ioctl command message.

EFAULT   if arg points, or the buffer area specified by ic_dp and ic_len (separately for data sent and data returned) is, outside the allocated space.

EINVAL   if ic_len is less than 0, or ic_len is larger than the maximum configured size of the data part of a message, or ic_timout is less than − 1.

ENXIO   if a hangup occurs on fd.

ETIME   if a downstream ioctl command timed-out before receiving an acknowledgment message.

I_STR can also fail while waiting for an acknowledgment if a message indicating an error or a hangup is received at the stream-head. In addition, an error code can be returned in the positive or negative acknowledgment message, in the event the ioctl command sent downstream fails. For these cases, I_STR fails and errno equals the value in the message.

The following two ioctl commands are used to connect and disconnect multiplexed STREAMS-configurations:

I_LINK   Connects two streams, where fd is a file-descriptor denoting the stream connected to the multiplexing-driver, and arg is a file-descriptor denoting the stream connected to another driver.

The stream denoted by arg gets connected below the multiplexing-driver. I_LINK requires the multiplexing-driver to send an acknowledgment message to the stream-head regarding the linking operation.

On success, I_LINK returns a multiplexer-ID number (an identifier used to disconnect the multiplexer [see I_UNLINK]); on failure, it returns − 1.

On failure, errno equals:

ENXIO   if a hangup occurs on fd.

ETIME   if time-out before receiving an acknowledgment message at the stream-head.

EAGAIN | if unable to allocate STREAMS storage to perform the I_LINK.

EBADF | if arg is not a valid open file-descriptor.

EINVAL | if the fd stream does not support multiplexing.

EINVAL | if arg is not a stream or is already linked under a multiplexer.

EINVAL | if the specified link operation would cause a "cycle" in the resulting configuration; that is, if a given stream-head is linked into a multiplexing configuration in more than one place.

I_LINK can also fail while waiting for the multiplexing-driver to acknowledge, if a message indicating an error or a hangup is received at the stream-head of fd. In addition, an error code can be returned in the positive or negative acknowledgment message. For these cases, I_LINK fails and errno equals the value in the message.

I_UNLINK | Disconnects the two streams denoted by fd and arg.

The argument fd is a file-descriptor denoting the stream connected to the multiplexing-driver.

The argument arg is the multiplexer-ID number returned by I_LINK when a stream is linked below the multiplexing-driver. If arg is – 1, then all streams linked to fd are disconnected.

As in I_LINK, this ioctl command requires the multiplexing-driver to acknowledge the unlink.

On failure, errno equals:

ENXIO | if a hangup occurs on fd.

ETIME | if time-out before receiving an acknowledgment message at the stream-head.

EAGAIN | if unable to allocate buffers for the acknowledgment message.

EINVAL | if the multiplexer-ID number is invalid.

I_UNLINK can also fail while waiting for the multiplexing-driver to acknowledge, if a message indicating an error or a hangup is received at the stream-head of fd. In addition, an error code can be returned in the positive or negative acknowledgment message. For these cases, I_UNLINK fails and errno equals the value in the message.

RETURN VALUE

Unless otherwise indicated, on success, `ioctl` returns 0; on failure, it returns −1 and `errno` is set as indicated above. In addition to those errors, `ioctl` fails, it does *not* process an `ioctl` command, and `errno` equals `EINVAL` if the stream denoted by `fd` is linked below a multiplexer or if `cmd` is not a valid value for a stream.

Since these STREAMS commands are a subset of `ioctl` commands, they are subject to the errors described in IOCTL(BA_OS). Also, as described in IOCTL(BA_OS), STREAMS-modules and drivers can detect errors. In this case, the module or driver sends an error message to the stream-head containing an error value. This causes subsequent system calls to fail with `errno` set to this value.

SEE ALSO

CLOSE(BA_OS), FCNTL(BA_OS), IOCTL(BA_OS), OPEN(BA_OS), READ(BA_OS), GETMSG(NS_OS), POLL(NS_OS), PUTMSG(NS_OS), SIGNAL(BA_OS), SIGSET(BA_OS), WRITE(BA_OS).

NAME

`termio` — general terminal interface

SYNOPSIS

```
#include <termio.h>

ioctl(fildes, request, arg)
struct termio *arg;

ioctl(fildes, request, arg)
int arg;
```

DESCRIPTION

The `termio` facility offers a general interface for asynchronous communications ports that is hardware-independent and that has the common features discussed in this section.

When a terminal file is opened, it normally causes the process to wait until a connection is established. Typically, these files are opened by the system initialization process and become the *standard input*, *standard output* and *standard error* files [see **stdio-stream** in VOCAB(BA_DEF)]. The very first terminal file opened by the process-group-leader but not already associated with a process-group becomes the *control-terminal* for that process-group. The control-terminal plays a special role in handling quit and interrupt signals [see below]. The control-terminal is inherited by a new process during a FORK(BA_OS) or EXEC(BA_OS) operation. A process can break this association by changing its process-group with the SETPGRP(BA_OS) routine.

A terminal associated with one of these files ordinarily operates in full-duplex mode. This means characters may be typed at any time, even while output is occurring. Characters are only lost when the system's character input buffers become completely full, or when an input line exceeds {MAX_CHAR}, the maximum allowable number of input characters. When the input limit is reached, all the saved characters may be thrown away without notice.

Normally, terminal input is processed in units of lines. A line is delimited by the new-line (ASCII LF) character, end-of-file (ASCII EOT) character, or end-of-line character. This means that a program attempting to read will be suspended until an entire line has been typed. Also, no matter how many characters may be requested in a read, at most one line will be returned. It is not, however, necessary to read a whole line at once; any number of characters may be requested in a read, even one, without losing information.

Some characters have special meaning when input. For example, during input, *erase* and *kill* processing is normally done. The ERASE character erases the last character typed, except that it will not erase beyond the beginning of the line. Typically, # is the default ERASE character. The KILL character kills (deletes) the entire input line, and optionally outputs a new-line character. Typically, @ is the default KILL character. Both characters operate on a keystroke basis independently of any backspacing or tabbing.

Special Characters

Some characters have special functions on input. These functions and their typical default character values are summarized below:

INTR   (Typically, rubout or ASCII DEL) generates an *interrupt* signal, which is sent to all processes with the associated control-terminal. Normally, each such process is forced to terminate, but arrangements may be made either to ignore the signal or to receive a trap to an agreed-upon location [see SIGNAL(BA_OS)].

QUIT   (Typically, control-\ or ASCII FS) generates a *quit* signal. Its treatment is identical to the interrupt signal except that, unless a receiving process has made other arrangements, it will not only be terminated but the abnormal termination routines will be executed.

ERASE   (Typically, the character #) erases the preceding character. It will not erase beyond the start of a line, as delimited by an EOF, EOL or NL character.

KILL   (Typically, the character @) deletes the entire line, as delimited by an EOF, EOL or NL character.

EOF   (Typically, control-d or ASCII EOT) may be used to generate an EOF, from a terminal. When received, all the characters waiting to be read are immediately passed to the program, without waiting for a new-line, and the EOF is discarded. Thus, if there are no characters waiting, which is to say the EOF occurred at the beginning of a line, zero characters will be passed back, which is the standard end-of-file indication.

NL   (ASCII LF) is the normal line delimiter. It can not be changed or escaped.

EOL   (Typically, ASCII NUL) is an additional line delimiter, like NL. It is not normally used.

STOP   (Typically, control-s or ASCII DC3) is used to temporarily suspend output. It is useful with CRT terminals to prevent output from disappearing before it can be read. While output is suspended, STOP characters are ignored and not read.

START   (Typically, control-q or ASCII DC1) is used to resume output suspended by a STOP character. While output is not suspended, START characters are ignored and not read. The START/STOP characters can not be changed or escaped.

MIN   Used to control terminal I/O during raw mode (ICANON off) processing [see the MIN/TIME Interaction section below].

TIME   Used to control terminal I/O during raw mode (ICANON off) processing [see the MIN/TIME Interaction section below].

The ERASE, KILL and EOF characters may be entered literally, their special meaning escaped, by preceding them with the escape character, \. In this case, no special function is performed and the escape character is not read as input.

When one or more characters are written, they are transmitted to the terminal as soon as previously-written characters have finished typing. Input characters are echoed by putting them in the output queue as they arrive. If a process produces characters more rapidly than they can be typed, it will be suspended when its output queue exceeds some limit. When the queue has drained down to some threshold, the program is resumed.

When a modem disconnect is detected, a *hang-up* signal, SIGHUP, is sent to all processes that have this terminal as the control-terminal. Unless other arrangements have been made, this signal causes the processes to terminate. If the hang-up signal is ignored, any subsequent read returns with an end-of-file indication. Thus, programs that read a terminal and test for end-of-file can terminate appropriately when hung up on.

IOCTL(BA_OS) Requests

The primary IOCTL(BA_OS) requests to a terminal have the form:

```
ioctl(fildes, request, arg)
struct termio *arg;
```

The requests using this form are:

TCGETA   Get the parameters associated with the terminal and store in the structure `termio` referenced by `arg`.

TCSETA   Set the parameters associated with the terminal from the structure `termio` referenced by `arg`. The change is immediate.

TCSETAW   Wait for the output to drain before setting the new parameters. This form should be used when changing parameters that will affect output.

TCSETAF   Wait for the output to drain, then flush the input queue and set the new parameters.

Additional IOCTL(BA_OS) requests to a terminal have the form:

```
ioctl(fildes, request, arg)
int arg;
```

The requests using this form are:

TCSBRK   Wait for the output to drain.
          If `arg` is 0, then send a break (zero bits for 0.25 seconds).

TCXONC   Start/stop control.
          If `arg` is 0, suspend output; if 1, restart suspended output.

TCFLSH   Flush queues
          If `arg` is 0, flush the input queue; if 1, flush the output queue; if 2, flush both the input and output queues.

Several IOCTL(BA_OS) requests apply to terminal files and use the structure termio which is defined by the <termio.h> header file. The structure termio includes the following members:

```
unsigned short c_iflag;    /* input modes */
unsigned short c_oflag;    /* output modes */
unsigned short c_cflag;    /* control modes */
unsigned short c_lflag;    /* local modes */
char           c_line;     /* line-discipline */
unsigned char  c_cc[NCC];  /* control chars */
```

The special control-characters are defined by the array c_cc. The symbolic name NCC is the size of the control-character array and is also defined by the <termio.h> header file. The relative positions, subscript names and typical default values for each entry are as follows:

0	VINTR	ASCII DEL
1	VQUIT	ASCII FS
2	VERASE	#
3	VKILL	@
4	VEOF	ASCII EOT
4	VMIN	
5	VEOL	ASCII NUL
5	VTIME	
6	reserved	
7	reserved	

Input Modes

The following values for c_iflag define basic terminal input control:

IGNBRK   Ignore break condition.
If IGNBRK is set, the break condition (a character framing error with data all zeros) is ignored (i.e., not put on the input queue and therefore not read by any process). Otherwise, see BRKINT.

BRKINT   Signal interrupt on break.
If BRKINT is set, the break condition generates an interrupt signal and flushes both the input and output queues.

IGNPAR   Ignore characters with parity errors.
If IGNPAR is set, characters with other framing and parity errors are ignored.

PARMRK   Mark parity errors.
If PARMRK is set, a character with a framing or parity error which is not ignored is read as the three-character sequence: 0377, 0, X, where 0377, 0 is a two-character flag preceding each sequence and X is the data of the character received in error. To avoid ambiguity in this case, if ISTRIP is clear, a valid character of 0377 is read as 0377, 0377.

If PARMRK is clear, a framing or parity error which is not ignored is read as the character ASCII NUL (ASCII code 0).

INPCK   Enable input parity check.
If INPCK is set, input parity checking is enabled.

If INPCK is clear, input parity checking is disabled allowing output parity generation without input parity errors.

ISTRIP   Strip character.
If ISTRIP is set, valid input characters are first stripped to 7-bits, otherwise all 8-bits are processed.

INLCR   Map NL to ASCII CR on input.
If INLCR is set, a received NL character is translated into a ASCII CR character.

IGNCR   Ignore ASCII CR.
If IGNCR is set, a received ASCII CR character is ignored (not read).

ICRNL   Map ASCII CR to NL on input.
If ICRNL is set, a received ASCII CR character is translated into a NL character.

IUCLC   Map upper-case to lower-case on input.
If IUCLC is set, a received upper-case alphabetic character is translated into lower-case.

IXON   Enable start/stop output control.
If IXON is set, start/stop output control is enabled. A received STOP character will suspend output and a received START character will restart output. All start/stop characters are ignored and not read.

IXANY   Enable any character to restart output.
If IXANY is set, any input character, will restart output which has been suspended.

IXOFF   Enable start/stop input control.
If IXOFF is set, the system will transmit START/STOP characters when the input queue is nearly empty/full.

The initial input control value is all bits clear.

Output Modes

The following values for c_oflag define system treatment of output:

OPOST   Postprocess output.
If OPOST is set, output characters are post-processed as indicated by the remaining flags; otherwise characters are transmitted without change.

OLCUC   Map lower case to upper on output.
If OLCUC is set, a lower-case alphabetic character is transmitted as the corresponding upper-case character. This function is often used in conjunction with IUCLC.

ONLCR   Map NL to ASCII CR-NL on output.
If ONLCR is set, the NL character is transmitted as the ASCII CR-NL character pair.

OCRNL   Map ASCII CR to NL on output.
If OCRNL is set, the ASCII CR character is transmitted as the NL character.

ONOCR   No ASCII CR output at column 0.
If ONOCR is set, no ASCII CR character is transmitted when at column 0 (first position).

ONLRET   NL performs ASCII CR function.
If ONLRET is set, the NL character is assumed to do the carriage-return function; the column pointer will be set to 0 and the delays specified for ASCII CR will be used. Otherwise the NL character is assumed to do just the line-feed function; the column pointer will remain unchanged. The column pointer is also set to 0 if the ASCII CR character is actually transmitted.

OFILL   Use fill-characters for delay.
If OFILL is set, fill-characters will be transmitted for delay instead of a timed delay. This is useful for high baud-rate terminals that need only a minimal delay.

OFDEL   Fill is ASCII DEL, else ASCII NUL.
If OFDEL is set, the fill-character is ASCII DEL, otherwise ASCII NUL.

The delay-bits specify how long transmission stops to allow for mechanical or other movement when certain characters are sent to the terminal. In all cases a value of 0 indicates no delay. The actual delays depend on line-speed and system-load.

NLDLY   New-line delay lasts about 0.10 seconds.

If ONLRET is set, the carriage-return delays are used instead of the new-line delays.

If OFILL is set, two fill-characters will be transmitted.

Select new-line delays:
NL0   New-Line character type 0
NL1   New-Line character type 1

CRDLY   Carriage-return delay type 1 is dependent on the current column position, type 2 is about 0.10 seconds, and type 3 is about 0.15 seconds.

If OFILL is set, delay type 1 transmits two fill-characters, and type 2, four fill-characters.

Select carriage-return delays:

CR0	Carriage-return delay type 0
CR1	Carriage-return delay type 1
CR2	Carriage-return delay type 2
CR3	Carriage-return delay type 3

TABDLY   Horizontal-tab delay type 1 is dependent on the current column position, type 2 is about 0.10 seconds, and type 3 specifies that tabs are to be expanded into spaces.

If OFILL is set, two fill-characters will be transmitted for any delay.

Select horizontal-tab delays:

TAB0	Horizontal-tab delay type 0
TAB1	Horizontal-tab delay type 1
TAB2	Horizontal-tab delay type 2
TAB3	Expand tabs to spaces.

BSDLY   Backspace delay lasts about 0.05 seconds.

If OFILL is set, one fill-character will be transmitted.

Select backspace delays:

BS0	Backspace delay type 0
BS1	Backspace delay type 1

VTDLY   Vertical-tab delay lasts about 2.0 seconds.

Select vertical-tab delays:

VT0	Vertical-tab delay type 0
VT1	Vertical-tab delay type 1

FFDLY   Form-feed delay lasts about 2.0 seconds.

Select form-feed delays:

FF0	Form-feed delay type 0
FF1	Form-feed delay type 1

The initial output control value is all bits clear.

Control Modes

The following values for c_cflag define hardware control for terminals:

HUPCL   Hang up on last close.
If HUPCL is set, the modem control lines for the port will be lowered when the last process with the line open closes it or terminates. In other words, the data-terminal-ready signal will not be asserted.

CLOCAL   Local line, else dial-up.
           If CLOCAL is set, the line is assumed to be a local, direct
           connection with no modem control. Otherwise modem control is
           assumed.

           Under normal circumstances, an OPEN(BA_OS) operation will
           wait for the modem connection to complete. However, if
           O_NDELAY is set, or CLOCAL is set, the OPEN(BA_OS)
           operation will return immediately without waiting for the
           connection. For those files on which the connection has not been
           established, or has been lost, and for which CLOCAL is clear,
           both READ(BA_OS) and WRITE(BA_OS) operations will return a
           zero character count. For the READ(BA_OS) operation, this is
           equivalent to an end-of-file condition. The initial hardware
           control value after the OPEN(BA_OS) operation is
           implementation-dependent.

CBAUD   Specify the baud-rate.
           The zero baud-rate, B0, is used to hang up the connection. If
           B0 is specified, the data-terminal-ready signal will not be
           asserted. Normally, this will disconnect the line. For any
           particular hardware, unsupported speed changes are ignored.

           Select baud rate:

B0	Hang up
B50	50 baud
B75	75 baud
B110	110 baud
B134	134.5 baud
B150	150 baud
B200	200 baud
B300	300 baud
B600	600 baud
B1200	1200 baud
B1800	1800 baud
B2400	2400 baud
B4800	4800 baud
B9600	9600 baud
B19200	19200 baud
B38400	38400 baud

CSIZE   Specify the character size in bits for both transmission and
           reception. This size does not include the parity-bit, if any.

           Select character size:

CS5	5-bits
CS6	6-bits
CS7	7-bits
CS8	8-bits

CSTOPB Send two stop-bits, else one.
If CSTOPB is set, two stop-bits are used, otherwise one stop-bit.
For example, at 110 baud, two stop-bits are normally used.

CREAD   Enable receiver.
If CREAD is set, the receiver is enabled. Otherwise no
characters will be received.

PARENB Enable parity.
If PARENB is set, parity generation and detection is enabled and
a parity-bit is added to each character.

PARODD Specify odd parity, else even.
If parity is enabled, PARODD specifies odd parity if set,
otherwise even parity is used.

Local Modes and Line Discipline

The line-discipline uses c_lflag to control terminal functions. The basic
line-discipline, c_line set to 0, provides the following:

ISIG   Enable signals.
If ISIG is set, each input character is checked against the
special control characters INTR and QUIT. If an input character
matches one of these control characters, the function associated
with that character is performed. If ISIG is clear, no checking
is done. Thus these special input functions are possible only if
ISIG is set. These functions may be disabled individually by
changing the value of the control character to an unlikely or
impossible value (e.g., 0377).

ICANON Canonical input (ERASE and KILL processing).
If ICANON is set, canonical processing is enabled. This enables
the ERASE and KILL edit functions, and the assembly of input
characters into lines delimited by the EOF, EOL or NL characters.
If ICANON is clear, read requests are satisfied directly from the
input queue. A read will not be satisfied until at least MIN
characters have been received or the time-out value TIME has
expired between characters [see the MIN/TIME Interaction
section below]. This allows fast bursts of input to be read
efficiently while still allowing single character input. The MIN
and TIME values are stored in the position for the EOF and EOL
characters, respectively. The time-value is expressed in units of
0.10 seconds.

XCASE   Canonical upper/lower presentation.
If both XCASE and ICANON are set, an upper-case letter is
input by preceding it with the character \, and is output
preceded by the character \.

With canonical upper/lower presentation, the following escape sequences are generated on output and accepted on input:

for:	use:
`	\'
¦	\!
~	\^
{	\(
}	\)
\	\\

A is input as \a, \n as \\n, and \N as \\\n.

ECHO   Enable echo.
If ECHO is set, characters are echoed back to the terminal as received.

When ICANON is set, the following echo functions are possible:

ECHOE   Echo the ERASE character as ASCII BS-SP-BS.
If both ECHOE and ECHO are set, the ERASE character is echoed as ASCII BS-SP-BS, which will clear the last character from a CRT screen.

If ECHOE is set but ECHO is clear, the ERASE character is echoed as ASCII SP-BS.

ECHOK   Echo the NL character after the KILL character.
If ECHOK is set, the NL character will be echoed after the KILL character to emphasize that the line will be deleted. Note that an escape character preceding the ERASE character or the KILL character removes any special function.

ECHONL   Echo the NL character.
If ECHONL is set, the NL character will be echoed even if ECHO is clear. This is useful for terminals set to local-echo (also called half-duplex). Because ASCII EOT is the default EOF character, the EOF character is not echoed unless escaped, to prevent terminals that respond to ASCII EOT from hanging up.

NOFLSH   Disable flush after interrupt or quit.
If NOFLSH is set, the normal flush of the input and output queues associated with the quit and interrupt characters will not be done.

The initial line-discipline control value is all bits clear.

MIN/TIME Interaction

MIN represents the minimum number of characters that should be received when the read is satisfied (i.e., the characters are returned to the user). TIME is a timer of 0.10 second granularity used to time-out bursty and short-term data transmissions.

The four possible values for MIN and TIME and their interactions follow:

1. MIN > 0, TIME > 0. In this case, TIME serves as an inter-character timer activated after receipt of the first character, and reset upon receipt of each character. MIN and TIME interact as follows:

   As soon as any character is received, the inter-character timer starts.

   If MIN characters are received before the inter-character timer expires, the read is satisfied.

   If the inter-character timer expires before MIN characters are received, the characters received to that point are returned to the user.

   A READ(BA_OS) operation will sleep until the MIN and TIME mechanisms are activated by the receipt of the first character; thus, at least one character must be returned.

2. MIN > 0, TIME = 0. In this case, because TIME = 0, the timer plays no role and only MIN is significant. A READ(BA_OS) operation is not satisfied until MIN characters are received.

3. MIN = 0, TIME > 0. In this case, because MIN = 0, TIME no longer serves as an inter-character timer, but now serves as a read timer that is activated as soon as the READ(BA_OS) operation is processed (in canon). A READ(BA_OS) operation is satisfied as soon as a single character is received or the timer expires, in which case, the READ(BA_OS) operation will not return any characters.

4. MIN = 0, TIME = 0. In this case, return is immediate. If characters are present, they will be returned to the user.

SEE ALSO

FORK(BA_OS), IOCTL(BA_OS), SETPGRP(BA_OS), SIGNAL(BA_OS).

Glossary

NAME

vocabulary — definitions of terms

DESCRIPTION

ASCII character set

The following maps of the ASCII character set give octal and hexadecimal equivalents for each character. Although the ASCII code does not use the eighth-bit in an octet, this bit should not be used for other purposes because codes for other languages may need to use it.

Octal map of ASCII character set.

```
000 nul 001 soh 002 stx 003 etx 004 eot 005 enq 006 ack 007 bel
010 bs  011 ht  012 nl  013 vt  014 np  015 cr  016 so  017 si
020 dle 021 dc1 022 dc2 023 dc3 024 dc4 025 nak 026 syn 027 etb
030 can 031 em  032 sub 033 esc 034 fs  035 gs  036 rs  037 us
040 sp  041 !   042 "   043 #   044 $   045 %   046 &   047 '
050 (   051 )   052 *   053 +   054 ,   055 -   056 .   057 /
060 0   061 1   062 2   063 3   064 4   065 5   066 6   067 7
070 8   071 9   072 :   073 ;   074 <   075 =   076 >   077 ?
100 @   101 A   102 B   103 C   104 D   105 E   106 F   107 G
110 H   111 I   112 J   113 K   114 L   115 M   116 N   117 O
120 P   121 Q   122 R   123 S   124 T   125 U   126 V   127 W
130 X   131 Y   132 Z   133 [   134 \   135 ]   136 ^   137 _
140 `   141 a   142 b   143 c   144 d   145 e   146 f   147 g
150 h   151 i   152 j   153 k   154 l   155 m   156 n   157 o
160 p   161 q   162 r   163 s   164 t   165 u   166 v   167 w
170 x   171 y   172 z   173 {   174 |   175 }   176 ~   177 del
```

Hexadecimal map of ASCII character set.

```
00 nul 01 soh 02 stx 03 etx 04 eot 05 enq 06 ack 07 bel
08 bs  09 ht  0a nl  0b vt  0c np  0d cr  0e so  0f si
10 dle 11 dc1 12 dc2 13 dc3 14 dc4 15 nak 16 syn 17 etb
18 can 19 em  1a sub 1b esc 1c fs  1d gs  1e rs  1f us
20 sp  21 !   22 "   23 #   24 $   25 %   26 &   27 '
28 (   29 )   2a *   2b +   2c ,   2d -   2e .   2f /
30 0   31 1   32 2   33 3   34 4   35 5   36 6   37 7
38 8   39 9   3a :   3b ;   3c <   3d =   3e >   3f ?
40 @   41 A   42 B   43 C   44 D   45 E   46 F   47 G
48 H   49 I   4a J   4b K   4c L   4d M   4e N   4f O
50 P   51 Q   52 R   53 S   54 T   55 U   56 V   57 W
58 X   59 Y   5a Z   5b [   5c \   5d ]   5e ^   5f _
60 `   61 a   62 b   63 c   64 d   65 e   66 f   67 g
68 h   69 i   6a j   6b k   6c l   6d m   6e n   6f o
70 p   71 q   72 r   73 s   74 t   75 u   76 v   77 w
78 x   79 y   7a z   7b {   7c |   7d }   7e ~   7f del
```

directory

Directories organize files into a hierarchical system of files with directories as the nodes in the hierarchy. A directory is a file that catalogs the list of files, including directories (sub-directories), that are directly beneath it in the hierarchy. Entries in a directory file are called links. A link associates a file-identifier with a file-name. By convention, a directory contains at least two links, . (*dot*) and . . (*dot-dot*). The link called *dot* refers to the directory itself while *dot-dot* refers to its parent-directory. The root-directory, which is the top-most node of the hierarchy, has itself as its parent-directory; thus, / is the path-name of both the root-directory and the parent-directory of the root-directory.

effective-user-ID and **effective-group-ID**

An active process has an effective-user-ID and an effective-group-ID that are used to determine file-access-permissions (see below). The effective-user-ID and effective-group-ID are equal to the process's real-user-ID and real-group-ID respectively, unless the process or one of its ancestors evolved from a file that had the set-user-ID bit or set-group-ID bit set [see EXEC(BA_OS)]. In addition, they can be reset with SETUID(BA_OS) and SETGID(BA_OS), respectively.

environmental variables

When a process begins, an array of strings called the *environment* is made available by EXEC(BA_OS) [see also SYSTEM(BA_OS)]. These strings take the form *variable=value*, for example, PATH=:/bin:/usr/bin. These environmental variables provide a way to make information about an end-user's environment available to programs [see ENVVAR(BA_ENV)].

file-access-permissions

Read, write and execute/search permissions [see CHMOD(BA_OS)] on a file are granted to a process if one or more of the following are true:

- The effective-user-ID of the process is super-user.

- The effective-user-ID of the process matches the user-ID of the owner of the file and the appropriate access-permission-bit of the *owner* portion of the file-mode is set.

- The effective-user-ID of the process does not match the user-ID of the owner of the file and the effective-group-ID of the process matches the group of the file and the appropriate access-permission-bit of the *group* portion of the file-mode is set.

- The effective-user-ID of the process does not match the user-ID of the owner of the file and the effective-group-ID of the process does not match the group-ID of the file and the appropriate access-permission-bit of the *other* portion of the file-mode is set.

Otherwise, the corresponding permissions are denied.

file-descriptor

A file-descriptor is a small integer used to identify a file for the purposes of doing I/O. The value of a file-descriptor is from 0 to {OPEN_MAX} – 1. An open file-descriptor is obtained from a call to functions defined in CREAT(BA_OS), DUP(BA_OS), FCNTL(BA_OS), OPEN(BA_OS) or PIPE(BA_OS). A process may have no more than {OPEN_MAX} file-descriptors open simultaneously.

A file-descriptor has associated with it information used in performing I/O on the file: a file-pointer that marks the current position within the file where I/O will begin; file-status and access-modes (e.g., read, write, read/write) [see OPEN(BA_OS)]; and close-on-exec flag [see FCNTL(BA_OS)]. Multiple file-descriptors may identify the same file. The file-descriptor is used as an argument by functions defined in READ(BA_OS), WRITE(BA_OS), IOCTL(BA_OS) and CLOSE(BA_OS).

file-name

Strings consisting of 1 to {NAME_MAX} characters may be used to name an ordinary file, a special file or a directory. {NAME_MAX} must be at least 14. These characters may be selected from the set of all character values excluding the characters *null* and *slash* (/).

Note that it is generally unwise to use *, ?, !, [or] as part of file-names because of the special meaning attached to these characters for file-name expansion by the command interpreter [see SYSTEM(BA_OS)]. Other characters to avoid are the hyphen, blank, tab, <, >, backslash, single and double quotes, accent grave, vertical bar, caret, curly braces and parentheses. It is also advisable to avoid the use of non-printing characters in file-names.

implementation-specific constants

In detailed definitions of components, it is sometimes necessary to refer to constants that are implementation-specific, but which are not necessarily expected to be accessible to an application-program. Many of these constants describe boundary-conditions and system-limits.

In the SVID, for readability, these constants are replaced with symbolic names. These names always appear enclosed in curly brackets to distinguish them from symbolic names of other implementation-specific constants that are accessible to application-programs by header files. These names are not necessarily accessible to an application-program through a header file, although they may be defined in the documentation for a particular system.

In general, a portable application program should not refer to these constants in its code. For example, an application-program would not be expected to test the length of an argument list given to EXEC(BA_OS) to determine if it was greater than {ARG_MAX}.

The following lists implementation-specific constants used in component interface definitions:

Name	*Description*
{ARG_MAX}	max. length of argument to `exec`
{CHAR_BIT}	number of bits in a `char`
{CHAR_MAX}	max. integer value of a `char`
{CHILD_MAX}	max. number of processes per user-ID
{CLK_TCK}	number of clock ticks per second
{FCHR_MAX}	max. size of a file in bytes
{INT_MAX}	max. decimal value of an `int`
{LINK_MAX}	max. number of links to a single file
{LOCK_MAX}	max. number of entries in system lock table
{LONG_BIT}	number of bits in a `long`
{LONG_MAX}	max. decimal value of a `long`
{MAXDOUBLE}	max. decimal value of a `double`
{MAX_CHAR}	max. size of character input buffer
{NAME_MAX}	max. number of characters in a file-name
{OPEN_MAX}	max. number of files a process can have open
{PASS_MAX}	max. number of significant characters in a password
{PATH_MAX}	max. number of characters in a path-name
{PID_MAX}	max. value for a process-ID
{PIPE_BUF}	max. number bytes atomic in write to a pipe
{PIPE_MAX}	max. number of bytes written to a pipe in a write
{PROC_MAX}	max. number of simultaneous processes, system wide
{SHRT_MAX}	max. decimal value of a `short`
{STD_BLK}	number of bytes in a physical I/O block
{SYS_NMLN}	number of characters in string returned by `uname`
{SYS_OPEN}	max. number of files open on system
{TMP_MAX}	max. number of unique names generated by `tmpnam`
{UID_MAX}	max. value for a user-ID or group-ID
{USI_MAX}	max. decimal value of an `unsigned`
{WORD_BIT}	number of bits in a `word` or `int`
{CHAR_MIN}	min. integer value of a `char`
{INT_MIN}	min. decimal value of an `int`
{LONG_MIN}	min. decimal value of a `long`
{SHRT_MIN}	min. decimal value of a `short`

parent-process-ID

The parent-process-ID of a process is the process-ID of its creator, for the lifetime of its creator [see EXIT(BA_OS)]. A new process is created by a currently active-process [see FORK(BA_OS)].

path-name and **path-prefix**

In a C program, a path-name is a null-terminated character-string starting with an optional slash (/), followed by zero or more directory-names separated by slashes, optionally followed by a file-name. A null string is undefined and may be considered an error.

More precisely, a path-name is a null-terminated character-string as follows:

       <path_name> ::= <file_name> | <path_prefix> <file_name> | / | . | . .
       <path_prefix> ::= <rtprefix> | / <rtprefix> | *empty*
       <rtprefix> ::= <dirname> / | <rtprefix> <dirname> /

where <file_name> is a string of 1 to {NAME_MAX} significant characters other than slash and null, and <dirname> is a string of 1 to {NAME_MAX} significant characters (other than slash and null) that names a directory. The result of names not produced by the grammar are undefined.

If a path-name begins with a slash, the path search begins at the root-directory. Otherwise, the search begins from the current-working-directory.

A slash by itself names the root-directory. An attempt to create or delete the path-name slash by itself is undefined and may be considered an error. The meanings of . and . . are defined under directory.

process-group-ID

Each active-process is a member of a process-group. The process-group is uniquely identified by a positive-integer, called the process-group-ID, which is the process-ID of the group-leader (see below). This grouping permits the signaling of related processes [see KILL(BA_OS)]. A process inherits the process-group-ID of the process that created it [see FORK(BA_OS) and EXEC(BA_OS)].

process-group-leader

A process-group-leader is any process whose process-group-ID is the same as its process-ID. Any process that is not a process-group-leader may detach itself from its current process-group and become a new process-group-leader by calling SETPGRP(BA_OS).

process-ID

Each active-process in the system is uniquely identified by a positive-integer called a process-ID. The range of this ID is from 0 to {PID_MAX}. By convention, process-ID 0 and 1 are reserved for special system-processes.

real-user-ID and **real-group-ID**

Each user allowed on the system is identified by a positive-integer called a real-user-ID. Each user is also a member of a group. The group is identified by a positive-integer called the real-group-ID.

Each active-process has a real-user-ID and real-group-ID that are set to the real-user-ID and real-group-ID, respectively, of the user responsible for the creation of the process. They can be reset with SETUID(BA_OS) and SETGID(BA_OS), respectively.

root-directory and current-working-directory

Each process has associated with it a concept of a root-directory and a current-working-directory for the purpose of resolving path searches. The root-directory of a process need not be the root-directory of the root-file-system [see CHROOT(BA_OS)].

special-processes

All special-processes are system-processes (e.g., a system's process-scheduler). At least process-IDs 0 and 1 are reserved for special-processes.

stdio-routines

A set of routines described as Standard I/O (*stdio*) routines constitute an efficient, user-level I/O buffering scheme. The complete set of Standard I/O, *stdio* routines is shown below [see also the definition of stdio-stream below]. Detailed component interface definitions of each can be found in either the Base System (BA_OS) routines or the Base Library (BA_LIB) routines.

(BA_OS)   `clearerr, fclose, fdopen, feof, ferror, fileno,`
                `fflush, fopen, fread, freopen, fseek, ftell,`
                `fwrite, popen, pclose, rewind.`

(BA_LIB)   `ctermid, fgetc, fgets, fprintf, fputc, fputs,`
                `fscanf, getc, getchar, gets, getw, printf, putc,`
                `putchar, puts, putw, scanf, setbuf, setvbuf,`
                `sprintf, tempnam, tmpfile, tmpnam, ungetc,`
                `vprintf, vfprintf, vsprintf.`

The Standard I/O routines and constants are declared in the `<stdio.h>` header file and need no further declaration. The following "functions" are implemented as macros and must not be redeclared: `getc, getchar, putc, putchar, ferror, feof, clearerr` and `fileno`. The macros `getc` and `putc` handle characters quickly. The macros `getchar` and `putchar` and the higher-level routines `fgetc, fgets, fprintf, fputc, fputs, fread, fscanf, fwrite, gets, getw, printf, puts, putw` and `scanf` all use or act as if they use `getc` and `putc`; they can be freely intermixed.

To use the *stdio* routines, an application-program must include the `<stdio.h>` header file to define symbolic constants the *stdio* routines use:

The defined constant NULL designates a nonexistent *null* pointer.

The integer constant EOF is returned upon end-of-file or error by most integer functions that deal with streams (see the individual component interface definitions for details).

The integer constant BUFSIZ specifies the size of the buffer required by SETBUF(BA_LIB).

stdio-stream

A file with associated *stdio* buffering is called a *stream*. A stream is a pointer to a type `FILE` defined by the `<stdio.h>` header file. The function `fopen` creates certain descriptive data for a stream and returns a pointer that identifies the stream in all further transactions with other *stdio* routines [see FOPEN(BA_OS)].

Most *stdio* routines manipulate either a stream created by the function `fopen` or one of three streams that are associated with three files that are expected to be open in the Base System [see TERMIO(BA_ENV)]. These three streams are declared in the `<stdio.h>` header file:

`stdin`	the standard input file.
`stdout`	the standard output file.
`stderr`	the standard error file.

Output streams, with the exception of the standard error stream `stderr`, are by default buffered if the output refers to a file and line-buffered if the output refers to a terminal. The standard error output stream `stderr` is by default unbuffered. When an output stream is unbuffered, information is queued for writing on the destination file or terminal as soon as written; when it is buffered, many characters are saved up and written as a block. When it is line-buffered, each line of output is queued for writing on the destination terminal as soon as the line is completed (that is, as soon as a new-line character is written or terminal input is requested). SETBUF(BA_LIB) may be used to change the stream's buffering strategy.

super-user

A process is recognized as a super-user process and is granted special privileges if its effective-user-ID is `0`.

tty-group-ID

Each active-process can be a member of a terminal-group that shares a control terminal [see DEVTTY(BA_ENV)] and is identified by a positive-integer called the tty-group-ID. This grouping is used to terminate a group of related processes upon termination of one of the processes in the group [see EXIT(BA_OS) and SIGNAL(BA_OS)].

SEE ALSO

CHMOD(BA_OS), CHROOT(BA_OS), CLOSE(BA_OS), CREAT(BA_OS), DEVTTY(BA_ENV), DUP(BA_OS), ENVVAR(BA_ENV), EXEC(BA_OS), EXIT(BA_OS), FCNTL(BA_OS), FORK(BA_OS), IOCTL(BA_OS), KILL(BA_OS), OPEN(BA_OS), PIPE(BA_OS), READ(BA_OS), SETBUF(BA_LIB), SETBUF(BA_LIB) , SETGID(BA_OS), SETPGRP(BA_OS), SETUID(BA_OS), SIGNAL(BA_OS), SYSTEM(BA_OS), TERMIO(BA_ENV), WRITE(BA_OS).

NAME

vocabulary — definitions of terms

DESCRIPTION

ipc-permissions

The Kernel Extension includes three mechanisms for inter-process communication (ipc):

1. messages.

2. semaphores.

3. shared-memory.

All of these use a common structure type, `ipc_perm`, to pass information used in determining permission to use an ipc-operation.

The `<ipc.h>` header file defines the `ipc_perm` structure that includes the following members:

```
ushort cuid; /* creator user-ID */
ushort cgid; /* creator group-ID */
ushort uid;  /* user-ID */
ushort gid;  /* group-ID */
ushort mode; /* r/w permission */
```

The `<ipc.h>` header file also defines the following symbolic constants:

Name	Description
IPC_CREAT	create entry if key does not exist
IPC_EXCL	fail if key exists
IPC_NOWAIT	error if request must wait
IPC_PRIVATE	private key
IPC_RMID	remove identifier
IPC_SET	set options
IPC_STAT	get options

message-queue-identifier

A message-queue-identifier `msqid` is a unique positive integer created by MSGGET(KE_OS). Each `msqid` has a message-queue and a data structure `msqid_ds` associated with it. The `msqid_ds` structure contains the following members:

```
struct ipc_perm msg_perm;   /* operation perms */
ushort          msg_qnum;   /* no. of messages on q */
ushort          msg_qbytes; /* max no. of bytes on q */
ushort          msg_lspid;  /* pid, last msgsnd call */
ushort          msg_lrpid;  /* pid, last msgrcv call */
time_t          msg_stime;  /* last msgsnd time */
time_t          msg_rtime;  /* last msgrcv time */
time_t          msg_ctime;  /* last change time */
                            /* time in secs since */
                            /* 00:00:00 GMT 1 Jan 70 */
```

msg_perm an `ipc_perm` structure [see ipc-permissions] that specifies the message-operation-permission.

msg_qnum the number of messages currently on the queue.

msg_qbytes the maximum number of bytes allowed on the queue.

msg_lspid the process-ID of last process to use `msgsnd`.

msg_lrpid the process-ID of last process to use `msgrcv`.

msg_stime the time of last `msgsnd` operation.

msg_rtime the time of last `msgrcv` operation.

msg_ctime the time of last MSGCTL(KE_OS) operation to change a member of the above structure.

message-operation-permissions

In MSGOP(KE_OS) and MSGCTL(KE_OS), the permission required for an operation is determined by the bit-pattern in `msg_perm.mode`, where the type of permission needed is interpreted as follows:

00400	Read by user
00200	Write by user
00040	Read by group
00020	Write by group
00004	Read by others
00002	Write by others

The Read and Write permissions on a `msqid` are granted to a process if one or more of the following are true:

- The effective-user-ID of the process is super-user.

- The effective-user-ID of the process matches `msg_perm.cuid` or `msg_perm.uid` in the `msqid_ds` structure and the appropriate bit of the *user* portion (0600) of `msg_perm.mode` is set.

- The effective-user-ID of the process does not match `msg_prm.cuid` or `msg_perm.uid`, and the effective-group-ID of the process matches `msg_perm.cgid` or `msg_perm.gid`, and the appropriate bit of the *group* portion (0060) of `msg_perm.mode` is set.

- The effective-user-ID of the process does not match `msg_perm.cuid` or `msg_perm.uid`, and the effective-group-ID of the process does not match `msg_perm.cgid` or `msg_perm.gid`, and the appropriate bit of the *other* portion (0006) of `msg_perm.mode` is set.

Otherwise, the corresponding permissions are denied.

semaphore

A semaphore is a data structure with the following members:

```
ushort semval;  /* semaphore value */
short  sempid;  /* pid of last operation */
ushort semncnt; /* no. awaiting semval > cval */
ushort semzcnt; /* no. awaiting semval = 0 */
```

semval   a non-negative integer.

sempid   the process-ID of last process to use a semaphore operation on this semaphore.

semncnt   a count of the suspended-processes currently waiting for the semval of this semaphore to exceed its current value.

semzcnt   a count of the suspended-processes currently waiting for the semval of this semaphore to equal zero.

semaphore-identifier

A semaphore-identifier semid is a unique positive integer created by SEMGET(KE_OS). Each semid has a set of semaphores and a data structure semid_ds associated with it. The semid_ds structure contains the following members:

```
struct ipc_perm sem_perm;  /* operation perms */
ushort          sem_nsems; /* count of sems in set */
time_t          sem_otime; /* last operation time */
time_t          sem_ctime; /* last change time */
                           /* time in secs since */
                           /* 00:00:00 GMT 1 Jan 70 */
```

sem_perm   an ipc_perm structure [see ipc-permissions] that specifies the semaphore-operation-permission.

sem_nsems   the number of semaphores in the set. Each semaphore in the set is denoted by a positive integer, sem_num, that runs sequentially from 0 to the value of sem_nsems-1.

sem_otime   the time of last SEMOP(KE_OS) operation.

sem_ctime   the time of last SEMCTL(KE_OS) operation to change a member of the above structure.

semaphore-operation-permissions

In SEMOP(KE_OS) and SEMCTL(KE_OS), the permission required for an operation is determined by the bit-pattern in sem_perm.mode, where the type of permission needed is interpreted as follows:

00400	Read by user
00200	Alter by user
00040	Read by group
00020	Alter by group
00004	Read by others
00002	Alter by others

The Read and Alter permissions on a `semid` are granted to a process if one or more of the following are true:

- The effective-user-ID of the process is super-user.

- The effective-user-ID of the process matches `sem_perm.cuid` or `sem_perm.uid` in the `semid_ds` structure and the appropriate bit of the *user* portion (`0600`) of `sem_perm.mode` is set.

- The effective-user-ID of the process does not match `sem_perm.cuid` or `sem_perm.uid`, and the effective-group-ID of the process matches `sem_perm.cgid` or `sem_perm.gid`, and the appropriate bit of the *group* portion (`0060`) of `sem_perm.mode` is set.

- The effective-user-ID of the process does not match `sem_perm.cuid` or `sem_perm.uid`, and the effective-group-ID of the process does not match `sem_perm.cgid` or `sem_perm.gid`, and the appropriate bit of the *other* portion (`0006`) of `sem_perm.mode` is set.

Otherwise, the corresponding permissions are denied.

shared-memory-identifier

A shared-memory-identifier `shmid` is a unique positive integer created by SHMGET(KE_OS). Each `shmid` has a segment of memory (referred to as a shared-memory-segment) and a data structure `shmid_ds` associated with it. The `shmid_ds` structure contains the following members:

```
struct ipc_perm shm_perm;    /* operation perms */
int             shm_segsz;   /* size of segment */
ushort          shm_cpid;    /* pid, creator */
ushort          shm_lpid;    /* pid, last operation */
short           shm_nattch;  /* no. of current attaches */
time_t          shm_atime;   /* last attach time */
time_t          shm_dtime;   /* last detach time */
time_t          shm_ctime;   /* last change time */
                             /* times in secs since */
                             /* 00:00:00 GMT 1 Jan 70 */
```

`shm_perm`   an `ipc_perm` structure [see ipc-permissions] that specifies the shared-memory-operation-permission.

`shm_segsz`   specifies the size of the shared-memory-segment.

`shm_cpid`   the process-ID of the creator of `shmid`.

`shm_lpid`   the process-ID of last process to use `shmat` or `shmdt`.

`shm_nattch`   the number of processes with the segment currently attached.

`shm_atime`   the time of last `shmat` operation.

`shm_dtime`   the time of last `shmdt` operation.

`shm_ctime`   the time of last SHMCTL(KE_OS) operation to change one of the members of the above structure.

shared-memory-operation-permissions

In SHMOP(KE_OS) and SHMCTL(KE_OS), the permission required for an operation is determined by the bit-pattern in `shm_perm.mode`, where the type of permission needed is interpreted as follows:

00400	Read by user
00200	Write by user
00040	Read by group
00020	Write by group
00004	Read by others
00002	Write by others

The Read and Write permissions on a `shmid` are granted to a process if one or more of the following are true:

- The effective-user-ID of the process is super-user.

- The effective-user-ID of the process matches `shm_perm.cuid` or `sem_perm.uid` in the `shmid_ds` structure and the appropriate bit of the *user* portion (0600) of `shm_perm.mode` is set.

- The effective-user-ID of the process does not match `shm_perm.cuid` or `sem_perm.uid`, and the effective-group-ID of the process matches `shm_perm.cgid` or `sem_perm.gid`, and the appropriate bit of the *group* portion (0060) of `shm_perm.mode` is set.

- The effective-user-ID of the process does not match `shm_perm.cuid` or `sem_perm.uid`, and the effective-group-ID of the process does not match `shm_perm.cgid` or `sem_perm.gid`, and the appropriate bit of the *other* portion (0006) of `shm_perm.mode` is set.

Otherwise, the corresponding permissions are denied.

SEE ALSO

MSGCTL(KE_OS), MSGGET(KE_OS), MSGOP(KE_OS), SEMCTL(KE_OS), SEMGET(KE_OS), SEMOP(KE_OS), SHMCTL(KE_OS), SHMGET(KE_OS), SHMOP(KE_OS), VOCAB(BA_DEF).

NAME

vocabulary — definitions of terms

DESCRIPTION

active transport-user

The transport-user that initiates a connection.

asynchronous execution

The mode of execution in which transport-service functions do not wait for specific asynchronous events to occur before returning control to the user, but instead return immediately if the event is not pending.

connection-mode

A circuit-oriented mode of transfer in which data is passed from one user to another over an established connection in a reliable, sequenced fashion.

connectionless-mode

A mode of transfer in which data is passed from one user to another in self-contained units with no logical relationship required among multiple units.

ETSDU

The Expedited Transport Service Data Unit, which is the expedited data transmitted over a transport-connection and whose identity is preserved from one end of a transport-connection to the other (i.e., an expedited message).

implementation-specific constants

In addition to the values listed under implementation-specific constants in VOCAB(BA_DEF), several values are defined here. The following lists implementation-specific constants used in component interface definitions:

Name	Description
{NS_RECOVER}	max. no. of minutes before domain name service recovery.
{RDESC_MAX}	max. no. of characters in a resource description.

netbuf structure

The netbuf structure is used by many of the library functions and is defined by the <tiuser.h> header file. This structure includes the following members:

```
unsigned int maxlen;   /* maximum buffer length */
unsigned int len;      /* length of data in buffer */
char *buf;             /* pointer to data buffer */
```

passive transport-user

The transport-user that listens for an incoming connect-indication.

protocol address

The address, also known as the Transport Service Access Point (TSAP) address, that identifies the transport-user. This interface places no structure or semantics on an address.

queue

Each stream-module contains two queues, one for messages moving in each direction. The queue structure defined for STREAMS I/O is important to the module-developer.

strbuf **structure**

The `strbuf` structure is used to contain data or control information and is used by the `getmsg`, `putmsg` and `ioctl` operating system service routines. This structure is defined by the header file `stropts.h` and includes the following members:

```
int maxlen;    /* maximum buffer length */
int len;       /* length of data */
char *buf;     /* pointer to data buffer */
```

stream

A stream is a full-duplex connection between a user-process and an open device or pseudo-device. The stream itself exists entirely within the kernel and provides a general character I/O interface for user-processes. It optionally includes one or more intermediate processing modules that are interposed between the user-process end of the stream and the device-driver (or pseudo-device-driver) end of the stream.

stream-head and **stream-end**

The stream-head is the beginning of the stream and is at the kernel/user boundary. This is also known as the upstream end of the stream.

The stream-end is the driver end of the stream and is also known as the downstream end of the stream.

Data generated as a result of a system call and destined for the driver end of the stream moves downstream; and data moving from the driver end of the stream toward the stream-head is moving upstream. Also, an intermediate module A is said to be upstream from module B when it is interposed between module B and the stream-head (upstream) end of the stream, and downstream from module B when it is between module B and the driver end of the stream.

stream-messages

STREAMS I/O is based on messages. Message types are classified according to their queueing priority and may be non-priority messages or priority messages. Non-priority messages are always placed at the end of the queue following all other messages in the queue. Priority messages are always placed at the head of a queue but after any other priority messages already in the queue. Priority messages are used to send control and data information outside the normal flow-control constraints. A user may access stream-messages that contain a data part, control part or both. The data part is that information which is sent out over the network and the control information is used by the local stream-modules. The other types of messages are used between modules and are not accessible to users.

stream-module and **stream-driver**

A STREAMS-component may be a module or a driver that conforms to the rules specified for STREAMS I/O. A STREAMS-device-driver or pseudo-device-driver is always "opened" and may be "linked" if it is a multiplexing-driver. A stream-module is any other type of software module such as a line discipline or protocol module and is always "pushed" onto the stream.

synchronous execution

The mode of execution in which transport-service functions wait for specific asynchronous events to occur before returning control to the user.

transport-provider

The transport-protocol that provides the services of the transport-interface.

transport-endpoint

The communication path, which is identified by a file-descriptor, between a transport-user and a specific transport-provider.

transport-user

The user-level application or protocol that is accessing the services of the transport-interface.

TSDU

The Transport Service Data Unit, which is the user-data transmitted over a transport-connection and whose identity is preserved from one end of a transport-connection to the other (i.e., a message).

SEE ALSO

VOCAB(KE_DEF), VOCAB(BA_DEF).

Appendices

NAME

STREAMS – Streams I/O Interface

OVERVIEW

"STREAMS" refers to a collection of system functions, kernel resources and
kernel utility routines that offer a general, flexible facility for developing UNIX
System V communication services. By defining standard interfaces for
character input/output within the kernel, STREAMS supports developments
ranging from complete networking protocol suites to individual device-drivers.
The standard interfaces and associated tools enable modular, portable
development and easy integration of high performance network services and
their components.

STREAMS provides a broad framework that avoids imposing any specific
network architecture. It implements an interface consistent and compatible
with the character I/O system available in UNIX System V. The interface
between a user-process and STREAMS is compatible with the existing
character I/O system, and both are available in UNIX System V Release 3.0.

The power of STREAMS resides in modularity that enables customers to retain
their investment in application software as they migrate to different
networking environments. Modularity allows these advantages:

- Application programs can be independent of any underlying protocols and
  physical communication media.

- Network architectures and higher-level protocols can be independent of
  any underlying protocols, device-drivers and physical communication
  media.

- Higher-level services can be created by selecting and connecting lower-
  level services and protocols.

- Protocol-modules can be independent of any underlying computer because
  portability is enhanced by well-defined structure and interface standards.

Each module represents a set of processing functions and communicates with
other modules via a standard interface. Using STREAMS, user-processes can
dynamically select and interconnect kernel-resident modules to implement the
layered designs of contemporary networking architectures such as Open
Systems Interconnection (OSI), Systems Network Architecture (SNA),
Transmission Control Protocol/Internet Protocol (TCP/IP) and Xerox*
Network Systems (XNS). For these protocol suites, developers have
traditionally faced problems arising from an absence of relevant standard
interfaces in UNIX System V.

The Streams I/O system defines standard mechanisms for modularly
implementing protocols. Implementing networking facilities and
communication capabilities using Streams I/O allows efficient, open-ended
products.

---

* Xerox is a registered trademark of Xerox Corporation.

A stream, as illustrated in Figure C-1, is a full duplex processing and data-transfer path in the kernel that is created with the *streamio* facility. The *streamio* facility provides a general character input/output interface for user-processes based on *messages*, which flow in both directions in a *stream*. A stream implements a connection between a *driver* in *kernel-space* and a *process* in *user-space*. Each *module* represents processing functions to be performed on the contents of messages flowing into the module on the stream.

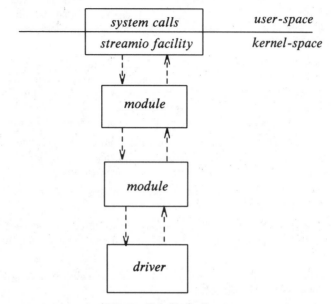

FIGURE C-1. Basic Stream

Each module is self-contained and functionally isolated from any other component in the stream except its two neighboring components. A module communicates with its neighbors by passing messages. The module receives the message, inspects the type, and processes it or just passes it on. A module can function, for example as, a communication protocol, line discipline or data filter.

There are many message types used by stream-modules and these are classified according to queueing priority.

Non-priority messages go to the rear of the queue behind all other messages in the queue.

Priority messages go to the head of a queue but after any other priority messages already on the queue.

Priority messages send control and data information outside the normal flow control constraints. However, to prevent congestion and resource waste due to lack of flow control with priority messages, only one priority message may be placed in the stream-head read queue at a time.

A user may access stream-messages that contain a data-portion, control-portion or both. The data-portion is information sent out over the network and the control information is used by the local stream-modules. The other types of messages are used between modules and not accessible to users. Messages containing only a data-portion are accessible via `putmsg`, `getmsg`, `read` and `write` system functions. Messages containing a control-portion with or without a data-portion are accessed by calling `putmsg` and `getmsg`.

ACCESSING STREAMS

Accessing STREAMS uses the traditional C functions `open`, `close`, `read`, `write` and `ioctl` as well as the new C functions `putmsg`, `getmsg` and `poll`.

Setting Up a Stream

Like conventional device-drivers, STREAMS device-drivers occupy a node in the file-system and may be "opened" and "closed". When a STREAMS device is opened, a stream is automatically set up. As shown in Figure C-2, this "open" sets up a stream with an internal module called the **stream-head** [see VOCAB(NS_DEF)]. The stream-head is closest to the user and the device-driver is *downstream* from the stream-head.

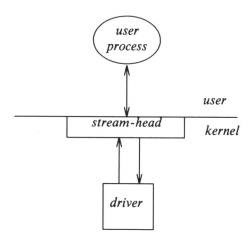

FIGURE C-2. Setting Up a Stream

A stream initially consists of the stream-head and a device-driver. To add other modules to the stream, the user calls `ioctl` to "push" a module. The syntax for this `ioctl` call is:

```
ioctl (fd, I_PUSH, "name")
```

where `fd` is the file-descriptor of the open stream, `I_PUSH` is the `ioctl` command, and "*name*" is the name of the module to be pushed.

The number of modules that may be pushed onto a stream is a configurable quantity. A new module is always pushed just below the stream-head so the order of "pushes" is important. After the module is pushed, the stream looks as shown in Figure C-3.

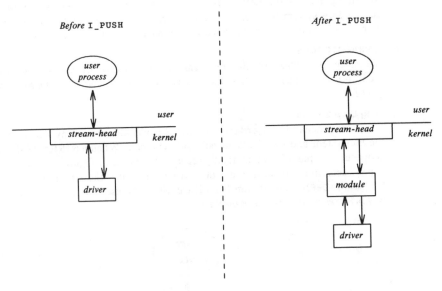

FIGURE C-3. Before and After a Module is Pushed

The user may "pop" modules off a stream using the `ioctl` call:

```
ioctl (fd, I_POP, 0)
```

This `ioctl` command removes the module most recently added to the stream designated by the file-descriptor `fd`; this is always the intermediate module closest to the stream-head. At the user level, drivers are operationally distinct from other modules; drivers are explicitly opened by device path-name, while modules are "pushed" onto the stream by module-name. Device path-names are ordinary UNIX System V file-names, but the names of pushable modules are internal to the system and are not opened or closed.

Sending and Receiving STREAMS Messages

To send and receive STREAMS messages containing control information*, requires the new functions `getmsg` and `putmsg`. These differ from `read` and `write` in that the traditional functions can access only non-priority STREAMS messages containing data alone, while `getmsg` and `putmsg` can access priority and non-priority messages containing a control-portion, data-portion or both.

---

* The control-portion carries interface information between modules and drivers.

For example, the transport functions of the Open Systems Networking Interfaces (NS_LIB) use `putmsg` to send service requests (e.g., to establish a connection), either with or without data, to the underlying STREAMS-based transport-protocol. The transport functions use `getmsg` to receive information back.

Polling STREAMS

The function `poll` provides a mechanism for multiplexing input/output over a set of file-descriptors which refer to open streams. It identifies those streams on which a user can send or receive messages or on which certain events have occurred. The syntax for `poll` is as follows:

```
int poll (pollfds, nfds, timeout)
```

where `nfds` specifies the number of file-descriptors to be examined, `timeout` specifies the number of msec that `poll` should wait for an event to occur, and `pollfds` is an array of `pollfd` structures where each structure contains the following members:

```
int fd;         /* file-descriptor */
short events;   /* requested events */
short revents;  /* returned events */
```

These structures specify the file-descriptors to be examined and the events of interest for each file-descriptor. The argument `fd` specifies an open file-descriptor and `events` and `revents` are bitmasks constructed by OR-ing any combination of the event specific to the function `poll`.

For each element of the array pointed to by `fds`, `poll` examines the given file-descriptor for the event(s) specified in `events`. The number of file-descriptors to examine is set by `nfds`.

The results of the `poll` query are stored in the `revents` field in the `pollfd` structure. Bits in the `revents` bitmask are set to indicate which of the requested events occur. If none occur, none of the specified bits in `revents` are set when `poll` returns.

If none of the defined events occurred on any selected file-descriptor, `poll` waits at least `timeout` msec for an event to occur on any of the selected file-descriptors.

If `timeout` is 0, `poll` returns immediately, effectively polling the file-descriptors.

If `timeout` is -1, `poll` blocks until a requested event occurs or until `poll` is interrupted.

MULTIPLEXING STREAMS

Until now, STREAMS has been described as linear connections of modules, where each invocation of a module is connected to at most a single upstream module and a single downstream module. While this configuration is suitable for many applications, others require the ability to multiplex STREAMS in a variety of configurations. Typical examples are internetworking protocols, which might route data over several subnetworks or terminal window facilities.

STREAMS provides the capability to dynamically build, maintain and dismantle multiplexing configurations. Two types of multiplexing are supported by STREAMS.

The first multiplexing type allows user-processes to connect multiple STREAMS to a single driver from *above*. This configuration can be established by opening multiple minor devices of the same driver, and does not require any special STREAMS facilities.

The second multiplexing type allows user-processes to connect multiple STREAMS *below* a pseudo-driver. This configuration must contain a multiplexing pseudo-driver recognized by STREAMS as having special characteristics.

A special set of `ioctl` commands is used to establish this multiplexing configuration. STREAMS allows a user to build complex, multi-level configurations by cascading multiplexing STREAMS below one another.

Setting Up a Multiplexer

A multiplexing driver is a pseudo-device, and is treated like any other software driver. It owns a node in the UNIX System V file-system, and is opened just like any other STREAMS device-driver. The `open` call establishes a single stream "above" the multiplexer, and the process that opened the multiplexer is returned a file-descriptor that can be used to access the stream that was opened. The file-descriptor `fd0` in Figure C-4 is an example of this.

Next, one of the drivers that is to exist "below" the multiplexer is opened. Once again, this is a driver, and is opened like any other UNIX System V device. The function `open` is used to open the driver, a stream is established between the driver and a stream-head, and the process that issued the `open` call is returned a file-descriptor that can be used to access the stream connected to the driver (e.g., `fd1` in Figure C-4).

If the eventual multiplexing configuration is to have intermediate protocol or line-discipline modules in the stream between the driver just opened and the multiplexer (e.g., between the MUX driver and *driver1* in the "After" section of Figure C-4), these modules should be added at this time to the stream just opened, using the `ioctl` command `I_PUSH`. The "push" operation must be done before the driver is attached below the multiplexer because, once connected, `ioctl` commands cannot be issued to the bottom driver in the normal way.

Using `I_LINK`, the driver just opened is connected below the multiplexing driver opened first as follows:

```
fd0 = open("/dev/MUXdriver", oflag);
fd1 = open("/dev/driver1", oflag);
mux_id = ioctl(fd0, I_LINK, fd1);
```

The `ioctl` call returns `mux_id` used by the multiplexing module to identify the stream just connected. Here, `fd0` is the file-descriptor for the stream connected to the multiplexing driver, and `fd1` is the file-descriptor for the stream connected to another driver. It should be noted that the placement of the first argument (fd0) and the third argument (fd1) is important; the first argument *must* be the file-descriptor of the stream connected to the multiplexing driver. Figure C-4A and 4B shows two drivers and a multiplexing driver *before* (4A) and *after* (4B) linking the two drivers below the multiplexer.

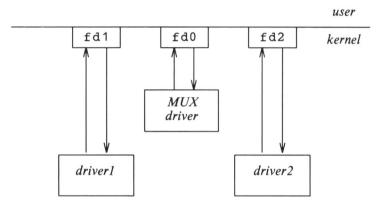

FIGURE C-4A. A multiplexing configuration *before* I_LINK ioctls

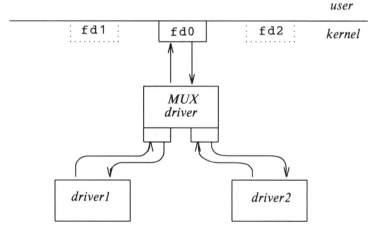

FIGURE C-4B. A multiplexing configuration *after* 2 I_LINK ioctls

Other device-drivers are opened and linked below the multiplexing driver in the same way, as in the example shown in Figure C-4:

```
/* open another driver */
fd2 = open("/dev/driver2", oflag);
/* link it below the MUX */
mux_id2 = ioctl(fd0, I_LINK, fd2);
```

The number of STREAMS that can be "linked" to a multiplexer depends on the particular multiplexer, and it is the responsibility of the multiplexer to keep track of the STREAMS linked to it. However, only one I_LINK operation is allowed for each "lower" stream; a single stream cannot be linked below two multiplexers simultaneously.

The order in which the STREAMS in the multiplexing configuration are opened is unimportant. It is only necessary that the two STREAMS referenced as arguments to the `ioctl` command `I_LINK` are both open when the `ioctl` command `I_LINK` is issued.

Once the configuration is established, the file-descriptors that point to the "bottom" device-drivers (e.g., `fd1` and `fd2` in Figure C-4) can be closed without affecting the way the multiplexer works; these closes will not cause the drivers to be unlinked from the multiplexer. Closing these file-descriptors is necessary sometimes when building large multiplexers, so that many devices can be linked together without exceeding the UNIX System V limit on the number of simultaneously-open files per process. If these file-descriptors (`fd1` and `fd2` in Figure C-4) are not closed, the multiplexer will work as expected, but all subsequent `read`, `write`, `poll`, `putmsg` and `getmsg` calls that use `fd1` and `fd2` will fail.

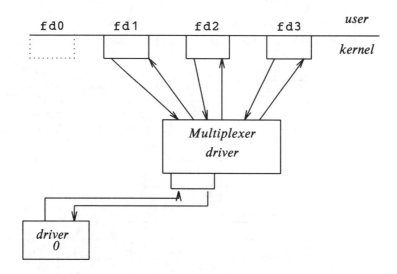

FIGURE C-5. Three STREAMS converging on one device-driver

Building a multiplexer that connects several STREAMS to a single driver, as in Figure C-5, is similar, except that only one driver is linked below the multiplexer. Additional STREAMS above the multiplexer would be established by issuing repeated `open` calls to the multiplexer on "related" minor devices. Again, the way the multiplexer handles these repeated `open`s is multiplexer-dependent, as is the number of STREAMS that a particular multiplexer will successfully handle.

More complex multiplexing configurations can also be created. It is possible to combine the examples of Figures C-4 and C-5 to create a configuration

with many STREAMS above and many drivers linked below the multiplexer.
STREAMS imposes no restrictions on the number of multiplexing drivers that
may be included in a multiplexing configuration or on the number of
multiplexers that data can pass through when moving from one end of the
stream to the other.

Dismantling a Multiplexer

Multiplexing configurations are taken apart using the `ioctl` command
`I_UNLINK`. Each of the bottom drivers linked below the multiplexing driver
(e.g., *driver1* and *driver2* in Figure C-4) can be individually disconnected:

```
ioctl(fd0, I_UNLINK, mux_id);
```

Here, `fd0` is the file-descriptor pointing to a stream connected to the
multiplexing driver, and `mux_id` is the identifier that was returned by the
`ioctl` command `I_LINK` when one of the bottom drivers was linked to the
multiplexing driver. Each bottom driver can be disconnected individually in
this way, or a special `mux_id` value of –1 will disconnect all bottom modules
from the multiplexer simultaneously. This unlinking occurs automatically on
the *last* close of the top stream through which the lower STREAMS were
linked under the multiplexer driver; all these bottom STREAMS are then
unlinked.

Multiplexed Data Routing

Processes use the normal UNIX System V `read`, `write`, `getmsg` and
`putmsg` calls to read data from and write data to an upper stream connected
to the multiplexer. When these data are routed through a multiplexer, the
multiplexer must use its own criteria to route the data moving in both
directions. For example, a protocol multiplexer might use protocol address
information found in a protocol header to determine over which subnetwork a
given packet should be routed. It is the multiplexing driver's responsibility to
define its routing criteria.

One option available to the multiplexer is to use the `mux_id` value to
determine which stream to route data to. The driver has access to this value,
and the `ioctl` command `I_LINK` returns this value to the user. The driver
can therefore specify that the `mux_id` value accompany the data routed
through it.

NAME

TLI — Transport Layer Interface

DESCRIPTION

The Transport Layer Interface defines a set of functions that provides a transport-service for user-processes that is independent of any specific transport-protocol. This transport-service enables two user-processes to transfer data between them over a communications channel.

In order to properly use the library functions defined, certain rules must be followed. This overview describes the relationship among the components and shows how a developer would write an application using these components. State tables are included to show the allowable sequences of function calls given a particular state and event.

The remainder of this component interface definition uses the concept of a **transport-endpoint**. A transport-endpoint specifies a communications path between a transport-user and a specific transport-provider, and is identified by a local file-descriptor (fd) which presents a transport-endpoint as an open device-special file. A transport-provider is defined to be the transport-protocol that provides the services of the transport-layer. All requests to the transport-provider must pass through a transport-endpoint. The T_OPEN(NS_LIB) component returns the file-descriptor fd used as an argument to subsequent functions to identify the transport-endpoint.

Modes of Service

The transport-service interface offers two modes of service:

1. connection-mode.

2. connectionless-mode.

A single transport-endpoint works in only one service-mode at a time.

The connection-mode transport-service is circuit-oriented and enables data to be transferred over an established connection in a reliable, sequenced manner. This service enables the negotiation of the parameters and options that govern the transfer of data. It provides an identification mechanism that avoids the overhead of address transmission and resolution during the data-transfer phase. It also provides a context in which successive units of data, transferred between peer users, are logically related. This service is attractive to applications that require relatively long-lived, datastream-oriented interactions.

In contrast, the connectionless-mode transport-service is message-oriented and supports data-transfer in self-contained units with no logical relationship required among multiple units. These units are also known as **datagrams**. This service requires only a pre-existing association between the peer users involved, which determines the characteristics of the data to be transmitted. No dynamic negotiation of parameters and options is supported, and all the information required to deliver a unit of data (e.g., destination-address) is presented to the transport-provider, together with the data to be transmitted, in a single service-access which need not relate to any other service-access. Also, each unit of data transmitted is entirely self-contained, and can be independently routed by the transport-provider. This service is attractive to applications that involve short-term request/response interactions, exhibit a high level of redundancy, are dynamically reconfigurable, or do not require guaranteed, in-sequence delivery of data.

Error Handling

The transport-interface defines two levels of error: The first level of error is the library function level. Each library function has one or more error returns. A return value of – 1 indicates failure. An external integer, t _ errno, holds the specific error number when a failure occurs. This value is set when errors occur but is not cleared on successful library calls, so it should be tested only after an error is indicated. A diagnostic component, T_ERROR(NS_LIB), is provided for printing out information on the current transport-error. The state of the transport-provider may change if a transport-error occurs.

The second level of error is the system function level. Each library function generates a special library level error number, TSYSERR, when a system function fails or some general error occurs. When a function sets t _ errno to TSYSERR, the external variable errno holds the specific system error code.

The transport-provider generates a new system error, EPROTO, when a protocol error occurs. If the error is severe, it may cause the file-descriptor and transport-endpoint to be unusable. To continue in this case, all users of the file must close it; then the file may be re-opened and initialized.

Synchronous and Asynchronous Execution Modes

The transport-service interface is inherently asynchronous; various events may occur independent of the actions of a transport-user. For example, a user may be sending data over a transport-connection when an asynchronous disconnect-indication arrives. The user must somehow be informed that the connection has been broken. The transport-service interface has two execution-modes for handling asynchronous events:

1. synchronous execution-mode.

2. asynchronous execution-mode.

The synchronous execution-mode requires transport-functions to wait for specific events before returning control to the user. While waiting, the user cannot perform other tasks. For example, a function that attempts to receive data in synchronous execution-mode waits until data arrives before returning control to the user. This is the default execution-mode. It is useful for user-processes that want to wait for events to occur, or for user-processes that have no other useful work to perform.

The asynchronous execution-mode, on the other hand, provides a mechanism for notifying a user of some event without forcing the user to wait for that event. Handling networking events in an asynchronous manner is a desirable capability of the transport-interface. This enables users to perform useful work while waiting for a particular event. For example, a function that attempts to receive data in asynchronous execution-mode returns control to the user immediately if no data is available. The user may then periodically poll for incoming data until it arrives. The asynchronous execution-mode is intended for those applications that expect long delays between events and have other tasks that they can perform in the meantime.

Functions that process incoming events have two execution-modes:

1. synchronous execution-mode.

2. asynchronous execution-mode.

The two execution-modes do not use separate interfaces or different functions. Instead, O_NDELAY specifies the desired execution-mode. O_NDELAY can be set when first opening the transport-provider, or before using FCNTL(BA_OS) to execute any specific function or group of functions.

Eight asynchronous events are defined in the transport-service interface to cover both connection-mode and connectionless-mode. The following defined symbolic names represent them as separate bits in a bitmask

T_LISTEN	Occurs when a transport-provider receives a connect-request from a remote-user (connection-mode only).
T_CONNECT	Occurs when a transport-provider receives a connect-confirmation (connection-mode only).
T_DATA	Occurs when a transport-provider receives normal data.
T_EXDATA	Occurs when a transport-provider receives expedited data (connection-mode only).
T_DISCONNECT	Occurs when a transport-provider receives a disconnect-indication (connection-mode only).
T_ORDREL	Occurs when a transport-provider receives an orderly-release-indication (connection-mode with orderly-release only).
T_ERROR	Occurs when a transport-provider generates a fatal error, thus making the transport-endpoint inaccessible.
T_UDERR	Occurs when a transport-provider finds an error in a previously sent data-unit (connectionless-mode only).

A process that calls functions in synchronous execution-mode must still recognize certain asynchronous events immediately and act on them if necessary. Transport-functions return a special transport-error TLOOK when an asynchronous event occurs. T_LOOK(NS_LIB) can then identify the specific event that occurred when this error was returned.

Asynchronous processing is done with polling. The polling capability enables processes to do useful work and periodically poll for one of the above asynchronous events. This facility is provided by setting O_NDELAY for the appropriate function(s) and by using T_LOOK(NS_LIB) to do the polling.

Overview of the Connection-mode Service

The connection-mode transport-service has four phases of communication:

1. initialization/de-initialization.

2. connection-establishment.

3. data-transfer.

4. connection-release.

Initialization/De-initialization Phase

Before a user tries to establish a transport-connection, the environment of the user must be initialized. Specifically, the user must create a local communication path to the transport-provider (i.e., create the transport-endpoint), obtain necessary protocol-specific information, and activate the transport-endpoint. A transport-endpoint is viewed as active when the transport-provider may accept or request connections associated with the endpoint.

After a connection is released, the transport-user must de-initialize the associated transport-endpoint, thereby freeing the resource for future use. Components that support initialization/de-initialization tasks described below perform local management functions; no information is sent over the network.

T_OPEN(NS_LIB)	Creates a transport-endpoint and returns protocol-specific information associated with that endpoint. It also returns a file-descriptor that serves as the local identifier of the endpoint.
T_BIND(NS_LIB)	Associates a protocol address with a given transport-endpoint, thereby activating the endpoint. It also directs the transport-provider to begin accepting connect-indications if so desired.
T_OPTMGMT(NS_LIB)	Enables the user to get or negotiate protocol options with the transport-provider.
T_UNBIND(NS_LIB)	Disables a transport-endpoint such that no further request destined for the given endpoint will be accepted by the transport-provider.
T_CLOSE(NS_LIB)	Informs the transport-provider that the user is finished with the transport-endpoint, and frees any local resources associated with that endpoint.

The following components are also local management functions, but can be called during any phase of communication.

T_GETINFO(NS_LIB)	Return protocol-specific information associated with the given transport-endpoint.
T_GETSTATE(NS_LIB)	Return the current state of the transport-endpoint.
T_SYNC(NS_LIB)	Synchronize the data structures managed by the transport library with the transport-provider.

T_ALLOC(NS_LIB)	Allocate storage for a given library data structure.
T_FREE(NS_LIB)	Free storage for a library data structure allocated by T_ALLOC(NS_LIB).
T_ERROR(NS_LIB)	Print out a message describing the last error of a transport library function.
T_LOOK(NS_LIB)	Return the current event associated with the given transport-endpoint.

Connection Establishment Phase

This phase enables two transport-users to establish a transport-connection between them. In the connection-establishment scenario, one user is considered active and initiates the conversation, while the second user is passive and waits for a transport-user to request a connection. The active-user requests a connection and then receives a response from the called user. The passive-user waits for connect-indications (i.e., indications of a connect-request) and then either accepts or rejects the request. The components that support these operations are:

T_CONNECT(NS_LIB)	Requests a connection to the transport-user at a given destination, and waits for the remote-user's response. This component may be used in either synchronous or asynchronous execution-mode. In synchronous execution-mode, the component waits for the remote-user's response before returning control to the local-user. In asynchronous execution-mode, the component initiates connection-establishment but returns control to the local-user before a response arrives.
T_RCVCON(NS_LIB)	Enables the active-user to determine the status of a previously sent connect-request. If the request was accepted, the connection-establishment phase is complete on return from this component. This component is used with T_CONNECT(NS_LIB) to establish a connection in an asynchronous manner.
T_LISTEN(NS_LIB)	Enables the passive-user to receive connect-indications from other transport-users.
T_ACCEPT(NS_LIB)	Used by the passive-user to accept a particular connect-request after an indication is received.

Data Transfer Phase

Once a transport-connection is established between two users, data may be transferred back and forth over the connection. Two components are defined to support data-transfer in connection-mode as follows:

| T_SND(NS_LIB) | Send either normal or expedited data over a transport-connection. |
| T_RCV(NS_LIB) | Receive either normal or expedited data over a transport-connection. |

Connection Release Phase

The connection-mode transport-interface has two forms of connection-release:

1. abortive-release.

2. orderly-release.

An abortive-release may be invoked from either the connection-establishment phase or the data-transfer phase. When in the connection-establishment phase, a transport-user may use the abortive-release to reject a connect-request. In the data-transfer phase, either user may abort a connection at any time. The abortive-release is not negotiated by the transport-users, and it takes effect immediately on request. The user on the other side of the connection is notified when a connection is aborted. The transport-provider may also initiate an abortive-release, in which case both users are informed that the connection no longer exists. There is no guarantee of delivery of user-data once an abortive-release is initiated.

The orderly-release capability is an optional feature of the connection-mode service. If supported by the underlying transport-provider, orderly-release may be invoked from the data-transfer phase to enable two users to gracefully release a connection. The procedure for orderly-release prevents the loss of data that may occur during an abortive-release.

The components that support connection-release are:

T_SNDDIS(NS_LIB)	Initiates the abortive-release of a transport-connection. Either transport-user may initiate abortive-release, and it may use it to reject a connect-request during the connection-establishment phase.
T_RCVDIS(NS_LIB)	Identifies the reason for the abortive-release of a connection, whether the connection is released by the transport-provider or another transport-user.
T_SNDREL(NS_LIB)	(Optional). Initiates an orderly-release. Either transport-user may initiate an orderly-release. The connection remains intact until both users use this component and T_RCVREL(NS_LIB).
T_RCVREL(NS_LIB)	(Optional). Informs the transport-provider that the user is aware of the remote-user's actions when a user is notified of an orderly-release-request.

Overview of the Connectionless-mode Service

The connectionless-mode transport-service has two phases of communication:

1. initialization/de-initialization.

2. data-transfer.

Initialization/De-initialization Phase

Before a user attempts to transfer data in connectionless-mode, the environment of the user must be initialized. Specifically, the user must create a local communication path to the transport-provider (i.e., create the transport-endpoint), obtain necessary protocol-specific information, and activate the transport-endpoint. A transport-endpoint is considered active when a transport-user may send or receive data-units on that endpoint.

When a transport-user no longer wishes to send or receive data-units on a given transport-endpoint, the endpoint must be de-initialized, thereby freeing the resource for future use. The functions that support the initialization/de-initialization tasks are the same functions used in the connection-mode service.

Data Transfer Phase

Once a transport-endpoint is activated, a user may send and receive data-units on that endpoint in connectionless-mode as follows:

T_SNDUDATA(NS_LIB)   Send a self-contained data-unit to the user at the given protocol-address.

T_RCVUDATA(NS_LIB)   Receive data-units from other users.

T_RCVUDERR(NS_LIB)   Retrieve error information associated with a previously sent data-unit.

Transport Interface State Machines

Figure B-1 describes all possible states of the transport-provider as seen by the transport-user. The service type may be connectionless-mode (T_CLTS), connection-mode (T_COTS) or connection-mode with orderly-release (T_COTS_ORD).

State	Description	Service Type
T_UNINIT	uninitialized — initial and final state of interface	T_CLTS T_COTS T_COTS_ORD
T_UNBND	unbound	T_CLTS T_COTS T_COTS_ORD
T_IDLE	no connection established	T_CLTS T_COTS T_COTS_ORD
T_OUTCON	outgoing connection pending for active-user	T_COTS T_COTS_ORD
T_INCON	incoming connection pending for passive-user	T_COTS T_COTS_ORD
T_DATAXFER	data-transfer	T_COTS T_COTS_ORD
T_OUTREL	outgoing-orderly-release (waiting for orderly-release-indication)	T_COTS_ORD
T_INREL	incoming-orderly-release (waiting to send orderly-release-request)	T_COTS_ORD

FIGURE B-1. Transport Interface States

Sequence of Functions

Figure B-2 shows a sequence of functions for an active-user and passive-user using connection-mode transport-service. Blank lines indicates use of a component by one user prior to use of a related component by the other user.

Active User	Passive User
t_open	t_open
t_bind	t_bind
	t_listen
t_connect	
	t_accept
t_rcvconnect	
t_snd	
	t_rcv
t_snddis	
	t_rcvdis
t_unbind	t_unbind
t_close	t_close

FIGURE B-2. Example of a Sequence of Transport Functions

Figure B-3 shows how events flow for connection-mode transport-service without orderly-release. Solid lines stand for the active-user, and dashed lines stand for the passive-user.

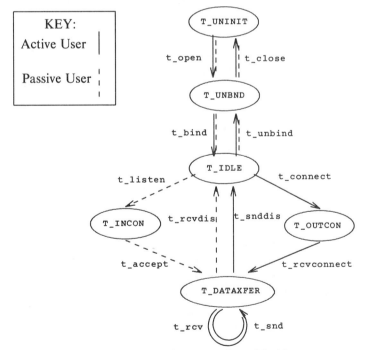

FIGURE B-3. Transport State Machine

This preceding example does not show all the functions that must be called, but rather highlights the important functions that request a particular service. For example, the active-user requests a connection using t_connect, and the passive-user receives an indication of the connect-request using t_listen, then uses t_accept. Figure B-9 details all possible states and events.

Figures B-5 through B-9 describe the incoming and outgoing events that may occur on any connection, and the allowable sequence of function calls. Given a current state and event, the transition to the next state is shown as well as any actions by the transport-user must take.

Incoming Events

The following incoming events correspond to the successful return of the specified user-level transport-functions, where these functions retrieve data or event information from the transport-provider. The only incoming event not associated directly with the return of a function on a given transport-endpoint is pass_conn, which occurs when a user transfers a connection to another transport-endpoint. This event occurs on the endpoint that is being passed the connection, despite the fact that no function is called on that endpoint. The state pass_conn is included in the state tables to describe what happens when a user accepts a connection on another transport-endpoint.

In Figure B-4, the rcvdis events are distinguished by the context in which they occur. The context is based on the value of ocnt, which is the count of outstanding connect-indications on the current transport-endpoint.

Event	Description	Service Type
listen	successful return of t_listen	T_COTS T_COTS_ORD
rcvconnect	successful return of t_rcvconnect	T_COTS T_COTS_ORD
rcv	successful return of t_rcv	T_COTS T_COTS_ORD
rcvdis1	successful return of t_rcvdis with ocnt <= 1	T_COTS T_COTS_ORD
rcvdis2	successful return of t_rcvdis with ocnt == 1	T_COTS T_COTS_ORD
rcvdis3	successful return of t_rcvdis with ocnt > 1	T_COTS T_COTS_ORD
rcvrel	successful return of t_rcvrel	T_COTS_ORD
rcvudata	successful return of t_rcvudata	T_CLTS
rcvuderr	successful return of t_rcvuderr	T_CLTS
pass_conn	receive a passed connection	T_COTS T_COTS_ORD

FIGURE B-4. Transport Interface Incoming Events

Outgoing Events

The following outgoing events correspond to the successful return of the specified user-level transport-functions, where these functions send a request or response to the transport-provider. In Figure B-5, the context distinguishes some events (e.g., `accept`*n*) based on the following values:

`ocnt`   count of outstanding connect-indications.

`fd`   file-descriptor of the current transport-endpoint.

`resfd` file-descriptor of the transport-endpoint to accept connection on.

Event	Description	Service Type
`opened`	successful return of `t_open`	`T_CLTS` `T_COTS` `T_COTS_ORD`
`bind`	successful return of `t_bind`	`T_CLTS` `T_COTS` `T_COTS_ORD`
`optmgmt`	successful return of `t_optmgmt`	`T_CLTS` `T_COTS` `T_COTS_ORD`
`unbind`	successful return of `t_unbind`	`T_CLTS` `T_COTS` `T_COTS_ORD`
`closed`	successful return of `t_close`	`T_CLTS` `T_COTS` `T_COTS_ORD`
`connect1`	successful return of `t_connect` in synchronous execution-mode	`T_COTS` `T_COTS_ORD`
`connect2`	`TLOOK` error due to a disconnect-indication arriving on the transport-endpoint, or `TNODATA` error on `t_connect` in asynchronous execution-mode.	`T_COTS` `T_COTS_ORD`
`accept1`	successful return of `t_accept` with `ocnt == 1` and with `fd == resfd`	`T_COTS` `T_COTS_ORD`
`accept2`	successful return of `t_accept` with `ocnt == 1` and with `fd != resfd`	`T_COTS` `T_COTS_ORD`
`accept3`	successful return of `t_accept` with `ocnt > 1`	`T_COTS` `T_COTS_ORD`
`snd`	successful return of `t_snd`	`T_COTS` `T_COTS_ORD`
`snddis1`	successful return of `t_snddis` with `ocnt <= 1`	`T_COTS` `T_COTS_ORD`
`snddis2`	successful return of `t_snddis` with `ocnt > 1`	`T_COTS` `T_COTS_ORD`
`sndrel`	successful return of `t_sndrel`	`T_COTS_ORD`
`sndudata`	successful return of `t_sndudata`	`T_CLTS`

FIGURE B-5. Transport Interface Outgoing Events

Transport User Actions

Some state transitions are accompanied by a list of actions the transport-user must take. These actions are represented by the notation [n], where n is the number of the specific action as described in Figure B-6.

[1] Set the count of outstanding connect-indications to zero.

[2] Increment the count of outstanding connect-indications.

[3] Decrement the count of outstanding connect-indications.

[4] Pass a connection to another transport-endpoint [see T_ACCEPT(NS_LIB)]

FIGURE B-6. Transport Interface User Actions

State Tables

Figures B-7, B-8 and B-9 describe the allowable sequence of functions. T_GETSTATE(NS_LIB), T_GETINFO(NS_LIB), T_ALLOC(NS_LIB), T_FREE(NS_LIB), T_LOOK(NS_LIB) and T_SYNC(NS_LIB) are excluded from the state tables because they do not affect the state of the interface. Each of these components may be used from any state except the uninitialized state. Similarly, T_ERROR(NS_LIB) is excluded from the state table because it does not affect the state of the interface.

Figures B-7, B-8 and B-9 describe possible states of the transport-provider as seen by the transport-user. The contents of each box represent the next state given the current state (column) and the current incoming or outgoing event (row). An empty box represents an invalid state/event combination. Along with the next state, each box may include an action list (as specified in Figure B-6). The transport-user must take the actions specified in the order specified in the state table. Separate table show initialization/de-initialization, data-transfer in connectionless-mode and connection-release/data-transfer in connection-mode.

state \ event	T_UNINIT	T_UNBND	T_IDLE
opened	T_UNBND		
bind		T_IDLE[1]	
optmgmt			T_IDLE
unbind			T_UNBND
closed		T_UNINIT	

FIGURE B-7. Initialization/De-initialization State Table

state \ event	T_IDLE	T_OUTCON	T_INCON	T_DATAXFER	T_OUTREL	T_INREL
connect1	T_DATAXFER					
connect2	T_OUTCON					
rcvconnect		T_DATAXFER				
listen	T_INCON [2]		T_INCON [2]			
accept1			T_DATAXFER [3]			
accept2			T_IDLE [3][4]			
accept3			T_INCON [3][4]			
snd				T_DATAXFER		T_INREL
rcv				T_DATAXFER	T_OUTREL	
snddis1		T_IDLE	T_IDLE [3]	T_IDLE	T_IDLE	T_IDLE
snddis2			T_INCON [3]			
rcvdis1		T_IDLE		T_IDLE	T_IDLE	T_IDLE
rcvdis2			T_IDLE [3]			
rcvdis3			T_INCON [3]			
sndrel				T_OUTREL		T_IDLE
rcvrel				T_INREL	T_IDLE	
pass_conn	T_DATAXFER					

FIGURE B-8. Connection/Release/Data-Transfer State Table for Connection-mode Service

state \ event	T_IDLE
sndudata	T_IDLE
rcvudata	T_IDLE
rcvuderr	T_IDLE

FIGURE B-9. Data-Transfer State Table for Connectionless-mode Service

The following rules govern the maintenance of the state of the interface.

- The transport-provider must keep record of the state of the interface as seen by the transport-user.

- The transport-provider must never process a function that places the interface out of state.

- The transport-provider must indicate through an error return of each function, where possible, when that function is called out of sequence, and the state should not change. When out of the T_DATAXFER state, the transport-provider must not accept or forward any data passed with a function.

- The uninitialized state (T_UNINIT) of a transport-endpoint is the initial state, and the transport-provider must initialize and bind the endpoint before considering it active.

- The uninitialized state is also the final state, and the transport-provider must consider the transport-endpoint unused. T_CLOSE(NS_LIB) closes the transport-provider and frees transport library resources for another endpoint.

- According to the state table in Figure B-7, T_CLOSE(NS_LIB) should only be used in the T_UNBND state. If it is used in any other state and no other user has that endpoint open, the action will be abortive, the transport-endpoint will be successfully closed, and the library resources will be freed for another endpoint. When T_CLOSE(NS_LIB) is used, the transport-provider must ensure that the address associated with the specified transport-endpoint is unbound from that endpoint. Also, the provider should send appropriate disconnects if T_CLOSE(NS_LIB) is not used in the unbound state.

The following rules apply only to the connection-mode transport-service:

- The transport-connection-release phase can be initiated at any time during the connection-establishment phase or data-transfer phase.

- The only time the state of a transport-service interface of a transport-endpoint may be transferred to another transport-endpoint is when the T_ACCEPT(NS_LIB) component specifies such action. The following rules then apply to the cooperating transport-endpoints:

  — The endpoint accepting the current state of the interface must be bound to an appropriate protocol address and be in the T_IDLE state.

  — The user transferring the current state of an endpoint must have correct permissions to use the protocol address bound to the accepting endpoint.

  — After completing the transfer when there are no more outstanding connect-indications, the transport-provider places the endpoint that transfers the state of the transport-interface into the T_IDLE state.

Guidelines for Writing Protocol-Independent Software

A primary goal of the user-level transport-interface is to be independent of any particular transport-protocol. More importantly, the interface is designed for users to write programs without knowing the particular transport-protocol to which they would interface. This enables networking applications to run in different protocol environments without change.

The user-level transport-interface offers protocol-independence for applications following these guidelines:

1. The user should not assume that logical data boundaries are preserved across a connection because not all transport-providers support the concept of a Transport Service Data Unit (TSDU) in connection-mode.

2. The user must not exceed the protocol-specific service limits returned by T_OPEN(NS_LIB) and T_GETINFO(NS_LIB). The user is responsible for accessing these limits and then adhering to the limits throughout the communication process.

3. The user should not look at or change options specific to the underlying protocol. The T_OPTMGMT(NS_LIB) component enables a user to access default protocol options from the transport-provider, which the user may blindly pass as an argument to the appropriate connection-establishment function. Optionally, the user may choose not to pass options as an argument to connection-establishment functions.

4. The user should not specify any protocol address on T_BIND(NS_LIB), but instead should allow T_BIND(NS_LIB) to assign an address to the user. In this way, details concerning protocol-specific addressing are hidden from the user.

    Similarly, the user must have some way of accessing destination addresses in an invisible manner, such as through a name-server. However, the details for doing so fall outside the scope of this interface definition.

5. The user should not interpret the reason codes associated with T_RCVDIS(NS_LIB) if protocol-independence is a concern because this information is protocol-dependent.

6. The user should not interpret the error codes associated with T_RCVUDERR(NS_LIB) if protocol-independence is a concern because this information is protocol-dependent.

7. Software should not have the names of devices hard-coded. While software may be written for a particular class of service (e.g., connectionless-mode service), it should not be written to depend on any attribute of the underlying protocol.

8. Software targeted for multiple protocol environments should not use the optional orderly-release facility of the connection-mode service (i.e., T_SNDREL(NS_LIB) and T_RCVREL(NS_LIB)) because this facility is not supported by all connection-based transport-protocols. In particular, using it prevents one from successfully communicating with ISO open-systems.

SEE ALSO

1. ISO 7498, *Information Processing Systems — Open Systems Interconnection — Reference Model*, 1983.

2. CCITT Recommendation X.200, *Reference Model of Open Systems Interconnection for CCITT Applications*, 1984.

3. ISO 8072, *Information Processing Systems — Open Systems Interconnection — Transport Service Definition*, 1984.

Indexes

C

D

E

G

J

K

L

N

O

P

S

C Language Interfaces   389